Feminist Perspectives

Peace Education

Pergamon Titles of Related Interest

Brock-Utne EDUCATING FOR PEACE
Russell EXPOSING NUCLEAR PHALLACIES

Related Journals

(Free sample copies available upon request)

REPRODUCTIVE AND GENETIC ENGINEERING: Journal of International Feminist Analysis
WOMEN'S STUDIES INTERNATIONAL FORUM

The ATHENE Series

General Editors
Gloria Bowles
Renate Klein
Janice Raymond

Consulting Editor
Dale Spender

The Athene Series assumes that all those who are concerned with formulating explanations of the way the world works need to know and appreciate the significance of basic feminist principles.

The growth of feminist research has challenged almost all aspects of social organization in our culture. The Athene Series focuses on the construction of knowledge and the exclusion of women from the process—both as theorists and subjects of study—and offers innovative studies that challenge established theories and research.

On Athene—When Metis, goddess of wisdom who presided over all knowledge was pregnant with Athene, she was swallowed up by Zeus who then gave birth to Athene from his head. The original Athene is thus the parthenogenetic daughter of a strong mother and as the feminist myth goes, at the "third birth" of Athene she stops being Zeus' obedient mouthpiece and returns to her real source: the science and wisdom of womankind.

Feminist Perspectives

Peace Education

by **Birgit Brock-Utne**

University of Oslo, Norway
University of Dar es Salaam, Tanzania

Pergamon Press
New York Oxford Beijing Frankfurt São Paulo Sydney

Pergamon Press Offices:

U.S.A.	Pergamon Press, Inc., Maxwell House, Fairview Park, Elmsford, New York 10523, U.S.A.
U.K.	Pergamon Press plc, Headington Hill Hall, Oxford OX3 0BW, England
PEOPLE'S REPUBLIC OF CHINA	Pergamon Press, Room 4037, Qianmen Hotel, Beijing, People's Republic of China
FEDERAL REPUBLIC OF GERMANY	Pergamon Press GmbH, Hammerweg 6, D-6242 Kronberg, Federal Republic of Germany
BRAZIL	Pergamon Editora Ltda, Rua Eça de Queiros, 346, CEP 04011, São Paulo, Brazil
AUSTRALIA	Pergamon Press Australia Pty Ltd., P.O. Box 544, Potts Point, NSW 2011, Australia
JAPAN	Pergamon Press, 8th Floor, Matsuoka Central Building, 1-7-1 Nishishinjuku, Shinjuku-ku, Tokyo 160, Japan
CANADA	Pergamon Press Canada Ltd., Suite 271, 253 College Street, Toronto, Ontario M5T 1R5, Canada

---

First edition 1989

Library of Congress Cataloging in Publication Data

Brock-Utne, Birgit, 1938-
Feminist perspectives on peace and peace education / by Birgit Brock-Utne.
p. cm. -- (The Athene series)
Bibliography: p.
Includes index.
ISBN 0-08-036568-X. -- ISBN 0-08-036567-1 (pbk.)
1. Women and peace. 2. Peace--Study and teaching. 3. Feminism.
I. Title. II. Series.
JX1965.B77 1989
303.6′6--dc19 88-37466
CIP

Printed in the United States of America

The paper used in this publication meets the minimum requirements of American National Standard for Information Sciences -- Permanence of Paper for Printed Library Materials, ANSI Z39.48-1984

To Gunnar,
my swimming and dancing partner,
my intellectual and emotional partner
who challenges me, cares
for me, and supports me.

Contents

PREFACE xi

1. THE PURPOSE OF THIS STUDY 1
How Do We Go About Studying the Questions We Have Posed? 4
Feminist Perspectives 6
Feminist Perspectives on Peace 7
Feminist Perspectives on Peace Education 9
Feminist Perspectives on Peace Education in the Nonformal Sector 10
Feminist Perspectives on Peace Education in the Formal Sector 11

2. FEMINIST PERSPECTIVES 14
A Feminist Perspective 14
Several Feminist Perspectives 16
The Conservative Perspective *17*
The Liberal Perspective *18*
The Marxist Perspective *20*
The Radical Feminist Perspective *22*
The Socialist Feminist Perspective *31*
Women of Color Perspective *34*
A Combination of Perspectives *35*

3. WOMEN AND PEACE: THE MEANING OF PEACE FOR WOMEN 39
What is Peace? 39
Negative Peace *41*
A Preliminary Table of the Peace Concept 43
Positive Peace *44*

A Table Summarizing the Discussion On Negative and Positive Peace 47

Cell 1: Absence of Unorganized, Personal, Physical, and Direct Violence 48
Cell 2: Absence of Organized, Personal, Physical, and Direct Violence 52
Cell 3: Absence of Unorganized, Indirect Violence Shortening the Life Span 58
Cell 4: Absence of Organized, Indirect Violence Shortening the Life Span 60
Cell 5: Absence of Indirect, Unorganized Violence Reducing the Quality of Life 61
Cell 6: Absence of Organized, Indirect Violence Reducing the Quality of Life 64

Summary Remarks 65
Two Groups of Feminist Peace Researchers 68
The Development of the Peace Concept Through Three UN Women's Decade Conferences 70

Plan of Action from Mexico 70
Programme of Action from Copenhagen 71
Forward-Looking Strategies from Nairobi 72

4. FEMINIST PERSPECTIVES ON PEACE EDUCATION 73

What Is Peace Education from a Feminist Perspective? 73
What Is Peace Education? 74
Education *for* Peace and Education *About* Peace 77
Peace Education as a Controversial Concept 79
Recent Developments in Peace Education 80

Taking Gender into Account 82
Level of Information and the Readiness to Act on the Information 83

Feminist Perspectives on Various Approaches to the Definition of Peace Education 84

The Structural Approach 85
The Dialectical Approach 85
The Evolutionary Approach 85

The Development of the Peace Education Concept Through Three UN Women's Decade Conferences 88

Plan of Action from Mexico 88
Programme of Action from Copenhagen 89
Forward-Looking Strategies from Nairobi 90
Can Peace Come About Through Peace Education? 92
Attitude Formation and Social Behavior 99

5. FEMINIST PERSPECTIVES ON PEACE EDUCATION IN THE NONFORMAL SECTOR 107
Peace Education Within the Family Institution 107
The Role of Mothers 107
Feminist Mothers of Sons 111
The "Ideal Mother" and the "Ideal Soldier" 116
Socialization into Violence and Aggression 119
The Role of Fathers 128
Education Through Choice of Toys 133
The Role of Television in Peace Education 135
Sports and Games: Power-over or Power-to? 143
Direct Violence—The Cult of Danger and Courage 146
Indirect Violence—The Cult of Power as Dominance 147
Physical Activity as Pleasure and Joy 149
Do We Educate Girls for Peace and Boys for War? 151

6. FEMINIST PERSPECTIVES ON PEACE EDUCATION IN THE FORMAL SECTOR 155
Peace Education in a Formal School Setting 155
The Typical Peace-Oriented School Student 159
What Attitudes Toward the World Are Shaped Through the Official Curriculum? 162
Through the Teaching of History 162
Through the Teaching of Science 164
What Attitudes Toward the World Are Shaped Through the Hidden Curriculum of the School? 169
The Learning of Obedience and Loyalty 170

The Learning of Competitiveness *171*
Is There A Light in the Tunnel? 172

REFERENCES 177

INDEX 193

Preface

This work is a follow-up to my book *Educating for Peace, A Feminist Perspective* (Pergamon Press, 1985). It is a further development and elaboration of thoughts found in that book, but a more critical analysis of them. This development and analysis would not have been possible without the constructive criticism and inspiration I have received from both male and female researchers belonging to the international peace research community, mostly within IPRA (the International Peace Research Association).

In this preface I describe how this book differs from *Educating for Peace* and what has led to the further development of my thoughts since I wrote that book. I do not mention all the people who have inspired my work the last two to three years nor all the exciting peace and peace research conferences I have been to in that period. But I do describe *some* environments that have been especially inspiring for my work, and acknowledge some people without whose keen interest in my thoughts and critical comments this work would not have been a new book.

Comments I have received from reviewers, translators, students and professors who have used the book as a textbook have been very valuable. I would especially like to thank Robin Burns from Australia, Elise Boulding and Betty Reardon from the United States and Berit Ås from Norway for their valuable and challenging comments on *Educating for Peace*. I would also like to thank those people who initiated the translations for their belief in the book—and the translators for their work and constructive comments. I want to thank Suh Young-Hee, who took the initiative to and actually made the translation into Korean (published in 1986); also, Ivar Johansen from the Norwegian branch of War Resisters International (Folkereisning mot krig) and Eleanor Brenna from the Norwegian branch of Women's International League for Peace and Freedom (WILPF) for the initiative which led to a Norwegian translation and Ellen Elster for the translation (published in 1987). An Italian translation is underway.

I would also like to thank Iftikhar Hassan from the Open University in Islamabad, Pakistan, for inviting me to lecture at her university and at the University of Peshawar in April 1985. The lectures were on topics taken from *Educating for Peace* and the discussions heated and challenging. I would also like to thank Govind Kelkar from Women's Center for Development Studies in New Delhi, India, where I spent some time in May 1985, for good discussions on the topic of my book.

Finnish peace groups have been especially interested in *Educating for Peace*, and I have lectured in Finland quite often since the book appeared. I would especially like to thank Helena Allahwerdi and Hilkka Pietilä from the Finnish UN Association for their valuable comments and their hospitality.

Another source of inspiration was my participation in the UN Women's Decade Conference in Nairobi in the summer of 1985. I wrote a background paper for the peace sections of the official document, and I participated in the official conference as an observer representing IPRA. Also, I participated in the forum on several roundtable discussions, gave lectures in the peace tent, and was on peace panels. I would like to thank the Norwegian Development Agency, NORAD, which paid for my trip, thus enabling me to participate. After the conference I received an inspiring assignment from the Swedish Ambassador for Disarmament, Maj-Britt Theorin, who was heading the World Women Parliamentarians for Peace, to analyze the peace sections in the Nairobi document. I would like to thank Maj-Britt and her secretary Bernt Jonsson for the assignment, which inspired me to further develop the analysis into a comparison of the final documents in the three women's decade conferences. This analysis, which I presented at the IPRA conference in Sussex in April 1986 (published as PRIO Working Paper 1/86 and also in: Alger, Chad, and Michael Stohl (eds). *A Just Peace through Transformation.* Boulder: Westview Press, 1988), provided a background for an analysis of the same documents in this book.

I had expected that *Educating for Peace* would be used primarily in women's studies and by women's peace groups. It has been used in these forums, but it has also been used extensively, and somewhat to my surprise, by male professors, teaching not only peace studies but also law and theology.

It was a great source of inspiration for me to be invited, in May 1986, by the student body to the University of Oregon to give the keynote lecture at the opening of their peace week and to meet Tom Hovet's class in irenology (who were using my book as their main textbook) and have discussions with them. These discussions further developed my thinking and started ideas growing in my mind for a new book.

It has been possible to develop these ideas and write this book only because I was granted a sabbatical year (covering fall 1986 and spring 1987) by the University of Oslo. I am very grateful to those people at my Institute who enabled me to have this year of grace, during which I had several challenges to clear my thinking on feminism and peace. I decided that the work would not only be a new book but should also be academically sound enough to be accepted as a doctoral dissertation at the University of Oslo—the first such dissertation in peace research. The thesis was defended at the University of Oslo on the 2nd of June, 1988. I would like to thank my two opponents Håkan Wiberg from the Institute for Peace and Conflict Studies at the University of Lund, Sweden, and Paul Smoker from the Richardson Institute for Conflict and Peace Research at the University of Lancaster, UK, for sound and constructive criticism. I would also like to thank them for the open mind with which they met this feminist work. Their comments from the opposition have been useful in rewriting the thesis into this book. So have the comments from Pergamon's consultant.

My first opponent Håkan Wiberg has also done a great job of commenting on earlier drafts of the manuscript. My understanding of the field of peace research has been considerably enhanced by his suggestions for literature to read and his critical comments, all given within the spirit of caring rationality. I here want to thank you, Håkan, for all the time you have spent advising me, for your encouraging remarks and your loud screams when you felt I was treading on your masculine toes. A dialogue between peace researchers and feminist researchers can only be conducted in a spirit of mutual openness and frankness. I also want to express my gratitude to my father, Gerhard Brock-Utne, whose encouragement in connection with my doctoral degree was what kept me going and to my mother, Gertrud Brock-Utne, who followed the whole ordeal with eagerness.

Yet another source of inspiration was the Second International Feminist Bookfair held in Oslo the end of June 1986. Here I was asked to give a keynote lecture on "Feminist Perspectives on Peace Research" (published as PRIO Report 11/86), which forced me to start structuring this book. That lecture I later repeated in Sweden, Finland, and the United States, and the discussions of it in the different forums where it has been presented have done much to enrich my thinking on the various feminist perspectives on peace.

While I was working with this manuscript in the academic year 1986–87 I was invited as a guest professor, first at the University of Umeå, Sweden, in the fall of 1986 and then at several universities in the United States in the spring of 1987. I would especially like to thank Ingegerd Lundstrøm from the Interdisciplinary Forum for Women Studies at the University of Umeå, for arranging my stay, giving me perfect conditions in which to work—a guest researcher flat with calm and peace—and for providing a stimulating environment for the discussion of my ideas and the further development of them.

The relationship between sports and aggression and the potential of sports, or rather of physical education, to contribute to peace has long interested me. I touch on this issue in *Educating for Peace*. What I wrote there led me into great discussions with sports researchers. I was asked to lecture and discuss with students at the College of Sports in Oslo. I was challenged to develop my thoughts further in a lecture to an international and multidisciplinary conference for sport sciences held at Lillehammer, Norway, in the middle of November 1986 (published as PRIO Report 1/87). The lecture and the discussions it led to form the basis for my discussion of this theme in this book. I would especially like to thank Kari Fasting, professor at the College of Sports and a fine feminist, for inviting me to speak and for lending her ear and seriously discussing this sensitive issue with me. It is good to meet athletes who are not afraid of questioning the fundamentals of what they are doing.

In *Educating for Peace* I left out the formal school system as a place where peace education could be taught or is being prevented; however, in this book I devote a whole chapter to the discussion of this topic. I have often lectured on the topic but the push to study it more seriously was given to me by peace researcher Arthur Westing, then at SIPRI in Stockholm, now at PRIO, who asked me to participate in a book project sponsored by UNEP and SIPRI called *Cultural Norms in Relation to War and the Environment*. A book with that title and edited by Arthur Westing was published by the Oxford University Press in 1988. My chapter there is called "Formal Education as a Force in Shaping Cultural Norms in Relation to War and the Environment." Working with this assignment has been a challenge and has also inspired my work with the chapter on formal education in this book. I am grateful to Arthur Westing for giving me the assignment, for valuable and thorough criticism, and for arranging an inspiring meeting of all the authors in Stockholm in the middle of March 1987.

The initiative for my lecture tour of the midwestern United States in the spring of 1987 came from three professors in Indiana: Jill Bystydzienski from Franklin College, and Hal Pepinsky and Jim Hart from Indiana University. Both Hal and Jim use *Educating for Peace* as required reading in their classes—Hal in his on feminist justice, and Jim in his on feminist theology. My discussions with the students in these classes meant a lot to the further development of my thoughts into this book. The students asked about my feminist perspective, which they found too implicit in the book. How would I explicate it? Was there just *one* feminist perspective or more? If there were several, how would they be related to various definitions of peace? Which of several perspectives would I find most valuable and why? I want to thank these students for the valuable discussions and challenges I met in Indiana, and I also want to thank Jill and Hal for their hospitality.

My first stop on this lecture tour was the University of Illinois, Champaign-Urbana, where I had last been 23 years ago when I took my Masters there (M.Ed.) and had also been a teaching assistant in Art Education. I had my eldest son, Karsten, with me at that time. He was 1 1/2 years old. It was strange to be back—so many memories, such a long time ago. I was well taken care of by Berenice Carroll and Clint Finch, she the chair, he the administrative secretary of COPRED, the U.S.-based Peace Research Association. Berenice also heads the Women Studies Program at the University of Illinois. I would like to thank Berenice and Clint for their hospitality, for the many good discussions and the interesting peace researchers and activists they introduced me to. I gave several lectures at the University of Illinois, a radio interview, and a co-lecture with Ruth Bleier on "sex differences in aggression." Even though Ruth is a biologist and I a social scientist we very much agreed that for the most part sex differences seem to be of social origin. At Illinois I also had lunches and discussions with WILPF (Women's International League for Peace and Freedom) and WID (Women in Development).

In Indiana I lectured at Indiana University, Earlham College, the experimental high school named "Harmony School," and at Franklin College. I participated in discussions with student groups and peace groups, had "brown bag lunches" and even "working breakfasts" with numerous groups who wanted to discuss my ideas with me. It was wonderful to be met with such enthusiasm and to see that my work meant a good deal to many people. (It is more difficult to become a prophet in your own country.) I also lectured to several church groups, was interviewed on television, and one of my lectures was also televised. Thanks to Jill, Hal, and Jim who made the wonderful stay possible; to Dagrun for a fantastic dinner for her colleagues at Franklin where I was the guest of honor.

My third stop was Ohio, where I was well taken care of by Suzanne Hyers of the Center for Women's Studies. The first several days and over Easter weekend I stayed with Pauline and Harold Pepinsky, who gave me a wonderful home away from home. They introduced me to very interesting people, and we had inspiring talks on peace issues. Thanks to Pauline and Harold. Later—when my lecturing started—I was the guest for three days of Governor Dick Celeste and First Lady Dagmar Celeste. Dagmar introduced me in the plenary talk I gave at Ohio State University, and we found in each other a mutual admiration for the great Austrian peace hero, Bertha von Suttner, "forgotten" in history and among most people. (She is dealt with extensively in *Educating for Peace*.) With Dick I had several good discussions on peace issues in their beautiful mansion. We seemed to agree a lot in our analysis of the world situation. Thank you both so much for the hospitality. It was inspiring to meet my IPRA-friend Chad Alger again and to lecture to and converse with his class in peace studies at the Mershon Center. It was also good to meet and converse with students at Ohio Wesleyan University, both formally and more informally over dinner at the House of Peace and Justice.

Another source of inspiration for this work and for the further development of it into a new project area was the grant given me by the Norwegian

Council for Research in the Social Sciences to conduct a research project on the education of sons. The grant was given for the years 1986, 1987, and 1988 and allowed me to employ a research assistant, Bjørnar Sarnes, who has been a joy to work with since he is also keenly interested in peace education and sees the implications of our project "Sons" for peace education. We have conducted 20 interviews with feminist mothers of sons, 20 with more traditional mothers of sons, 20 with more traditional fathers of sons, and 20 with fathers who have spent more than the normal amount of time with their sons and have a critical view of the male role. We are now in the process of analyzing the interviews, Bjørnar making a preliminary analysis of the fathers and I of the mothers. We are grateful to the Norwegian Research Council (NAVF) and also the official government committee on the study of the male role for granting us money to be able to conduct our research. We have published some of our preliminary results and thoughts about the topic in the book: Brock-Utne, Birgit, and Bjørnar Sarnes (eds.): *Når Gutter Blir Menn* (When Boys Grow Into Men). Oslo/Bergen/Tromsø: Universitetsforlaget, 1987. We shall continue working on this theme and the implications it has for peace education.

I have been fortunate to be invited as a keynote speaker by many organizations and to gathering places around the world the last years. Everywhere I have met friendly people and have had the opportunity to develop and discuss my thoughts further. It was a great inspiration to participate in the Women's Forum in Moscow in the last week in June 1987 and in the third Interdisciplinary Congress of Women's Studies in Dublin, Ireland, the first week of July the same year. Here I gave the introductory keynote speech on women and peace and later participated in several roundtables and debates on peace education, women and peace, and male role socialization. I here also met representatives from Pergamon and was encouraged to continue working on the new book. It was good to further meet again with Stephanie Boxall of Pergamon in London in the first week of August 1987 to discuss my work with her, with Renate Duelli-Klein and Dale Spender. I would like to thank all three for their constructive comments and Renate, also, for asking me to lecture on women and peace in the summer course at the Institute of Education, University of London.

I started my work as a Professor of Education at the University of Dar es Salaam on October 1, 1987, and have a contract with that University until January 1, 1990. I am teaching mostly social psychology and aspiring to teach a social psychology which is not British, American, or Norwegian but Tanzanian, or at least East African. This is a great challenge. It also enriches my views both on peace and on sex role socialization. I learn a great deal every day and am grateful to those people at the University of Oslo, the University of Dar es Salaam, and the Norwegian Development Agency, NORAD, who made this arrangement possible.

While finishing my doctoral dissertation, writing the required lectures for the doctoral promotion at the end of May 1988, and later making the necessary changes for turning the dissertation into this book in August 1988, I was provided a "home away from home" at the International Peace Research Institute of Oslo, PRIO. For this I would like to thank the staff at PRIO and especially its current director, Sverre Lodgaard.

I would also like to thank the Chilean peace researchers Inez Vargas and Maria Elena Valenzuela for giving me the opportunity to lecture to and discuss with Chilean peace researchers and feminists in Santiago in August 1988.

This book and *Educating for Peace* supplement each other and do not replace each other since there is hardly any overlap in the material presented. *Educating for Peace* contains a large chapter on women's work for peace, on women and peace movements, and on women peace heroes, especially Bertha von Suttner. This material is not repeated here. Those especially looking for this part of peace studies are advised to consult *Educating for Peace*. That book also contains more about women and peace research and about the conditions of women around the world. *Educating for Peace* has been said to raise consciousness about the relationship between gender roles and peace education. This book is more heuristic, pointing out the next steps and the problems for those who want to continue to work with peace issues from a feminist perspective.

The male peace researchers who have taken a keen interest in the potential contribution of feminist analysis to the development of peace studies have challenged me not only to make my feminist perspective more explicit but also to tie my work closer to the field of peace research. With their own great familiarity with peace research but less familiarity with feminist research, they have been able to give me good guidance when I took up this challenge. My gratitude is especially directed to Håkan Wiberg and also to the Swedish peace educator Stig Lindholm, who has commented on earlier drafts of the manuscript.

The task of making the feminist perspectives explicit and of showing their relevance to peace research and the field of peace education has been a great challenge. A challenge that certainly has developed my understanding of the field of feminist peace research and that will, I hope, develop the understanding of my readers.

While *Educating for Peace* is in many ways a collection of evidence showing that girls, much more than boys, are brought up as peaceful and nonviolent beings, this work is of a more analytical nature, the questions raised many more and the answers fewer. The conclusions drawn here are more tentative, and they may even seem to contradict those drawn with greater ardor in *Educating for Peace*. This is the function not only of a more analytical or more academic style of writing, but also of my own further work with the same topic for two additional years. I have been fortunate in these years to have by my side a husband who not only has a good knowledge of and keen interest in peace issues but who also is a feminist in practice, encouraging me to go on with my work and taking care of our youngest son when I am around the world lecturing. I would like to thank my husband, Gunnar Garbo, for his support during the years I have been working with this book.

When he read through the conclusions of this work, Gunnar said that he liked the conclusions of *Educating for Peace* better and thought they were more right. He said that women everywhere were much more peaceful than men, did not wage wars or develop nuclear bombs. He thought this was the result of a different upbringing, making them more peaceful individuals, and that if boys got a similar upbringing, the world would be better—or that if women were to lead this world, it would be a more peaceful world. This was also more of my conclusion in *Educating for Peace*. And maybe such conclusions are right. My doubts here are exactly that: doubts. My conclusions are not the opposite of those drawn in *Educating for Peace*, but they are more tentative. Going deeper into a topic does not necessarily mean that one comes up with more certain conclusions—it may mean that one becomes less certain and has more questions.

All of this has happened to me in the course of working with this topic. It is a topic that I shall go on working with and I may, in some years, reach conclusions other than those quite tentatively drawn here.

1

The Purpose of This Study

The main purpose of this study is to analyze peace and peace education from a feminist perspective. What does peace mean to women? Is peace the same for women as for men? I have reported some studies showing that women are generally more peace-oriented than men are. They are more inclined to want a more equal distribution of resources, to reduce military budgets, to advocate nonviolence, to go against war toys. Why is this so? Are women more cooperative by nature? (see Brock-Utne, 1989). Are men more aggressive by nature? Do they learn to become more aggressive than girls? How is this learning taking place? Are we educating girls for peace and boys for war? Would the world be a world without wars if boys were socialized the way girls are—or if girls in great numbers came into leading positions and went into science and technology? What attitudes relating to peace are shaped in girls and boys by their parents, by the media, by the games they play and leisure activities they participate in? And what attitudes are shaped by the official and the unofficial, or hidden, curriculum of the school? Would the whole question of what peace is and how it can come about and the field of peace education be viewed differently if feminist perspectives were applied to these fields under study? While there are many studies within peace research applying a Marxist perspective to the phenomena under study, there are few using a feminist perspective as a research approach. Most of the peace-related studies written from a feminist perspective are of very recent origin (see, for example, Boulding, 1984; Eisler & Loye, 1986; Nordland, 1985; Reardon, 1985, 1988a, 1988b; Roberts, 1983, 1984).

All of these studies are clearly written from feminist perspectives, perspectives where women matter and the gender neutrality of most social science, including peace research, is broken. The phrase *gender neutrality of social science* refers to a way of writing where the gender of the actors is overlooked. Gender is not looked at as a variable in the research. And what is more important: An implicit assumption is often made that the gender of the actors is an *irrelevant* variable. Such an assumption may lead researchers to draw general conclusions about, for example, "human nature," "human aggression," the development of the "self-concept," based on studies solely including human males.

The easiest way to break this gender neutrality is by deliberately trying to view the world through feminine eyes. And sometimes this is all that is meant by "a feminist perspective"—looking at the world through the eyes of women. Questions are posed such as: What would a feminist foreign policy look like? Is there a feminine alternative for the future in industrialized countries? (Pietilä, 1985). In most of these studies, including my own (Brock-Utne, 1985a), there is little conceptual work done to make the feminist perspective explicit, let alone to differentiate between the various feminist perspectives.

Yet there are quite substantial differences between the feminist perspective used by Nordland (1985), who ties security for women to women's traditional role as mothers and nurturers and sees the home as a place where security is given, and the feminist perspective of Roberts (1983), who ties security for women to an absence of male domination and patriarchal behavior. Barbara Roberts (1983) points to the fact that there is no place which is less secure for women than their own home. She makes a point out of the estimation that each year over 1.8 million U.S. wives are badly battered by their husbands. When asked if there had ever been physical violence in their relationship, 28 percent of couples in one survey said yes, but the researchers believe that the true rate for wives' "ever" being battered in the life of a relationship is closer to 50 percent for all U.S. couples (Straus, 1978, p. 36).

This discrepancy between what the wives reported and what the researchers estimate the rate of physical violence to be can probably be explained by both an unwillingness on the part of the wives to admit the violence to which they have been subjected and a disagreement between the wives and the researchers about the definition of physical violence. Most researchers, like myself, are likely to use a strict definition of physical violence including *any* physical assault and coercion. Among wives, one is likely to find various definitions of physical violence depending on the social class, culture, and background of the wives. Some wives who are used to much physical violence among their parents and in the neighborhood may tend to overlook the physical violence they themselves are subjected to by their husbands and let it go unreported because it is within limits they accept as "normal" in marriage, or they conclude that it is only what they deserve. I would even be willing to maintain that the more a system uses open physical violence to keep a group of people in their place—be it women, blacks, migrant workers, intellectual critics—the weaker is the system. The more women are beaten, the more the patriarchal system is under threat.

Barbara Roberts (1983) concludes that there is a war against women going on in the privacy of their homes and that "so long as men are at war against women, peace for all of humankind cannot exist, and there is no safe place on earth for any of us" (Roberts, 1983, p. 22).

While both Nordland (1985) and Roberts (1983, 1984) use a feminist perspective in their study of peace, insisting that women matter and the voice of women must be heard, their feminist perspectives are rather different. Barbara Roberts writes from a radical feminist perspective which can be differentiated from more conservative, liberal, and even Marxist perspectives through the way researchers using a radical feminist perspective insist that an analysis of patriarchy always has to be included in a feminist perspective, which shall serve as a fruitful research approach.

We shall return to a discussion of patriarchy. Suffice it to mention here that patriarchy has to do with power over—with male control and domination of—women. In a patriarchal system male control and even violence against women to keep them in their place is so much a part of the system as to render it invisible, even to well-meaning peace researchers. It can be argued that the less that male control is disputed, the more it is taken for granted and rendered invisible, the stronger the patriarchal system. Machiavelli talked about the good leader as someone who reigned through the love of the people. Likewise the good—here meaning effective—patriarch is the one who can make people behave the way he wants them to behave without using negative sanctions or violence. So the absence of physical violence against women in a given setting does not necessarily mean that the patriarchal system is weak and women are not oppressed. On the contrary, it may mean that patriarchy is so strong it has invaded all institutions and all thinking so that no violence is required on the side of the patriarchy to keep people in their place. No oppression is more effective than the one in which the oppressed has internalized the norms of the oppressor. When this is not done, the oppressor easily resorts to threats and violence.

Using a feminist perspective, a lot of regular mainstream (usually male) peace research would be criticized and would need to be rewritten. For instance, a study by Fabbro (1978) of societies which he classifies as "peaceful" does not disqualify those in which violence against women is routine. One can argue that violence against women, especially so-called private violence going on in the "privacy" of the home, has not been included in the peace concept.

In our discussion of the peace concept we shall look at the advantages and disadvantages of including private and personal violence at the microlevel in this concept. Are there tendencies that indicate a radical feminist perspective on peace is gaining ground and that a conquering of the peace concept by radical feminists is taking place within the intergovernmental community? I shall, at the end of Chapter 3, look at some such tendencies which especially can be found in the Nairobi document from the last UN Women's Decade Conference. If so, what would this new orientation mean for the development of peace research and for the integration of feminist research and peace research?

Applying a feminist perspective, whether a liberal, radical, or socialist one, means it would not be possible to write about social inequality without mentioning the fact that for women the daily consequences of inequality in health, education, income, and wealth are different than for men. For instance, a study by Höivik (1971) about social inequality fails to mention this fact and therefore gives a less complete and varied picture of the populations under study than would be given had his study been supplemented with analysis from a feminist perspective. Whether social inequality shall be made part of the peace concept is also under debate among peace researchers and will have to be dealt with under our discussion of the peace concept. I shall here also make use of the concept of structural violence, a well-known concept within peace research. We shall see that by structural violence we do not mean *all* types of social inequality. Rather, we mean *certain* consequences of *certain* types of social inequality.

What is meant by "a feminist perspective" and "peace" needs to be defined before we can look at women's relations to peace, peace education, and peace research. How fruitful is it to look at these relations from a feminist perspective—from just one feminist perspective—and which one—or from several? What would applying a feminist perspective to the fields of peace studies and peace education mean?

HOW DO WE GO ABOUT STUDYING THE QUESTIONS WE HAVE POSED?

I have asked the question whether the whole concept of peace and the fields of peace studies and peace education would be viewed differently if they were analyzed through a feminist perspective. If so, *how* would they be viewed differently? What would be gained from such an analysis? Would the gain depend on which of the feminist perspectives was used? What disadvantages and problems would develop from applying such a perspective to existing research? Is there reason to believe that the field of peace studies, including peace education, would benefit from an analysis from a feminist perspective or would the field be even more unwieldy? How can women's attitudes and behavior toward peace and war be understood? Would an analysis from a feminist perspective help us understand the gender gap (see, for example, Abzug, 1983; Boulding, 1984) between women's and men's attitudes toward military spending, arms buildup, war toys, stationing of cruise missiles, social security, and social expenditures? Could a feminist analysis be used to study the way women work against war, some by joining the army or the guerrilla fighters alongside men, some by joining the mixed-sex peace movements or by starting peace movements of their own, and some by participating in disarmament negotiations?

Such a variety of penetrating questions cannot be answered by one big empirical study. Peace studies, like most research, do not lack surveys, data, exploratory, empirical studies. What is lacking, as in most social science, is studies which seek to make sense out of some or all the knowledge already available in the field. This has to be done by explicitly applying a defined perspective as a research approach when scrutinizing the subject matter under research. The one used here is based on feminist thinking.

The main sources for our study will be other studies, data, and research gathered by other researchers who will sometimes, but not always, be writing from various feminist perspectives. Like studies in history or philosophy, for instance, we are building on existing sources, combining them in new ways, and analyzing them from another perspective. Our method of study is not unlike the one used by Stig Lindholm (1985) in his most recent research. By those who see firsthand data gathering as the only real research, this method has been condescendingly named "compilation research" and the researchers using it, "comp researchers." Be that as it may, I agree with the women peace researchers in Elise Boulding's study (1980) who claim that there has been too much mindless data gathering in peace research and too little analysis making the data worth having. (I could add that this generalization seems also to be valid for other parts of social science research.)

It would be correct here to make a distinction between two different ways of making an analysis built on existing sources:

- *Reanalysis* of primary data, a so-called secondary analysis. This means that data which have been gathered are reanalyzed from a different perspective. Such secondary analysis, important as it may be, could not have been made had not a primary analysis and data gathering taken place. Researchers who use mostly secondary analysis are indebted to those who gathered the original data and are often met by what to me seems to be reasonable demands to test their secondary analysis through primary data gathering.
- Using existing texts, sometimes reports and analysis, as *primary* data. Here a hermeneutic approach is used and the point is to gain an understanding of the texts, to interpret them. One tries to find out what the texts tell and—often more important—what they *do not* tell. To be able to do this type of analysis one has to have a picture of what the texts *could* or *ought to* tell, according to the frame of reference the researcher uses. To accuse a researcher using a hermeneutic approach of "compilation research" is missing the point.

In the following study both ways of using existing sources are employed for our analysis: Some studies are used for secondary analysis and here ideas for further empirical research to gather primary data are given. Other studies are used for a primary analysis through which I attempt to interpret the underlying perspective and show what perspectives are missing.

It is my hope that this study will stimulate the thinking of both peace scholars and feminist researchers, possibly building a bridge between the two groups.

FEMINIST PERSPECTIVES

What does it mean to make an analysis from a feminist perspective? *Is* there such a perspective or are there maybe several feminist perspectives? Have I chosen one of these perspectives or a combination of them?

In the next chapter I go through the main elements in six different feminist perspectives. I outline the conservative perspective with its emphasis on biological determinism, the liberal perspective with concepts such as equality and no discrimination. I go on to discuss the Marxist feminist perspective with its class analysis and a change in the ownership of the means of production. The radical feminist perspective is given somewhat more space than the other perspectives as it is mainly on this that I build my analysis. I here discuss the concept of power and make the radical feminist distinction between power over and power to, between power as dominance and power as competence, as pleasure and joy. Another important concept in radical feminist thinking is that the personal is political. Radical feminist thinkers do not readily accept statements about "the privacy of the home" without asking who profits by hiding some phenomena under the "private" label. The concept of patriarchy is also an important concept in radical feminist thinking, meaning not only the power of men over women but also the power of some men over other men, women, and children. The socialist feminist perspective tries to combine Marxist thinking with the concept of patriarchy developed by radical feminists. Gender and male dominance are as important to these feminist thinkers as is class analysis. Some of them insist that women have to seize the means of reproduction as the workers, according to Marxist theory, have to seize the means of production. Women should do away with the sexist institution of childbearing and child rearing. The women of color perspective is under development mostly by black American feminists who insist that race or color is just as important a variable as sex or class, and by Indian feminists who insist that not only race, class, and sex but also caste must be considered in an analysis.

The feminist perspective I am using for my analysis has most in common with the radical feminist perspective, but it also has elements from the socialist perspective, when the class background of mothers who encourage their sons to go to the military is analyzed, and from the women of color perspective, when the racist type of science taught is discussed. I also use concepts derived from more liberal feminist thinking, such as equality and no discrimination.

Looking at peace and peace education from any of the feminist perspectives I am using implies making an analysis from the viewpoint that women matter. It implies looking at the world from the underside, from the side of women, who as a group are oppressed by patriarchy on a macrolevel and experience male dominance at the meso- and microlevels. The oppression of women has great consequences for peace and peace education. There is the whole question of the meaning of peace for women. Can there be peace when women as a group are exploited by patriarchy, when individual women are raped and beaten by their husbands, are burnt and mutilated? What about a liberal human right like freedom of speech when women are made invisible, not asked to speak, or interrupted and silenced? Looking at peace education from a feminist perspective means making a scientific point out of the fact that education is gender-specific, that in our part of the world boys and girls are socialized differently according to the gender and the class they belong to. This gender-specific socialization cuts across classes and is seen by radical feminists as the most fundamental. To me it seems essential that the gender-specificity of all education and socialization be recognized and taken as a point of departure in a field like peace education. Through this education, both in school and at home, girls normally learn to be feminine in the sense of playing a secondary role, to wait on men, and to please them. Studies show that girls think more in terms of relationships than boys do, that they care more for other human beings, show more empathy, and think more about the human and social consequences of acts. These capabilities one would think would be important ingredients in any peace education. What does it mean for peace education that these capabilities are cultivated most in the gender that is most oppressed? Would it be better for the world if women, socialized the way they are today, were to rule the world or if men got the same socialization as women get today? Or is this socialization just a function of the oppressed state women are in?

The fact that gender-specific learnings have clear implications for education for peace or war, for sharing, cooperation, and caring, as well as for violence, exploitation, and dominance, has so far received little notice in the literature on peace education. This work is an attempt to enrich the field of peace education through insights developed in feminist thinking, by using feminist perspectives.

FEMINIST PERSPECTIVES ON PEACE

The exploration of the peace concept—what should be included in it, what excluded—is an intrinsic part of peace research itself. In Chapter 3 I show how the peace concept has been widened over the last decade from a more Eurocentric concept placing the main emphasis on nonwar to a more global concept including, also, the absence of indirect or so-called structural violence. As new groups have entered the peace research community there has also been a gradual conquering of the peace concept by these groups. This has made for a wider and in many ways more complete understanding of the phenomenon of peace in our world. The advantages of this are discussed, but at the same time, some of the problems of an unwieldy peace concept meaning almost everything are also scrutinized. An exploration of the peace concept from feminist perspectives is likely to widen the field even more, making it both more complete and more unwieldy.

Discussing various definitions of peace I have ended up by the normal distinction made by peace researchers between negative peace, defined as the absence of personal, physical, and direct violence, and positive peace, defined as the absence of indirect or structural violence. To have peace there must be both positive and negative peace. Within the category of structural violence I have grouped phenomena into two groups, those leading to a shorter life span and those leading to a less fulfilling life. I have introduced another distinction cutting across both the negative and the positive peace categories, that between unorganized and organized violence. These distinctions make for six cells; the cells are logically independent, but empirically relationships between them do exist. For each of the six cells research questions can be asked which are of particular relevance for women. And they can be asked from any of the six feminist perspectives outlined in the first chapter, making for thirty-six combinations. Many of these questions are raised in this chapter. Some tentative answers to a few of them are attempted on the basis of existing feminist research and reanalysis of existing studies. It is only when a vast number of studies pertaining to all the six cells, and studied from various feminist perspectives, are gathered that a complete feminist analysis of peace can be given. This chapter raises more research questions than it answers but tries to outline a direction for a continued exploration of the peace concept from a feminist perspective. I attempt to show through this chapter that the rewriting of peace research to include a feminist perspective will normally lead to a more complete picture, to better research. In such a way a feminist perspective may be perspective transforming. Some peace researchers may find it fruitful to use a feminist perspective on some parts of their research or to combine it with other perspectives. I am not advocating a purist position. My main point is that a feminist perspective is important in peace research. I use some space in this chapter to discuss the two groups of researchers most likely to build the bridge between feminist research and peace research, either feminist researchers, mostly women, entering the field of peace research or peace researchers, mostly men, entering feminist research. I discuss the likelihood that the latter group will receive a warmer reception than the former, but I am looking forward to fruitful meetings of the two groups.

At the end of Chapter 3 I make a primary analysis of the texts from the three UN Women's Decade conferences. By applying feminist perspectives to the analysis of these texts, I find that it is only in the final document from the Nairobi conference (in 1985) that a radical feminist perspective can be found. With the Nairobi document the feminist understanding of the necessity of including the absence of so-called private violence in the peace concept has been acknowledged by the UN and the intergovernmental community. It is the radical feminist perspective with its analysis of patriarchy which is reflected in this conceptual shift or "conquest" of the peace concept, as some may term it, but a conquest which I think will make for a better understanding of the whole field of peace research.

FEMINIST PERSPECTIVES ON PEACE EDUCATION

Chapters 4, 5, and 6 all deal with peace education. The first of them, Chapter 4, is a more theoretical chapter, discussing the concept of peace education. What is peace education, and why is it so controversial?

Peace education has mostly been spoken of as part of the *school* curriculum and as a subject—a controversial subject—to be introduced in schools. There have been various approaches to the definition of peace education within schools. A differentiation can be made between the structural approach, the dialectical approach, and the evolutionary approach. In Chapter 4 I make a reanalysis of these approaches from various feminist perspectives showing how various feminist perspectives will be well suited to analysis from the three respective approaches.

I make a primary analysis of the final texts from the three UN Women's Decade conferences to trace development of the peace education concepts in these documents. The concept of peace education is first introduced in the Nairobi document in 1985, although elements normally included in the concepts can also be found in the two earlier documents. There has, according to my analysis, been a shift of perspective from a liberal feminist perspective on peace education in earlier documents to a radical feminist one in the forward-looking strategies from Nairobi.

In Chapter 4 I also discuss the difficult question of analogies between different analytical levels and show that people who display aggressive conduct in interpersonal relationships do not necessarily display the same type of conduct when they are representatives of their nation and vice versa. I make a theoretical discussion of human aggression and attempt to show its relevance for peace education.

FEMINIST PERSPECTIVES ON PEACE EDUCATION IN THE NONFORMAL SECTOR

In Chapter 5 the aim is to throw light on the question: Do we educate girls for peace and boys for war? I look at the role of mothers, their attitudes, behavior, and wishes. I look at the role of fathers and their aspirations for their sons. I look at the toys given to girls and the toys given to boys. What do these toys teach? One of the main questions this chapter raises is why we are so afraid of influencing boys to develop traits of tenderness and caring, of nonviolence and sharing—traits normally associated with girls. And one of the main insights of the chapter is the urgency of legitimizing a new male role and a new male socialization.

In this chapter I also look at the role television plays in the lives of youngsters in the western world, what role models they get through this medium. What do the boys watch and how does it affect them? What do the girls watch? I also take a closer look at the most important leisure activity when it comes to the shaping of male identity, the institution of sports. This institution is analyzed from a radical feminist perspective. Does the institution reflect patriarchal thinking and power as dominance? Could it reflect a more feminist thinking with power as competence, pleasure, and joy?

The training girls get not to display aggressive conduct in microsettings is important in itself and more of it should be given to boys too, but that training, in itself, does not suffice to decrease the likelihood of wars' breaking out. It is also necessary to encourage critical thinking and disobedience to authorities who conduct politics likely to lead to war or to structural violence. So my new insight and question after having analyzed and reanalyzed a lot of empirical studies is that maybe we are not educating girls for peace and boys for war, but rather are educating both girls and boys for war—though boys to a higher degree and in a different way than girls. Merely giving the socialization now given to girls also to boys is not enough to make the world a safer place. I show that there is reason to believe that girls, even more than boys, are trained to be obedient and to take orders, to be loyal and not to question the philosophy of their superiors.

Through my analysis I have found that maybe one of the most important faculties to train in youngsters in order to make them equipped to work for a more just and peaceful world is critical thinking, which also implies civil courage and the capacity to stand up for one's rights and the rights of others. This may mean being disloyal to authority and disobeying orders. This is a training that contradicts the whole socialization of girls today. Girls are trained to be loyal, to obey, to take orders, which may be the reason they are regarded as good soldiers—they are easy to command. According to NATO officials girls take orders more easily than boys. Girls are trained for obedience from their earliest days, and they get this training in the family institution more than boys do, since the family is a patriarchal institution. Boys get their training in group loyalty and obedience to rules and superiors more through the institution of organized sports and through the military. These institutions seem to be more important in instilling patriarchal values in boys than the family is. For girls it may be the family and later the school that instill patriarchal values, such as obedience, in them, teaching them their secondary place.

Even though it is shown that girls are taught to care more than boys are, are trained to think more in relationships and about human and social consequences, this training does not necessarily mean that if women were in power there would be no wars. First of all the whole culture of caring rationality may be function of the oppressed state women are in. If women were no longer oppressed, the caring rationality might also disappear. And even if we suppose that women would still care more than men do and be more concerned about human relationships, this might mean only that women might wage wars for different reasons than men do—which seems to be indicated by one study I discuss.

Even if this is so, I still believe that it is in the socialization of girls that we have to look when we want to locate the seeds for the construction of a genuine peace education. And in this socialization it is the relational thinking of girls, their training to think in relationships and in human and social consequences, which gives the most promise. Girls are socialized to look after other human beings, to care and to think especially of children and their well-being. Girls are not given war toys, not trained to use weapons at any time in their lives. They are not encouraged to use physical violence as a legitimate way of solving conflicts, either at a micro- or a macro-level. But then I look at the oppressed position of women in patriarchy and how little choice they have when it comes to changing the education of their sons from their oppressed position, especially if they are also poor working-class women. I am using a socialist feminist analysis to understand why some working-class mothers wish for a military career for their sons, sons who would otherwise be without education and employment. It is difficult to blame these mothers and easy to shift the blame to capitalist and patriarchal structures which seem to decide their lives.

FEMINIST PERSPECTIVES ON PEACE EDUCATION IN THE FORMAL SECTOR

Chapter 6 starts with a report on a study of school students' attitudes toward peace and war, showing the greater peace-orientation of girls. I put forward some reflections on the fact that another study found that the most peace-oriented girls were those with the strongest self-concept. A strong self-concept is not the normal outcome of a typical feminine socialization. This finding may raise a new and important research question: Are the more peace-oriented the less sex-role stereotyped?

When analyzing peace education within the formal school setting I look both at the official curriculum and the more hidden curriculum. When it comes to the official curriculum two subjects have been chosen: history and science. What do youngsters learn in the history lessons about the use of violence in international disputes and about nonviolence? What do they learn about patriarchy and the role of women? Is patriarchy assumed and are women made invisible? And what about science? A feminist analysis of science finds it not only male-centered but also dominated by the views of an elite of white males experimenting on people from the third world (with nuclear testing) or women from the third world (contraceptives and some drugs). While an analysis from a liberal feminist perspective might lead to the conclusion that we must get more girls and women to go into science, analysis from a radical feminist perspective, as I am using here, leads to the conclusion that such a policy might have detrimental effects. It is more important to change the basic recipe of the pie than to get a larger share of a bad pie. More important to change science and technology than to have girls assimilate to it as it is. According to my analysis the hidden curriculum teaches obedience and loyalty to rules and to superiors, and this teaching is more pronounced for girls than boys; girls have to be more quiet, wait more, demand less. In co-educational classes they are taught to keep silent while the teachers and the boys in the class do the talking. The hidden curriculum of the school teaches a lesson in verticality and dominance, which is a core lesson in patriarchy, but which the solemn declarations in the official curriculum contradict. The hidden curriculum is often much stronger than the official one, especially since the first one is reinforced through a powerful system of grades and other sanctions. Through competitions and enforcement of rules children are taught to conform and obey.

An education for peace, I conclude, would be not merely an education giving girls more of a boy's education and boys more of a girl's education. It would be a different type of education, of socialization, for both boys and girls. It would entail the development of competence in nonviolent conflict solutions, in power-to and the doing-away with strong competition, power-over. It would mean girls' refusing to become feminine in the sense that femininity means the acceptance of playing a serving and secondary role, obeying husbands and other men having power over them. It would mean boys' refusing to become masculine when masculine means having power over other people, mostly women, being aggressive, and not showing emotions.

Having looked at peace education from a feminist perspective I find it important that definitions of peace education contain an understanding of the importance of doing away with rigid sex role socialization and the training into femininity or masculinity. Doing away with rigid sex role socialization is not just a woman's question. It is, equally, a male question, a task for humankind—an essential task for any peace education.

2

Feminist Perspectives

A FEMINIST PERSPECTIVE

The word *perspective* comes from the Latin word *perspectus*, which again derives from *perspicere*, meaning "look through, look into, see thoroughly, try out, investigate." The Swedish researcher Stig Lindholm defines a perspective as that which helps him to see aspects of reality (Lindholm, 1981, ch. 7). He quotes Susanne Langer (1958, p. 288), who claims that all thought processes start by seeing. And by seeing she does not necessarily mean looking through the eyes, but discovering phenomena through the powers of all the senses. A perspective can be simple, optical, or part of a paradigm or a whole world view.

We all apply various perspectives when we interpret reality around us. The perspectives help us make sense out of what we see and give direction and guidance to our focus. They also limit what we see, since when we focus on one part of reality, we have trouble seeing another. Our perspectives are built up from our values, beliefs, and assumptions, which may be more or less substantiated and well founded.

Researchers within any field view the world and their own research from a certain perspective which they—so it seems to me—very often do not bother to make explicit and even may not be aware of. Much research seems to have been conducted from a male perspective without the researchers' being aware of that fact. What to them has looked like gender neutrality may, through feminist analysis, be revealed as being male biased. As feminist researchers have made clear, this has been true for philosophy, psychology, law, economics, political science, history, education, science (see, for instance, Langland & Grove, 1981; Spender (ed.) 1981b; Spender, 1982). It should not surprise us at all that a research field which is composed of and cuts across several male-biased disciplines will also be male biased. I do not find it surprising that the male perspectives which are implicit in most research and which make up *all* academic disciplines will be multiplied in a multidisciplinary research field.

By this I am not saying that multidisciplinary studies, such as peace studies or ecological studies, are *more* male biased than other studies. I am merely stating that the multidisciplinarity in itself is no guarantee that the studies will include feminist understandings.

Through our early socialization processes men and women are trained to view the world differently. We are socialized into different perspectives on reality (see, for instance, Gilligan, 1982). To be able to view the world differently, a systematic change of perspective is necessary. Carol Gilligan finds, as many other feminists do (for instance, Brock-Utne, 1984; Deem, 1978; Spender, 1982), that women, more than men, are socialized in relational thinking, to think more about human relationships and the social consequences of actions.

Using a feminist perspective as an analytical tool—any feminist perspective—means insisting that women matter. The way women live, think, organize, matters. This is what one has to do systematically in women's studies. In the introduction to the book *A Feminist Perspective in the Academy*, Elizabeth Langland and Walter Grove (1981, p. 3) state: "The fact that our understanding of homo sapiens has incorporated the perspective of only half of the human race makes it clear that women's studies is not an additional knowledge merely to be tacked on to the curriculum. It is, instead, a body of knowledge that is perspective transforming and should therefore transform the existing curriculum from within and revise the common notion of what constitutes an "objective" or "normative perspective."

Since—as I see it—we are all taught through academic training to view the world through male eyes and are led to believe that the knowledge we have acquired is objective and gender neutral, it should not surprise us that most researchers, whether male or female, go on viewing the world through this implicit perspective. They have all been good students, excelling in male studies. But it is easier for female researchers to become critical of the implicit male perspective. It is easier for them to feel an uneasiness about the fact that women's experiences are made invisible in the curricula.

Because of earlier socialization, inspiration from the women's movement, and feminist consciousness raising, women researchers are more likely than their male colleagues to enter women's studies and read research written from a feminist perspective. But certainly men *can* hold a feminist perspective. Certainly the Canadian researcher Alan Silverman (1986) as well as the British researcher, mathematical physicist Brian Easlea (1981, 1983), are good examples of this. So is the historian Carl Degler (1981), who in his essay "What the Women's Movement Has Done to American History" writes that he has found his scholarship enriched by the understanding and insights that have emerged as historians have paid increasing attention to women.

SEVERAL FEMINIST PERSPECTIVES

So far I have used the words "feminist perspective" rather synonymously with "insight gained through women's studies." This is the way those words are used, for instance, in *A Feminist Perspective in the Academy* (Langland and Grove, eds., 1981). But within women's studies analysis is done from *several* feminist perspectives. What Etzioni (1967, p. 807) held to be true for peace research—the absence of a unified grand theory and the existence instead of *several* perspectives for analysis—seems to be true for feminist research now.

The mere seniority of the peace research field over feminist research has led to more of a selection process where some early perspectives in peace research have vanished while others have passed the test of time as more fruitful for theory formation and empirical research. This is likely to happen also with feminist research, especially feminist peace research, which is such a new area. The reasons that several perspectives have been and are used within both feminist research and peace research are probably the same: the interdisciplinarity and value orientation of the two research fields, coupled with their marginality and freshness and the urgency of actions in the fields under study. Life is short, but research is long.

Standard textbooks on feminist theory frequently operate with five or six feminist perspectives, sometimes called frameworks or theoretical accounts. Alison Jaggar and Paula Rothenberg (1984) make a distinction between six feminist frameworks:

1. *Conservatism,* in which women's oppression is looked at as biologically determined. (This is a framework which radical feminists including myself would not call feminist even though some biological determinists like, for example, Laurel Holliday want changes, sometimes even drastic changes, in the power distribution between women and men.)
2. *Liberalism,* in which women's oppression is looked at as unfair discrimination.
3. *Traditional Marxism,* in which women's oppression is seen as a result of the class system.
4. *Radical feminism,* in which women's oppression is seen as the most fundamental oppression.
5. *Socialist feminism,* which has grown out of traditional Marxism and sees an inseparability of gender and class oppression.

6. *Feminism and women of color,* in which the inseparability of gender, class, and race oppression is stressed.

Indian feminist researchers might add a seventh perspective, taking caste as another dividing category.

The Conservative Perspective

The conservative perspective has been applied by researchers like Sigmund Freud (1964, originally 1933) and by psycho- and sociobiologists like Lionel Tiger and Robin Fox (1971). Analysis from this perspective tries to explain the differences in behavior between women and men in terms of innate biological characteristics. Often analogies are drawn from the lives of animals showing the greater aggressiveness in most male animals. The most important role for a woman is believed to be the one of mother and nurturer. This role, or the lack of it (the "barren" woman), guides all her thoughts and actions. Sigmund Freud (op. cit.) in his writings on femininity tends to see only that woman as truly feminine whose highest wish is a baby. He sees the girl's wish for a baby develop already in her doll play; in fact, that is the whole reason, as he sees it, for the doll play by girls: they are already wishing for a baby. The real woman then tries to make the surroundings as safe and good for her offspring as possible. First she tries to find a mate who will provide her offspring and herself with the best possible surroundings.

Edward Wilson (1978), writing from the same perspective and drawing parallels between humans and other animals, holds that in all species that rear young, it is important for the females to select males who are more likely to stay with them after insemination and provide them with the necessities of life. He finds it quite logical that males are characteristically aggressive, especially toward one another, and that in most species assertiveness is the most profitable male strategy. In order to make for the best composition of genes it will pay males to be aggressive, hasty, fickle, and undiscriminating so that they can fertilize females. Likewise it is more profitable, according to him, for females to be coy and to hold back until they can identify those males with the best genes.

A female psychobiologist, Laurel Holliday (1978), who regards herself as a feminist (I do not agree) reasons along with the male scholars in the field and finds that males generally, especially human males, are biologically determined to be more aggressive. She looks at the composition of the right and the left parts of the brain in males and females, at hormone levels and chromosomes, and concludes that males are more aggressive by nature. But, unlike other psychobiologists, she does not use her findings only to try to explain why we find most men in governing and dominant positions and women as caretakers, worrying and caring for their offspring. She tries to find biological means to make men less aggressive by administering drugs to them as babies or marijuana later or by limiting the number of males on earth. The last chapter in her book gives advice on how to conceive only daughters—a logical conclusion if men are that violent by nature.

Another conclusion, which she does not draw but which might be just as logical if one adheres to a biological deterministic framework, would be to outlaw men from all governing and deciding positions, since we cannot have our world ruled by such aggressive beings.

It is not difficult to find traces of thoughts stemming from this perspective in the peace debates and in women's work for peace. Analysis from this perspective may lead to sexist conclusions—biased in favor of men in most cases but, as is demonstrated in Holliday's writings, which could be biased in favor of women. This perspective is mostly used to explain and defend the existing oppression of women by men and the status quo. It does not lend itself easily to the work for change unless one plays with the type of drastic changes Laurel Holliday suggests. But limiting the number of male children in the world I see as being just as sexist as limiting the number of females by selective gestation techniques, a practice feminists condemn.

But it is not only because of the sexist bias that I see this perspective as bearing little fruit. A perspective may lead to conclusions one does not like and still be fruitful. My main objection has to do with the fact that in an analysis from a biological determinist perspective, biological and genetic factors are looked at as extremely decisive. Some researchers using this perspective indeed leave no space for cultural influences whatsoever. I see cultural attitudes and norms as quite decisive in creating an atmosphere leading to war or to the halting of the arms race (Brock-Utne, 1988a). In fact such a belief is the cornerstone on which this work rests.

Biological determinists who, like Laurel Holliday, want to see drastic changes in the way our world is governed point at ways to bring about changes in the genetic makeup of people. The means they propose are of a biological nature, not of an educational or cultural nature such as the ones I would propose.

The Liberal Perspective

The roots of *liberal* feminism are first traced to the work of Mary Wollstonecraft (1759–1797). Her essay, *A Vindication of the Rights of Women,* first published in London in 1779, was so provocative that editions of it quickly appeared in Dublin, Paris, and New York. Further development of liberal feminism was done by Harriet Taylor Mill (1807–1858) and her collaborator John Stuart Mill (1806–1873). "On The Subjection of Women," first published in 1851, was the philosophical inspiration for the British suffrage movement. The liberal feminists are concerned with the unfair discrimination of women, with doing away with discrimination, with equality and the equal rights of women.

In John Stuart Mill's "On the Subjection of Women" (Mill, 1979, originally 1851, and which he really wrote together with Harriet Taylor Mill), he claims that the principle which regulates the existing social relations between the two sexes—the legal subordination of one sex to the other—is wrong in itself and one of the chief hindrances to human improvement, and that it ought to be replaced by a principle of perfect equality admitting no power or privilege on the one side, nor disability on the other.

Any grouping of writings placing them under a certain perspective or framework is bound to be somewhat inadequate. In Mill's writings there are passages which would qualify him to be grouped among the radical feminists as his analysis of patriarchy as the root of oppression of women is quite clear. He finds that all causes, social and natural, combine to make it unlikely that women should be collectively rebellious to the power of men. They are so far in a position different from all other subject classes that their masters require something more from them than actual service.

Men do not want solely the obedience of women, they want their sentiments. He claims that all men desire a woman to be not a *forced* slave, but a *willing* one. Men have therefore put everything in practice to enslave the minds of women.

> The masters of women wanted more than simple obedience, and they turned the whole force of education to effect their purpose. All women are brought up from their very earliest years in the belief that their ideal character is the very opposite to that of men: not self-will, and government by self-control, but submission and yielding to the control of others. (Here taken from Mill, 1970, p. 125.)

The reason that it may be justified to categorize Mill under liberal feminism, even though he includes an analysis of patriarchy, is the fact that he sees liberation from oppression for women as a question of women being able to occupy the same positions as men and being equal to men. Likewise Shere Hite (1976) has been placed in this tradition by Jaggar and Rothenberg (1984) for her work on redefining sex where she sees sexual liberation for women as being able to have as many sexual partners as men have and look at men as sex objects the way men look at women. (Many women belonging to liberal political parties will probably object to the categorization of Hite in the liberal tradition and especially object that the reason cited above should qualify for that categorization.)

People who call themselves liberal vary tremendously in political outlooks. Among them one finds both people adhering to a Manchester ideology of political liberalism and more radical liberals with a social and ecological outlook. Most liberals, especially the traditional ones, can be distinguished from other ideologists, for instance socialist or Marxist ones, by the way they define the concept "equality." To them that concept means "equality of opportunity." They find that when all privileges and discriminatory practices of a legal, ideological, or market economical kind are done away with, there is equality. The equality of opportunity doctrine helps to sort the gifted from the ungifted. The fact that the gifted are, through this sorting process, given new privileges and rewards does not seem to bother liberals as long as the initial position, the starting line, is the same for everybody. They do not question the basic rules of the game, which we could also call the recipe for the pie, the competitive system creating winners and losers; nor do they question the end result of the race. Socialists, on the other hand, look more at the results of equality of opportunity. They may look at equality as *equity*, meaning that people should receive rewards in proportion to the efforts they make or be given *equal rewards* no matter the efforts or type of work done, or—in keeping with traditional Marxism—as rewards distributed according to needs.

Jaggar and Rothenberg (1984) see big women's organizations like NOW (National Organization of Women) in the United States as adhering to a liberal feminist ideology. I would claim that state councils like the Norwegian Council for Equality may also be run by a liberal way of thinking. Analysis from this perspective may, for instance, lead to the conclusion that women should enter the military. This is seen as a matter of equality.

The question, Equal to do what?, is not asked. My main criticism of a liberal perspective—which may have been very important at one time—is that it does not carry the analysis far enough. It can be used as a partial analysis to look at discriminatory practices, but as the *only* perspective it misses more fundamental points. I am here criticizing the liberal perspective not only the way socialists and Marxists do, pointing to the fact that researchers using the liberal perspective tend to define equality as equal chances to obtain rewards not taking into consideration the final distribution of rewards. I am also criticizing the liberal perspective from a radical feminist stand, questioning the rewards themselves. Applying a liberal feminist perspective to reality, one is concerned with the opportunity women and men have to compete equally for a share of the pie, but not with the distribution of the pie and not with, what to me is more important, the basic recipe that the pie is made from.

The Marxist Perspective

The traditional *Marxist* perspective subscribes to Marxist analysis of capitalism and Engels' (1942) classic explanation of the origins of women's oppression. It came about through the development of a class society, founded upon the family, private property, and the state. Traditional Marxism sees women's oppression as a reflection of the more fundamental form of oppression by class. Thus, sexism is a secondary phenomenon and, presumably, will disappear with a revolution in class relations. It is on this point that socialist and radical feminists depart from classical Marxist feminists, because they would argue that the oppression of women itself is fundamental (Jaggar & Struhl, 1978). By fundamental I mean the type of relationship, here oppression, on which other types of relationships/oppression are based. Because class relationships are seen as fundamental or primary, gender relationships are secondary. By fundamental I do not mean to make a normative statement saying that sexual oppression is worse than class oppression or that *all* women are more oppressed than *all* men.

Even though Engels wrote that "the first class opposition that appears in history coincides with the development of the antagonism between man and woman in monogamous marriage, and the first class oppression coincides with that of the female sex by the male" (Engels, here from 1970, p. 121), he does not take this insight further and does not combine an analysis of class oppression with an analysis of the oppression of women by males. A more recent Marxist theorist, Evelyn Reed (1970, pp. 64–76), holds that any analysis of women's oppression is false if it leads to the false conclusion that it is not the capitalist system but men who are the prime enemy of women. Evelyn Reed claims that it requires a class struggle—of all the oppressed, male and female alike—to consummate women's liberation along with the liberation of all the oppressed masses. To me it seems that she overlooks the fact that within all oppressed groups there are males *and* females and in most cases the woman is more oppressed than the man. This does not mean that *all* women are more oppressed than *all* men. On the contrary, women belonging to the higher socioeconomic classes live in better material wealth than men coming from lower economic classes; their influence may also be higher. My point here is the relative inferiority of women, how women are kept in a position inferior to their spouses and to the males of their respective class or group. Interesting research illuminating this point has been done by the Norwegian psychologist Hanne Haavind (1982) showing how marriages function to keep women in place—that means somewhat under their men. A woman in an academic career may, for instance, earn quite a bit more than many men, but usually *not* more than her *own* husband.

To me a Marxist perspective, if it is not supplemented by other perspectives, will make for an incomplete analysis for several reasons. Marx and Engels divide work into production and reproduction and place reproduction solely within the family. In their analysis they subordinate reproduction and the family to economic systems of production. The use of the words production and reproduction seems to imply the importance of production over reproduction. There is certainly a male bias in naming what women do—for instance, producing babies—as reproduction and naming what men do—for instance, manufacturing weapons—as production, no matter how useless the products are.

Categories such as unpaid and paid work or useful and useless products are extremely important to both feminist and peace scholars. These categories can also be found in Marxist thinking, but here they mean something else. When a Marxist talks about unpaid work he is talking about the profit the capitalist makes on the products. The profit stems from the fact that the capitalist uses less money to produce something than he gets when the product is sold. Some of the profit he makes by paying low wages to the workers. In this sense one can say that part of the work in the productive sector is unpaid. But when Marxists talk about unpaid work they are normally not thinking about unpaid housework, work in the so-called private reproductive sector. It is through this type of unpaid work that many *women* are exploited all over the world. It is an exploitation of a labor force that is almost entirely female. This exploitation is not much of an issue in classical Marxism.

Marxists make a distinction between goods that are used and goods having solely a trading value. But the usefulness lies in the fact that the goods are wanted by groups of consumers. In the classical Marxist discussion there is no discussion of what would be useful to have to create a better society. For instance, weapons are useful for Marxists if there is a demand for them, that is, if they can be sold. Then they are produced. Feminist scholars or peace scholars will use the word useful differently and will be asking questions such as: For what is this product useful? Is it meant to improve living conditions and health or to destroy life?

An analysis from a classical Marxist perspective will lead us to a discussion of who should own the pie—the state or private enterprise? To be fair to Marxists we must admit that they see formal ownership only as a necessary step for the workers to gain the real control of production. And when the workers have gained this control they can use it to produce goods, not primarily to make profits, but because there is a need for them. But classical Marxists lack a theory of basic needs. What do people really need? What is needed to make someone happy? How are false needs created? These basic questions are asked by feminists but are of little importance in classical Marxism. Just as with a liberal perspective, the Marxist perspective does not lend itself easily to a discussion of the basic recipe.

Both radical feminism, Marxist feminism, and socialist feminism locate the cause of sexism in the economic and political institutions. Both radical feminism and socialist feminism pose a challenge to the very basis of our social existence by suggesting that revolutionary changes need to be made in the systems of *both* capitalism and patriarchy.

The Radical Feminist Perspective

The radical feminist perspective asks us to look at the structure of consciousness—not just as it is reproduced through sex roles but specifically as it reflects the patriarchal organization of society. Much of the strategy of radical feminist programs for change has been to redefine social relations by creating a woman-centered culture. Radical feminists emphasize the positive capacities of women by focusing on the creative dimensions of women's lives, specifically because women's culture and experience are seen as fundamental alternatives to patriarchal institutions and ways of thinking.

Of all the perspectives mentioned here, radical feminism is to my mind the one most concerned with changing the basic recipe of the pie, with analyzing the ingredients going into it and not just distributing it differently.

The character Ada in one of Arnold Wesker's plays looks at the world from a radical feminist perspective when she accuses her fellow male workers of not questioning the *values* of our society but just wanting to own the values themselves. The male workers view the fact that a man is serving the same monotonous machine eight hours a day, day in and day out, as a crime, only because the man does not *own* the machine. But she asks them what is the point of owning a machine. A discussion of this type can also be found in writings by some Marxist thinkers, especially by Kolakowski (1966), who writes about the alienation of workers in countries where the state owns the means of production.

The most thorough outline and discussion of the theory of radical feminism that has been written so far is the voluminous book (740 pages) by Marilyn French (1986) called *Beyond Power* and with the subtitle: *On Women, Men and Morals*. The book summarizes and discusses the radical feminist thinking that has developed, mostly over the last 15 years, though some works date back earlier. Many believe that her book will have the same impact on feminist thinking as *das Kapital* by Karl Marx had on Marxist thinking.

To Marilyn French, as to many feminists, "feminism" is synonymous with what I have here called "*radical* feminism," and "feminist thinking" or a "feminist perspective" means "*radical* feminist thinking" or a "*radical* feminist perspective" (1986, p. 477). She writes about those who believe they consider women equal to men but see women as fettered by their traditional socialization and by the expectations of the larger world. These people, she believes, see women as large children who have talent and energy, but who need training in male modes, male language, and an area of expertise in order to "fit in" in the male world. She refers to a philosopher who has commented that women are "not yet ready" for top government posts. This she sees not only as patronizing, but also as a lack of comprehension of feminism.

> For although feminists do indeed want women to become part of the structure, participants in public institutions, although they want access for women to decision-making posts, and a voice in how society is managed, *they do not want women to assimilate to society as it presently exists but to change it.* Feminism is not yet one more of a series of political movements demanding for their adherents access to existing structures and their rewards. . . . Feminism *is* a political movement demanding access to the rewards and responsibilities of

> the "male" world, but it is more—it is a revolutionary moral movement, intending to use political power to transform society, to "feminize" it. For such a movement assimilation is death. (French, 1986, p. 478)

She then outlines what I have called "changing the recipe of the pie." And I agree with her that if women who enter higher positions behave and think like men, they will not be able to change society. In that sense she is right that assimilation means the co-option of feminism, even its death. But staying *outside* the existing power structures will also mean death for feminism, as far as I can see it. So the integration of women into these structures should not be deplored, but looked at as a *necessary* first step.

The women who form almost 50 percent of the Norwegian government hopefully have a much greater chance of influencing Norwegian policy in a feminist direction than they would have had, had they not been in the leading political positions in the country. How much they are able to govern the male-dominated ministries they are running, as well as the rest of the government, remains to be seen. As is well-known also for male ministers, formal power positions are not always real power positions. It may be difficult for a new head at the top to move strong and well-established bureaucracies in other directions than they are used to going, even to change usual procedures. (They started with some extra built-in handicaps by having been given the "softer" ministries such as consumer affairs, social affairs, education, and so forth, and not the "harder" ones such as finance, industry, defense, and foreign affairs. Women seem to be expected to work in the repair and reproductive sectors even as ministers. But these ministries are important and dispose of large sums of money.)

Of the many fruitful concepts and ideas discussed in Marilyn French's great work we shall here concentrate on two because they are relevant to this particular study. The first is the concept of *power*, the second the idea that the personal is political—and what follows from that—the idea that ends and means should be closely connected.

The concept of *power* which has caused a lot of debate among political scientists has also troubled many feminist thinkers. To be able to change structures, we must have power—woman power. But if women, too, strive for power, do they have any guarantee that they will not change on their road to power or that they will use their power in any other way than men do? Will not power itself corrupt any human being, whether male or female? Marilyn French finds that the result of the many revolutions against various patriarchal forms that have taken place over the past three or four thousand years is only the succession of one oppressive structure by another oppressive structure.

"This is inevitable", she claims, "because, regardless of the initial ideas and ideals of rebellious groups, they come to worship power, only their greater power can bring them victory over an enemy. But each victory has increased human oppression" (French, 1986, p. 479).

I agree with her basic line of argument here, although I find that her last sentence contains a too-sweeping generalization which also, in some cases, is false. Examples can be found in which the overthrow of one government has decreased human oppression for the great masses (for instance, the overthrow of Hitler and his Nazi government and the Russian revolution of 1917). But it seems like those who get to power through military force also rely on military force to stay in power.

And maybe the whole way we elect political leaders to powerful positions in our democracy assures us that we will get people who enjoy power over other people and that "the meek will not inherit the earth." Hanna Newcombe (1986) discusses this in a recent paper. She does not think that women will be much different from men if they are elected the same way men are. We must look at other ways to elect our leaders, she claims, and analyzes ways used by some Indian tribes and by the Bahai faith.

Radical feminist thinkers have tried to deal with the concept of power by pointing out that there really are two separate kinds of power: the normal male-defined power concept—*power as dominance*—and a female-defined power concept—power as *competence*; the first is a *power over*, the other a *power to* (see, for instance, Eisler & Loye, 1986, with further references to Jean Baker Miller's works; see also Vellacott, 1982). Already Talcott Parsons (1964), who by no stretch of the imagination can be labeled a feminist, made a distinction between *power over* somebody—a relation—and *power to* be able to get something done. The first type of power often leads to a zero-sum game: the more power A gets over B, the less power B gets over A. The second type of power deals more with the power or the capacity of a given society to fulfill the collective aims of that society. Feminist thinkers see power-as-dominance as inextricably linked to violence; indeed the potential for physical, economic, and psychological violence is, according to Vellacott (1982, p. 32), "almost the traditional definition of power." "Mainstream peace research has, I think, tended to take that definition for granted. Berenice Carroll (1972) in her critique of the "cult of power" in peace research addresses the necessity and difficulty of redefining power:

> Breaking out of the mental straightjacket of the cult of power is one of the most difficult intellectual tasks one can set for oneself today. To think of power as *competence*, rather than as *dominance*, and to explore the implications of that shift, to shake off the preoccupations with the powerful and look for the power and the competence in the allegedly "powerless," to free oneself from the confines of living and thinking in the value universe of the topdogs—these are remarkably painful undertakings. (Carroll, 1972, p. 604)

Analyzing Berenice Carroll's critique of the "cult of power" I agree with her that we need a study of the competence in the allegedly "powerless." Gene Sharp (1980) in his book on *Social Power and Political Freedom* makes much the same point. He maintains that all rulers are dependent for their positions and political powers upon the obedience, submission, and cooperation of their subjects. By stressing this point he suggests that the ruler's power is not monolithic or permanent, but is instead always based on an intricate and fragile structure of human and institutional relationships (Sharp, 1980, p. 25). The reason for the fragility of the power of the ruler is that the allegedly powerless may unite against him.

We need more studies of the powers which have come and could come from normal people, from grass-root movements working through nonviolent means. Yet at the same time there is also a need for studies of the power used by ruling persons or groups.

It can be argued that the traditional power concept—power as dominance—is ultimately an expression of powerlessness (Rubin, 1981; Stiehm, 1982; Vellacott, 1982). This is correct insofar as the traditional power concept includes the use of physical violence or the threat of such use in order for one party to get his will through. Research on violence against women supports this view (Roberts, 1984). It may be absurd to see a rapist/batterer as powerless. Yet many violent men may be looked at as emotionally crippled, pathetic, and incompetent human beings. If power is competence, they have little. When a state, a regime, or a person has to build his power on violence, this may be seen as a symptom of a weak normative power base. Power based on violence can ultimately be seen as an expression of resourcelessness. It can be seen as a separation from the source of life, creation, joy, from the human spirit and cooperation.

Marilyn French takes this whole argument a step further by substituting the whole concept of *power* with the concept of *pleasure*. Her only reference to the feminist discussion of power, which she does not make explicit, is when she says that it is frequently difficult to distinguish between power-to and power-over, since the latter is often seen as a means to the former. She takes up the power discussion among radical feminist thinkers by suggesting that: "*Power-to* primarily increases *pleasure,* and power-over primarily increases *pain*" (French, 1986, p. 478).

Marilyn French sees the only true revolution against patriarchy as one which removes the idea of power from its central position and replaces it with the idea of *pleasure*.

> Despite the contempt in which this quality has been held for several millennia, pleasure, felicity—in its largest and deepest sense—is actually the highest human good . . . To restore pleasure to centrality, requires restoring the body, and therefore nature, to value. The restoration of *body* and *nature* to value would preclude the treatment of both bodies and nature that pervades our world—the torture and deprivation of the one, the erosion and pollution of the other.
>
> Cooperation with nature would replace exploitation of it, which is the model for other forms of exploitation, exploitation of any sort would become illegitimate. Lacking transcendent goals, we would have no reason to sacrifice

> well-being, harmony, sharing, cooperation and pleasure to symbolic superiority, the very notion of superiority of one kind over another would disappear, although differences among kind would remain. (French, 1986, pp. 479–480)

But the pleasure concept may give rise to other analytical problems which Marilyn French does not discuss. Is pleasure a subjective category or a more objective category built on some norms and ideals? If pleasure is taken as a subjective category, anything that gives *me* pleasure *is* pleasure. Such a view, which it is rather obvious that Marilyn French does *not* hold since she is so concerned with the sad way in which nature is exploited, could mean that car racing, for instance, should be encouraged since it gives some people pleasure. Our consumer society with smart advertising creates demands for an artificially produced and false pleasure. Though this point is not discussed much by Marilyn French, she makes it clear that there must be some norms for true pleasure. She talks about pleasure "in its largest and deepest sense." What this is may need further elaboration and discussion.

Marilyn French says little about how one should go about substituting power with pleasure, but she stresses that the feminist movement is not aimed at overthrow of any particular government or structure, but rather at the displacement of one way of *thinking* with another.

"This means that the tools of feminism are naturally *non-violent*: it moves and will continue to move by providing an alternative to the cul-de-sacs of patriarchy" (French, 1986, p. 480). With this I can agree as long as she defines nonviolent as nonuse of *physical* violence (which does not preclude the use of negative sanctions like strikes, boycotts, sit-downs, and so forth), but the great challenge remains: Even if we get nonfeminist men and women to read feminist writings (which they mostly do not), how do we have any guarantees that this reading will change their own writings, let alone their thinking and actions? You can lead the horse to water, you may even make him thirsty, but you cannot make him drink.

The idea that *the personal is political*, which is a central idea in radical feminist thinking, is also adhered to by Marilyn French and discussed in her last work. I shall spend some time on that idea here since it is important for my later definitional work on the peace concept. French (1986, p. 477) puts it this way: "feminists believe the personal is the political—that is, that the value structure of a culture is identical in both public and private areas, that what happens in the bedrooms has everything to do with what happens in the boardroom, and vice versa, and that at present the same sex is in control in both places."

Proclaiming to adhere to some values in one setting and behaving according to other values in another setting is contrary to feminist ideology.

Marilyn French puts it this way: "Such a split between pronounced value and actual value, between what is said and what is done, is not acceptable to feminists" (French, 1986, p. 477). She scorns patriarchal language which calls lethal weapons "peacekeepers" and an invading force backed by elite monied interests, "freedom fighters." Radical feminism is in a state which French calls "blessed" because its ends and its means are identical.

Marilyn French here uses the idea that the personal is political in two different ways, both as a statement and as a norm. In the first case she does not make a normative judgment. She just claims that this is so whether we like it or not. This she does when she claims that most personal questions have larger political implications or are manifestations of a political power structure in the society at large, as in the example with the bedroom and the boardroom. In that case it is a fact that the same sex is in control in both places, a fact we do not like. Maybe it would be okay that men are in control in the bedroom if women were in control in the boardroom? Or rather, the control should be evenly divided in both places. On the other hand, Marilyn French also looks at the idea that the personal is political as a normative statement. This she does when she claims that a split between pronounced value and actual value is not acceptable to feminists. She means to say that such a split *ought* not to be acceptable and that it is not enough to say nice things if they are not followed up in actual practice. A man who claims to be a co-feminist, for instance, has not deserved that label if he just *preaches* feminism while he at the same time exploits his wife, lets her take care of the children and do the housework. When French holds that the ends and the means of radical feminism are identical, I see this as a normative statement claiming that they *should* be identical, that feminists are striving to make them identical.

The split French talks about between public and private areas is a split typical of western capitalist societies over the last four to five hundred years. Sexual oppression existed long before such a split became common and may even be of a graver kind in societies where the split between the private and the public hardly exists. To many people in our societies privacy is a cherished value. We want to keep some things for ourselves and do not want everything we do to be a public matter. To many, the thought that Big Brother sees everything seems to be a nightmare. But feminists have started to question the advantages of privacy, especially privacy of the home. What goes on under the cover of privacy? To whom is this privacy an advantage? Maybe we should also ask the question: Is there a type of privacy feminists would adhere to?

Since the radical feminist perspective is here taken to be the most fundamental of the feminist perspectives, it has also been the most thought-stimulating and provocative perspective, causing the most debate and research from feminist scholars over the past ten years. Research has been carried out and continues to be carried out on the old peaceful matriarchies (for instance, Davis, 1971). Did they exist or did they not exist? Were they truly peaceful?

Norwegian feminist researchers have organized whole seminars around concepts like women's culture. There is no doubt that that concept has had an important political function within the feminist movement. It gave women something to be proud of and served much the same function that the slogan "black is beautiful" did for black people. But is it also meaningful as an analytical tool? Is women's culture just a function of the oppressed conditions women live under in patriarchy and will the culture then cease to exist when and if the oppression of women ends? I will return to these questions later on (for a discussion of the analytical use of this concept see Ås, 1975, 1981; Haukaa, 1982a; and issue no. 1/80 of the feminist academic journal *Kjerringråd*). Radical feminists coin new women-centered words and try to find "woman-made solutions to man-made problems." We find that also new words and concepts are needed in order to come up with solutions to old problems.

The concept and analysis of *patriarchy* is essential to radical feminism (see, for instance, Daly, 1979; French, 1986; Janssen-Jurreit, 1976). Patriarchy is a form of social organization founded on the force-based ranking of the male half of humanity over the female half. Patriarchy has to do with *power-over* other people, mostly power to control women and nature. "Patriarchy can be defined as a set of social relations between men, which have a material base, and which, though hierarchical, establish or create interdependence and solidarity among men that enable them to dominate women" (Hartmann, 1984, p. 177).

Though patriarchy is hierarchical and men of different classes, races, or ethnic groups have different places in the patriarchy, they are united in their shared relationship of dominance over their women, and, further, they are dependent on each other to maintain that domination. In the hierarchy of patriarchy, most men, whatever their rank in the patriarchy, are bought off by being able to control at least some women. It is important to note that patriarchy has to do *both* with a hierarchical structure—where some men rule over other men as well as over women, children, nature—*and* with solidarity between men in their domination of women.

The theory of patriarchy builds on the main assumption that the material base upon which patriarchy rests lies most fundamentally in men's control over women's labor power. Men maintain this control by excluding women from access to some essential productive resources (in capitalist societies, for example, jobs that pay living wages) and by installing in women the belief that they should do unpaid housework "for love."

Men also keep their control by restricting women's sexuality. The particular ways in which men control women's access to important economic resources and restrict their sexuality vary enormously, both from society to society, from subgroup to subgroup, and across time.

Jessie Bernard (1981) describes how in patriarchal systems there are two separate and not equal worlds: the main or man's world and a subsidiary, also male-controlled, female world. These worlds have in the course of time developed two different sets of governing values, which Bernard terms the "male ethos" of competition and power, and the "female ethos" of love and duty. In today's world, Bernard notes, "the power-driven male, operating on a never ending one-upmanship basis, who has to be victorious over all others no matter what, may be analogous to the stag with maladaptive horns" (Bernard, 1981, p. 538). Patriarchy means, she says, male dominance of women in the work place as well as at home.

Since women, according to UN statistics, are oppressed everywhere, in all classes though in different ways and to different degrees, we may look at this oppression as the most fundamental oppression there is. Some women who are eager not to alienate men as potential supporters of women claim that there ought to be an alliance of all "outsiders"—not just women, but also children, the unemployed, blacks, working classes, and so forth (see, for instance, Eglin, 1982). This position overlooks the fact that all the other groups mentioned also include women: girls, unemployed women, black women, working-class women—and in each of the instances mentioned the women in the named group are worse off than the men. They are exploited and oppressed by those they are asked to form an alliance with. The Australian researcher Robin Burns (1982) puts it this way:

> Women not only have to overcome the structural barriers that other marginalised or oppressed groups face, including the language, consciousness and sense of identity, which they have accepted from the wider society in exchange for alternative rewards, but to face the consequences of male frustration, especially oppressed men whose only way to maintain some sense of worth is through keeping women out or even lower.

The fact that one can find more expressed racism and sexism among oppressed men should not surprise us. When a man has a low ranking on most status-giving factors like position, wealth, education, housing, his only sense of worth will be built on his ascribed status: that he is white, a man, and so forth. Also, the white men who are most oppressed by the hierarchy of patriarchy are the ones who can only get jobs that black men or women might be even more likely to get because they can be given less pay. So these men experience both black men and white lower-class women as real threats. It is easier to hold a liberal and nondiscriminatory attitude to other groups when these groups cannot threaten one's own position.

A recent study by Riane Eisler and David Loye (1986) indicates that there are structural correlations between male dominance, a generally hierarchic and authoritarian social organization, and a high degree of institutionalized social violence, including warfare. Likewise, William Eckhardt (1980) found the militarist to be an emotionally blunt personality with high scores on scales like misanthrophy, lack of empathy with others, social irresponsibility, and egoism. Eisler and Loye have shown that the more rigidly male dominated a society is, the more heavily it will rely on violence in both interpersonal and intergroup relations. They show this through historical studies. A dramatic modern example is Nazi Germany, where the reimposition of rigid male dominance went hand in hand with the militarization that culminated in World War II.

From a radical feminist perspective the oppression of women lies in *cultural systems* that create *male solidarity*, not simply in systems of economic production. As the feminist anthropologist Gayle Rubin (1975, p. 163) has written, "No analysis of the reproduction of labour can explain footbinding, chastity belts, or any of the incredible array of Byzantine, fetishized indignities, let alone the more ordinary ones, which have been inflicted upon women in various times and places." It can be argued that most of the atrocities mentioned by Rubin have been inflicted upon women from the higher socioeconomic classes. Through these customs women from the higher classes have been kept away from the possibility of threatening the men of their own class or forming a solidarity with women and men from lower classes. But examples of other sexist customs which cut across the class barriers could be given like the infibulation practices in great parts of Africa. In an analysis of the usefulness of various feminist perspectives as analytical instruments Margaret Andersen (1983, p. 284) finds that the radical feminist perspective is best able to explain male violence against women and the many cultural practices designed to control female sexuality and birth giving.

I see insights developed through the use of a radical feminist perspective as essential in an analysis of peace and peace education. The discussion of power (personal and political) as well as the discussion of the concept of patriarchy seems to me to be necessary in an analysis of peace and peace education from a feminist perspective. I would, however, like to combine these insights with thoughts more prominent in the socialist feminist perspective.

The Socialist Feminist Perspective

The socialist feminist perspective builds on the Marxist premise that the economic mode of production is the defining factor of social organization, but departs from Marx and Engels when they assume that the liberation of women will occur automatically with the transition from capitalism to socialism. Socialist feminists ask embarrassing questions such as: Why does women's oppression continue even in socialist societies and predate the capitalist mode of production? And where, in advanced capitalist societies, do women fit into the Marxist definition of class?

Marxist theory can explain women's usefulness to capitalism, the necessity in a capitalist economy of having a group of people who can be made to enter the labor market and to withdraw from it according to fluctuations in the economy. But Marxist theory does not explain why this group of people consists mostly of women. The Marxist analysis of what in Marxist terminology is called "the reproduction of labor power" does not explain why it is women, rather than men, who do domestic work in the home.

One of the first theorists writing from a socialist feminist perspective was Shulamith Firestone (1970). In her book *The Dialectic of Sex* she uses the method of dialectical materialism to analyze the status of women. She argues that Marx and Engels are mistaken in giving a strictly economic interpretation to the oppression of women. She argues that just as the underclasses must seize the means of production as a way to eliminate economic classes, so women must control the means of *reproduction* if they are to eliminate sexual classes. She advocates technological innovation through artificial reproduction and the elimination of what she sees as the patriarchal institutions of childbirth and child rearing.

Other socialist feminists like Juliet Mitchell (1974), Nancy Chodorow (1978), and Gayle Rubin (1984) try to combine Marxist analysis with a revised version of psychoanalytic theory. They find that the oppression of women is so deep that, in Gayle Rubin's words, "equal pay, equal work and all of the female politicians in the world will not extirpate the roots of sexism" (Rubin, 1984, p. 167).

Like Juliet Mitchell, they are arguing that the oppression of women will continue as long as women are expected to have the prime responsibility for child rearing. But they are not, as Mitchell is, advocating new reproductive technologies whereby men can have children; rather, they are insisting that men must share equally in child rearing. They argue this point not primarily because of their belief in equality but because of their theories on identity formation in the oedipal phase. Gayle Rubin argues that men's fear of women, maybe their later need for domination and retaliation, stems from the fact that in their formative childhood years they have been completely dependent upon and dominated by a woman. Brian Easlea (1983), in his book on masculinity and the arms race, draws on insights developed through this perspective to try to explain a masculine arms race which has highly sexual overtones. Sexual and birth imagery is used in weapons research in a way that, when seen from a socialist feminist perspective, makes it likely that military research and the arms race can be explained partly as men's envy of women's childbearing capacities and also as their retaliation on the once omnipotent mother who decided over them as *they* now decide over "mother nature."

Marilyn French (1986, pp. 492–495) in her rather stern criticism of socialist feminism, which she does not even like to term "feminism," makes what to me seems to be a too-easy equation between socialist feminism and how women are treated in so-called socialist countries (especially the Soviet

Union). The only feminist socialist thinker she mentions is Barbara Ehrenreich, whom she accuses of having found a cause "worth *dying* for" instead of what feminists (that is, radical feminists) are searching for: "a cause worth *living* for." But it is rather unfair to compare the *ideas* of radical feminism with the *practice* of a socialism, which most feminist socialists would agree does not correspond to the *ideas* of socialist feminism.

It is, for instance, a major point in Nancy Chodorow's writings (especially Chodorow, 1978) that child care has to be divided evenly between the father and the mother. But Marilyn French criticizes socialist feminism on the grounds that in socialist countries fathers do not take any more care of their children nor participate more in housework than they do in capitalist countries.

She further holds that socialism is as dedicated as any other patriarchal form to the domination of nature. This may be true if one looks at the existing so-called socialist (or rather state-capitalist) states in the industrialized countries with heavy industry, pollution, oil technology, and weapons testing and research, but these policies have not been shaped by socialist feminists nor by the green feminist, the so-called ecofeminists, who can, to some extent, be found within social democratic parties in western Europe as well as in special parties (like "the Greens" in West Germany and some small radical liberal parties).

But if we look at just the theory of socialist feminism, disregarding the way women live in so-called socialist countries, how can it best be differentiated from Marxist and from radical feminist thinking? The question is not easy to answer because Marxist, socialist, and radical feminism all have several versions. There are variations of Marxist theory, especially orthodox Marxist thinking where the oppression of women as gender receives little attention, and other more modern variations where this oppression is focused more. While radical feminism had its birth in the United States around 1968–69, socialist feminism developed in Europe around the same time (Haukaa, 1982b). The early radical feminists had no class analysis and saw the question of social classes as of little relevance to the analysis of sexual oppression. From the start, however, they were already concerned with racism and the exploitation of blacks. They developed the theory of patriarchy, and accused socialist feminists of having been misled by using categories like social class, into which women do not easily fit, and of having no theory of patriarchy. Socialist feminists on the other hand accused radical feminists of having no class analysis. Over the last 20 years many socialist feminists have included an analysis of patriarchy and a discussion of power in their work. Likewise, many radical feminists have included an analysis of class and of the economic institution in their work. These theorists, using concepts from both these perspectives, may be hard to classify as either radical feminists or socialist feminists. They use a combined perspective, the one I also use.

When we look at the normative side, at practices recommended by various schools of feminists, we may find greater differences.

There are, for instance, variations of socialist feminism, such as the one advocated by Firestone, where women in order not to be oppressed by men have to become like men, even biologically, and have to do away with the institution of childbirth. Such a thought would never be adhered to by a radical feminist who finds that we should respect nature, not force her through artificial means. Radical feminists see the fact that women bear children as a fundamental fact of life, a fact on which other things should be based. It should not be used to degrade women. On the contrary, work life should be centered around the fact that women menstruate, get pregnant, bear children, and breast-feed. It is important for the new generation that society is organized in order for women to be able to fulfill their biological tasks as well as possible. This means also that fathers must take their part in child care and child rearing.

As shown, there are various schools of socialist feminism. Among radical feminists there are also several schools, stretching from those who see an economic analysis of patriarchy as important and who are hard to discern from some variations of socialist feminists, to those radical feminists who put their whole blame on individual males. Radical feminists are usually more concerned than socialist feminists are with seeing the differences between women and men as groups having different cultures, other ways of relating, different values and norms. The difference between the sexes is normally regarded as bigger than the differences between groups belonging to the same sex.

Women of Color Perspective

What feminist perspective will best explain the situation of women of color? (The category "women of color" is used by Jagger and Rothenberg, 1984, and really means women of other color than white: women of various color shades, from light brown and yellow to black. We may do well here to take note of the fact that the black African writer Kihumbu Thairu (1975) calls white people the pink race.) Women of color have started to ask this question and to develop their own feminist perspective. In so doing they also take a look at perspectives developed by white feminists.

So far it looks like they find a socialist feminist perspective as less problematic than either a liberal or a radical one. One of the leading black feminists, Bell Hooks (1984), explains well why she finds the radical feminist perspective, assuming that gender is the primary form of oppression, problematic. As a black woman she has experienced racism and sexism as equally fundamental facts of her life. She has experienced the powerlessness that minority men and women experience together and which also gives them racism as a common cause to fight against. She sees that her black brothers and male friends are victimized by racism although sexism allows them to act as exploiters and oppressors of women. White women, on the other hand, may be victimized by sexism, but racism enables them to act as exploiters and oppressors of black people, especially black women.

Bell Hooks (1984, p. 15) concludes: "As long as these two groups (black men and white women) or any group defines liberation as gaining social equality with ruling class white men, they have a vested interest in the continued exploitation and oppression of others." She deplores the fact that feminism may mean most anything and feels that the term should be reserved for an ideology bent on ending sexist oppression. But this has to be done in a way so that the aim is also to eradicate the whole ideology of domination that permeates Western culture on various levels "as well as a commitment to reorganizing society so that the self-development of people can take precedence over imperialism, economic expansion and material desires" (Hooks, 1984, p. 25). Here Bell Hooks joins white radical and socialist feminists in wanting not only a redistribution of the pie but also a reformulation of the whole basic recipe going into the pie.

I find that the perspective used by Bell Hooks is rather similar to perspectives used by some researchers who call themselves socialist feminists and also by some who call themselves radical feminists. Like socialist feminists, she sees how the oppression of both women and blacks is built into the economic structures, and she is bent on ending both racist and sexist oppression. Like some radical feminists, she is concerned about the fact that patriarchal institutions oppress both women and men. Her perspective to me does not seem much unlike my own perspective. Yet she may view this differently and insist on working out what she sees as a black feminist perspective, which may eventually be different from both socialist and radical feminist perspectives.

A Combination of Perspectives

Just as Third World women working out their own perspective draw on various feminist perspectives which have been and are developing, so also many white feminist thinkers draw on several perspectives in their analytical writings. They may use concepts from liberal feminism, such as equality of rights, discrimination, unfair treatment, and at the same time include an analysis of patriarchy developed by radical feminists and an analysis of capitalism deriving from Marxism.

In our book *Knowledge without Power* about the effects of education on women's lives, Runa Haukaa and I (Brock-Utne & Haukaa, 1980) have applied three of the feminist perspectives to our analytical work and tried to show how the socialist feminist perspective is best suited to explain oppression on a macrolevel while the radical feminist perspective is especially useful for an analysis of how institutions like the school and the family work.

The concept of male power and patriarchy are useful here; also, feminist concepts such as caring rationality. We did even find that the liberal perspective offered an understanding of the discrimination an individual would feel.

On an individual level a person may feel a discrimination that can be explained by the liberal concepts, norms, and roles. A woman who is not behaving according to the norms set for the female role is likely to be met by sanctions. In order to see how such norms function to "keep women in their place" one has to look at the interpersonal or institutional level. Here the concept of patriarchy is useful. When we move our analysis to the macrolevel showing the need, for instance, of a group of people entering and being drawn out of the paid labor market an analysis having its roots in Marxist theory may be most fruitful.

To me at this point in time the most fruitful feminist perspective lies in a combined socialist and radical feminist perspective. I stress "at this point in time" because the women of color perspective might prove especially useful when it is more fully developed by women of color themselves. This means a socialist feminist perspective incorporating an analysis of patriarchy developed by radical feminists. This combined perspective is also the one I see as best suited for feminist peace research in industrialized countries, especially when one is trying to understand direct and indirect violence on the macrolevel, as well as large-scale or collective violence. A study of the organized, collective, and direct violence called wars, from a socialist and radical feminist perspective, would include a study both of capitalism, with competition and profit seeking, and of patriarchy, with male domination and oppression of women and women's struggle against war.

A socialist feminist perspective would emphasize how different classes of women play their specific roles in supporting the military as mothers training boys to compete and be strong, as military wives, camp followers, army prostitutes in camp brothels, and ammunitions workers. A radical feminist perspective would emphasize how women unite and struggle against men's wars many places around the world, how women think differently from men when it comes to military questions and the use of violence. Both perspectives are needed to get a fuller picture of women and war and, therefore, a fuller picture and analysis of war as a phenomenon.

I have here outlined six essential feminist perspectives through which we may see the world and analyze it. Such an outline will never be satisfactory. Over the past 20 years, many thousands of pages have been written on feminist theory. Some feminist thinkers, as Dale Spender (1982) has shown, got their writings published several centuries ago but have been "forgotten" by history. Some of these pages may be categorized under one of the perspectives outlined, some under several; some will be difficult to categorize under any of the perspectives. Categories help us structure our reality, but they also do some injustice to it.

I have spent more time on some of the perspectives than on others because I have seen them as more important for the study I am undertaking. Likewise, I have made a halt at some basic concepts, not at others. This has again been done because I find some feminist concepts, such as the concepts of patriarchy, of power and of woman's culture, more fruitful than others.

I have mentioned that I would place myself somewhere between a radical feminist thinker and a socialist feminist thinker. This is especially true when I use feminist perspectives and concepts for analysis. In that case it is not enough for me that I agree with the political ideas and values incorporated in the perspectives, that there are *normative* arguments for my choice. I must also try to find the most *analytically useful* tools, concepts, and analyses that I find useful to explain the matter under study. As a feminist activist it might suffice to adhere solely to the radical feminist perspective because, as I see it, this perspective gives more directions for actions to promote a feminist and a more human world than any of the other perspectives. But as a researcher trying to *understand* and analyze phenomena, I find that certain concepts important in socialist feminism and stemming from Marxism are useful to explain the phenomena under study.

I see, for instance, an analysis of how capitalism functions as essential in understanding why in some periods with unemployment we get studies saying it is best for the children if the mother stays at home and day-care centers are shut, while in periods when "man" power is wanted the day-care centers are opened and studies say it is so healthy for children to be in such centers—it makes them independent and even intelligent. Women are asked to enter and withdraw the paid labor market according to fluctuations in capitalist economy.

As I shall show, various parts of the peace concept can be analyzed from various feminist perspectives. So can the whole field of peace education. I see the socialist feminist perspective building on Marxist theory as useful when analyzing the qualifications needed in a labor force suited to the capitalist mode of production (see, for instance, Brock-Utne, 1982b, p. 6). The radical feminist perspective is especially suited to analyzing the institution of patriarchy. The concept of power as competence instead of dominance, developed by radical feminists, is important in a peace education written from a feminist perspective. So is the radical feminist idea that the personal is political.

Analyzing peace issues from a feminist perspective we cannot do without radical feminism with its analysis of patriarchy, its insistence that the personal is political, and its criticism of man's power over woman and nature. These are *scientific* arguments for using a radical feminist perspective. Apart from these arguments I find that there are good *normative* arguments for using a radical feminist perspective for analysis. As I see it, radical feminism is the one perspective that best questions the values the current patriarchies are built on and tries to substitute one way of thinking with another, offering us such a utopia of a peaceful world.

And a peaceful world to me is not a matriarchy, not a world where women start dominating men as they themselves have been dominated, not a world where women own the means of production, control armies, and maybe possess some nuclear bombs all by themselves. Sexism is a creed based on the believed superiority of the one sex (usually males) over the other. Any domination of one sex over the other may turn into sexism. I envision a world freed from sexism and racism, class oppression, and oppression on grounds of caste, color, or creed—a world where men and women share child care and housework evenly and are able to use their time outside their home or collective for manufacturing useful products. My vision of a world is one in which neither human beings nor animals nor herbs nor nature is exploited, a world ruled by the principles of ecological balance, equality, cooperation, and pleasure.

How and to what extent can such a world come about through peace education? How would the nonformal and the formal educational sector have to be organized or, rather, reorganized to serve peace education? What values are instilled in children through the nonformal education they receive at home, through parents and siblings, through television and sports? What are youngsters taught in schools and other parts of the formal educational sector that is in harmony with or contradicts a feminist peace education? How would both formal and nonformal education have to be changed to be geared to the teaching and promotion of peace from a radical and socialist feminist perspective? Before I turn to these questions and the others I have asked, I shall spend some time on a discussion of the peace concept itself.

3

Women and Peace: The Meaning of Peace for Women

WHAT IS PEACE?

Naturally, "peace," as the central concept in peace research, is and has been the object of much controversy among peace researchers. Peace is not only a controversial concept among peace researchers. It is also an essentially contested concept, used not only for analytical but also for political purposes. The word *peace* (or *fred, Frieden, pax, irene, shalom, mir, paix*) has positive connotations almost everywhere. People want peace. But what they mean by that concept may vary greatly from one culture to another. This variance mirrors differences in political concerns, in what is *here* and *now* seen as the greatest evil. Any discussion of definitions of peace will naturally have political implications and, for a peace researcher, also implications concerning research priorities. The exploration of the peace concept, what should be included in it, what excluded, whether the peace concept is Eurocentered or male-centered, is likely to go on and to be an intrinsic part of peace research itself. (For a discussion of how the peace concept has been used in the *Journal of Peace Research* in the first 17 years of its existence, see Wiberg, 1981a. For another overview of the peace concept in various cultures, see Galtung, 1981a, and Ishida, 1969.)

In the early forties, the American international lawyer and researcher Quincy Wright (1942), in his well-known two-volume study of war, was already discussing the difficulties in defining what peace *is* rather than what it is *not*. This difficulty has stayed with peace research to the point that even so-called positive peace (to which we shall return) is defined along lines of what it is *not*—a way of defining which, to people outside the peace research community, seems contradictory.

The splitting up of the peace concept into "negative" and "positive" peace has been with the peace research field for a long time. In the editorial of the first issue of the *Journal of Peace Research*, the Norwegian peace researcher Johan Galtung (1964) sets the torch to a virtual inferno of debate by introducing his definition of "negative" peace as the absence of violence, of war. This, he finds, does not limit peace researchers working with the negative peace concept to dealing with international conflict alone, there being so many other borderlines that divide mankind. He mentions religion, race, class, but not the one radical feminists see as most important—sex. "Positive" peace is, in this article, defined in terms of "the integration of human society" and "functional cooperation." At this early stage we see "positive peace" defined in a positive way, as the *presence* of some desirable conditions in society. This may be more in line with the way people outside the peace research community think about peace. But after some debate on the positive peace concept, Johan Galtung (1969) himself redefined it as the *absence of structural violence*.

In his article on "What We Have Learnt About Peace" Håkan Wiberg (1981a) shows that the definition of positive peace as the absence of structural violence has also been controversial. He refers to the fact that some have criticized the concept because of its normative character, but he replies to this criticism that it is in the very line of peace research that a concept is normative as long as it can be given empirical operationalizations. He summarizes the discussion on the positive peace concept by stating "that it appears that, by now, the notions of structural violence and positive peace are rather firmly entrenched in the peace research movement" (Wiberg, 1981a, p. 113).

But the fact that these notions seem to be "rather firmly entrenched in the peace research movement" has not erased the controversy surrounding them. The fruitfulness of these concepts is constantly discussed. Some peace researchers find them distinctly unhelpful and feel that more than anything the concepts of structural violence and positive peace have distracted peace research. The American peace researcher Kenneth Boulding seems to adhere to this view. When discussing these concepts in an interview in the Australian journal *Social Alternatives* he maintains that the field of peace research got distracted from studying the most vital questions, those belonging to peace research proper, by the use of a concept like positive peace. And he blames Galtung for being the creator of this distraction: "Partly, this is my good friend Johan Galtung's fault. I am very fond of Johan but he really perverted the peace research movement into something that is too grand to manage: the idea of positive peace, etc. I am not going to throw it out of the window altogether, by any means—but it seems to me that negative peace is much more important, that is, just the prevention of war. In a certain sense, the movement has rather lost interest in this and I think that was unfortunate" (Redner, 1982, p. 19). In an article in another journal Galtung answers Boulding in this way: "I disagree doubly with my equally good friend Kenneth Boulding: there are so many states of affairs that do not include war but cannot possibly be said to include peace either; and the peace research movement has been very active in the field of war prevention and arms race research the last five years, after a focus during the 1970s on problems of development. When it comes to priorities, particularly for peace researchers in the first and second worlds right now, in our present desparate situation, I could easily agree with Kenneth, but I do not want to erect any barriers saying 'here, not further—that territory belongs to someone else'" (Galtung, 1985, p. 157). In an earlier article Galtung maintains that to reveal and unmask the subtle mechanisms of structural violence and explore the conditions for their removal or neutralization is at least as important as doing research on war and other direct violence, "although," he admits, "comparisons of the two types of violence in terms of priorities seems a little bit like discussing whether medical research should focus on cancer or heart diseases" (Galtung, 1969, p. 190).

I agree with Galtung that both types of research are needed—both of direct and indirect, or structural, violence. These are needed not only because we have to alert ourselves to the fact that there are other causes of premature deaths than wars, but also because it is important to see that the various types of violence are sometimes related and how they are related.

In somewhat earlier writings of less polemic nature Kenneth Boulding (1978) merely stresses that there has been an important controversy within the peace research movement between what might be called the narrow view, which stresses the importance of negative peace (peace as the absence of war), and the broad view, which stresses positive peace or the elimination of structural violence. Boulding claims that there "is some tendency for the broad view to be European, the narrow view to be American" (Boulding, 1978, p. 134). That tendency is strengthened here with my contribution, which is also within the European paradigm adhering to the broad view of peace. (I assume that by "European" here, he means west European.) Boulding himself seems to adhere to the narrow view, claiming that "peace and war are alternative states of human behavior" (Boulding, 1985, p. 129)—and that if human beings "are not participating in war, they are at peace" (Boulding, 1985, p. 130).

Negative Peace

In his newest revision of his textbook on peace and conflict studies, Wiberg (1987) defines *negative peace* as "the absence of organized, personal violence, that is approximately the same as nonwar" (translated by me from the Swedish edition) and positive peace as "requiring the absence of structural violence."

Peace he defines as a state of both negative and positive peace. He seems to find the positive peace concept as far more unweildy to work with than the negative one, which he likes to reserve for nonwar. But as I shall show here, even the negative peace concept can get unwieldly if one includes in it what I see as a quite essential feminist perspective on the concept, one which was already included in it in Galtung's (1969) early discussion of the negative peace concept. He says here: "when one husband beats his wife, there is a clear case of personal violence, but when one million husbands keep one million wives in ignorance, there is structural violence" (Galtung, 1969, p. 171).

What if one million husbands beat their wives? That must also be a clear case of personal violence, even of a collective kind. In a society where this happens, there is an absence of negative peace. Barbara Roberts (1983) calls it "the war against women," and some radical feminists criticizing women's "peace" work at Greenham Common (*Breaching the Peace*, 1983) claim that women are constantly "at war" with male society. Even in so-called peace times women live in fear of being burned (in India), raped, mutilated, and killed by their so-called protectors. One of the radical feminists says about women and peace:

> Because the violence of the war against women is so widespread, it is not seen as such by many of its victims and certainly not defined as such by those who do the naming—the war makers. It is the very personalized nature of the war against women that allows it to be so normal as to render it invisible . . . As far as I am concerned the ultimate act of male violence happens everyday. And when I am walking around thinking of this and I hear phrases like "Women for Life on Earth" and "Women for Peace" I feel completely bemused. What on earth do they mean? What peace? (Green, 1983, p. 9)

In the negative peace concept I want to include the absence of collective, personal violence against women, termed "war" by these feminists. But I also have some of the same ambition as Håkan Wiberg (1987) to have at least as clear a *war* concept as possible to work with. These combined wishes have made me try to solve the conceptual problem by creating a fourfold table (see Brock-Utne, 1986a, 1986b, 1986c). In this fourfold table I have divided both the negative and the positive peace concepts into two—the micro- and the macrolevel.

I have reserved the term war for the absence of personal, direct, and collective violence at the macrolevel. What has been called the war against women I have placed at the microlevel, thus including it in the negative peace concept but excluding it from the war concept. But this division may be criticized. Is not the collective violence against women violence at the macrolevel? More so than internal wars? Through further studying and reflection I see another way of solving the conceptual problems we have run into, wanting both to include the personal violence against women yet keeping a more conventional war concept within the same negative peace concept. A

A PRELIMINARY TABLE OF THE PEACE CONCEPT

	NEGATIVE PEACE	POSITIVE PEACE
	Absence of direct violence	Absence of indirect violence
MICROLEVEL Individual		
MACROLEVEL Collective		

possible solution lies in the word "organized" in Wiberg's negative peace concept. By insisting that "negative peace is the same as the absence of *organized* (stressed by me) personal violence" Wiberg excludes the example Galtung gave in his article of personal violence where a husband beats his wife. That beating has not been organized. Even when one million men beat one million wives, that brutality is not organized in the same way as when soldiers are trained to kill (or defend themselves) or when police are trained to combat riots (though some organized gang rapes may be on the definitional borderline).

After this discussion I would like to extend Wiberg's negative peace definition thus: "Negative peace means the absence of both organized (usually 'war') and unorganized personal violence." War is then defined as organized, collective, personal violence, usually between states but possibly within one nation-state—so-called domestic wars.

It is an advantage not to include violence against women in the war concept when one wants to analyze women's work to uphold as well as to uproot the institution of war, meaning collective violence between states. There is an advantage in having a concept that is relatively precise. The advantage of including violence against women in the war concept may be that peace researchers would have to study this phenomenon as much as they study war in the more conventional sense. While I seriously doubt that that would be the effect of such a widening of the war concept, I find that we may keep some of the advantage mentioned by including the absence of unorganized violence against women (but also against children and men) in the negative peace definition.

I see this inclusion as important because some of the same mechanisms are at work in both cases. The U.S. National Conference on Child Abuse and Neglect reported in 1981 that 1 of 4 girls in the U.S. is sexually abused before she is 18. Over 500,000 such cases are reported annually and an estimated 1,500,000 more are not reported. Some studies report that sexual abuse of children is more frequent than other physical abuse: one ten-year study found eight times more sexual abuse than other physical abuse. Nearly all victims are girls: 1 in 10 are boys (from studies referred to by Roberts, 1983).

In a study of the final documents from the three UN Women's Decade conferences (Mexico, 1975; Copenhagen, 1980; and Nairobi, 1985), I have shown how the peace concept has changed within these same types of UN documents through the decade to include in it, also, the absence of violence against women (Brock-Utne, 1986b). I shall return to these more official intergovernmental documents and a criticism of them after we have discussed the other side of the peace concept, the "positive" peace concept or the absence of structural violence, a concept that is even more difficult to handle and has caused peace researchers even more problems than the negative concept.

Positive Peace

Håkan Wiberg (1987) admits that it is not enough to say that *positive peace* requires the absence of structural violence. What about cultural freedom, identity? he asks. And I further ask: What about Galtung's million husbands keeping a million wives in ignorance as an example of structural violence? To keep someone in ignorance can be done both by actively denying them access to information and by denying them an environment conducive to consciousness raising. It certainly is a different kind of violence from the one committed by the industrialized countries or the multinational companies toward the Third World or from the violence going on internally in a country through structures built up in a way where the few may prosper but the many die of starvation.

Maybe the distinction between organized and unorganized violence would help our thinking here too? The multinationals, ministries of commerce, and the elites in each country are certainly organized. The million husbands *need* not be organized but they may behave the same way as if they had been because patriarchal thinking is so much part of their value structure (even maybe of their laws and educational system). Galtung uses the example of one million husbands and one million wives, but what about *one* husband keeping his wife in ignorance? As, for instance, Friedrich Engels whose "wife" (they never actually married, which was the reason why Karl Marx would never invite the two of them to his home) was analphabetic when he first met her and still was so after having lived with him for more than 20 years (for further documentation, see Janssen-Jurreit, 1976). That example creates some problems for us because, more than in the case with the one million husbands, it seems clear here that there is an actor or rather a non-actor and a victim (one could, of course, also think of the million husbands and wives as individual couples where the actor and the victim likewise would stand out as persons). The *personalized* nature of the repression mentioned here should in a way qualify it to be dealt with in the absence of *negative* peace category where the actors and victims are easily identified. Yet that category we have left for a more direct, physical violence (beatings, torture, rapes, physical and sexual assaults, killings).

So this leaves us with the necessity of including the million wives (or the one) under the structural violence category. This category will have to include all types of repression and exploitation, whether organized or unorganized, leading to premature death because of lack of food or because of breathing contaminated air, drinking contaminated water, or just living a more miserable life where human potentials are crippled and not used to their fullest extent. Keeping a wife in ignorance will normally not kill her, while providing her with an inadequate basic diet eventually will. And here we have another distinction between direct and structural violence—violence of the direct kind normally kills more quickly.

The categories aid our thinking, but also create problems for us. Where should we, for instance, place the violence built into the use and misuse of private cars in our part of the world? People are killed daily on our roads. The names of the victims are in the newspapers, normally also the names of the "actors." One could argue that traffic accidents are cases of direct, physical, and personal violence but there is also traffic violence built into the system, the structures of society. For instance, even though there are more people living in Sweden than in Norway, three times as many children are killed on their way to school in Norway as in Sweden.

Traffic "accidents" need not happen. Like wars they are products of human beings, built into structures and eased by a cult of the dangerous. I am giving the example to show how difficult the division between direct and structural violence, negative and positive peace, can get. There may be reasons to categorize traffic "accidents" under direct, physical violence of an *unorganized* kind admitting that those "accidents" certainly have system character. There is an actor, sometimes two, and one or more victims involved; the deaths and maiming are usually sudden; hence there is direct, physical violence. What differentiates this violence from other types of unorganized, direct, and physical violence is the fact that traffic accidents are normally *not intended.* There is no intention to hurt or to kill on the part of the actor, who may even die unintentionally. Because of this lack of intention it may be more correct to categorize traffic accidents under unorganized, indirect violence. In some cases, however, the car is used intentionally as an instrument of murder or for suicide. Such cases would be classified as instances of unorganized, direct violence.

I have mentioned that within the structural violence category we have to do with two rather separate groups of phenomena, the one which leads to premature deaths, to unequal life chances, the other which leads to a life of lesser quality, of unused potentialities. Phenomena in the first group are much easier to operationalize for empirical studies and may therefore attract more research attention, which does not necessarily mean that they are more important. Some people believe, for instance, that it is better to be dead than red or blue. An interesting example, which measures the first type of structural violence, is given by the Norwegian researcher Tord Höivik (1971) in a study of Mexico where he relates infant mortality and death of preschool children at various socioeconomic levels to the density of doctors, availability of drugs, and the basics of an adequate diet (enough proteins). On the basis of these data he makes a rough calculation of what infant and preschool mortality would have been like had the already available resources been distributed more evenly. He finds that the number of preschool children who actually die in Mexico per year is 90,000 higher than it would have been had the resources been distributed more evenly. He points out that this number is about the same as the number of deaths per year during the great Mexican revolution around 1910, which is known to have been one of the bloodiest in world history. This study has been widely cited by peace researchers and is a good example of how structural violence can be operationalized for empirical research. But Höivik does not ask some interesting empirical questions such as: Do more girls or more boys die in their preschool years? Is the sex ratio different in different socioeconomic classes? Was it the case in Mexico, as has been shown in India (Newland, 1979), that among the poorest socioeconomic groups, girls got more diseases from malnutrition than boys, but boys were hospitalized and administered drugs and vitamins more often than girls? If this was the case, we would have an example of patriarchal structural violence. Such questions were not asked by Höivik and cannot be answered from his study. Before I go on posing research questions and breaking up the gender neutrality of peace research any further, I shall summarize my discussion on the negative and positive peace concepts through the table shown on page 47.

This table distinguishes between negative and positive peace and between direct and indirect violence, as is normally done in peace research, but for our purpose it elaborates somewhat on the categories and introduces the distinction between unorganized and organized violence as well as between structural violence leading to a shorter life span and structural violence leading to a less fulfilling life. Peace is here, in my definition as in Wiberg's (1987), a state where both negative and positive peace exists. But it is important to note, as he also does, that the different concepts of violence are logically independent. Analytically there may be negative peace without

A TABLE SUMMARIZING THE DISCUSSION ON NEGATIVE AND POSITIVE PEACE

	Negative peace	*Positive* peace	
	Absence of personal, physical, and direct violence	Absence of indirect violence shortening life span	Absence of indirect violence reducing the quality of life
Unorganized	(1) Absence of wife batterings, rapes, child abuse, street killings	(3) Absence of inequalities in microstructures leading to unequal life chances	(5) Absence of repression in microstructures leading to less freedom of choice and fulfillment
Organized	(2) Absence of war	(4)Absence of economic structures built up within a country or between countries so that the life chances of some are reduced. Also the effect of damage on nature by pollution, radiation, etc.	(6) Absence of repression in a country of free speech, the right to organize, etc.

positive peace and positive peace without negative peace. As far as I can see it, all six cells are logically independent of one another. It is, for instance, possible that a man may keep his wife in ignorance, locked up in the house, not allowed to read or watch television in a country where the right to free communication is widely enjoyed. Likewise, there may be war in a country and no wife battering, or wife battering and no war.

It is important to be aware of this logical independence when one does research on one or more of the cells, an independence which is frequently not recognized by the UN consensus texts on peace, as we shall later see. In these texts peace is often taken to mean "the absence of war" in one paragraph whereas in the next paragraph it is said that peace cannot exist without the full participation of everyone in decision making, without the enjoyment of human rights, equality, development, and so on. Thus peace is suddenly defined in the much broader sense and not taken to mean only our cell 2.

But the logical independence of the cells does not preclude the possibility of some connections between the cells—indeed there may be many. Whether such connections exist is an empirical question, and we shall give some examples of studies which show, for instance, that in periods with high political unrest women are even more likely to be beaten and raped than in other periods.

For each of the six cells there may be research questions of particular relevance for women and arising from one or more of the feminist perspectives just outlined. One or more of the cells may attract more interest and attention from a researcher using a particular feminist perspective for analysis than from a researcher using one of the other perspectives. Only when we have gathered a vast number of studies pertaining to all six cells and from various feminist perspectives shall we have given a complete feminist analysis of peace, an analysis which will widen the field and give it greater objectivity, making it possible to see sides of the problems.

Such a task is not the main purpose of this study and would also be too big for one researcher to carry out all by herself. But let us take a brief look at the type of research questions that *could* be asked from feminist peace researchers for each of the six cells and take a look also at the findings we do have.

Cell 1: Absence of Unorganized, Personal, Physical, and Direct Violence

What is the extent of unorganized, personal, physical, and direct violence in different cultures and at different times and in different socioeconomic groups? Who are the ones committing this type of violence, and who are the victims?

Especially researchers with a radical feminist perspective will be drawn to this cell, as an analysis of patriarchy and macho attitudes is important to an understanding both of rapes and wife battering as well as street killings (where more *males* than females are victims). We have a vast amount of research and data in this area, mostly giving facts and statistics about the presence of this type of violence against women. Centers for battered women have been opened in many places, and writings coming out of these centers may teach us something about male dominance and violence in males (Janssen-Jurreit, 1976; Pizzey, 1974).

The British government appointed a committee in 1975 to look into the question of wife beatings. At that time the committee members were faced by the fact that of the 6,680,000 wives in Britain, more than 5,000 per year were known to have been severely injured and molested by their husbands. After 23 hearings the committee concluded that the 5,000 wives constituted only the tip of the iceberg. The actual number was much higher. The committee also reported on the prejudices with which their work had been met (House of Commons, 1976). They admitted that they had met many men, especially in leading positions, who did not want to acknowledge that the fact that women are beaten by their husbands constitutes a problem warranting official recognition and action.

They had met phrases like "nobody should inquire into the privacy of the home." And also: "If a man beats his wife, she has probably deserved it." Questions for further study would be: Who are the men who find that wife beatings belong to the "privacy" of the home? What other attitudes do they have concerning the use or threat of use of violence in other relationships, for instance in foreign policy? The American peace researcher Betty Reardon (1982, p. 47) describes such attitudes in this way:

> A society which deems wifebeating to be a private matter between spouses, not subject to civil interference, is not likely to perceive excessive exploitation of female labor as a significant problem of economic equity. . . . The degree to which violence operates in the relations between men and women is becoming more apparent as feminist research begins to reveal how many experiences formerly deemed "seduction" were in fact consummated through various forms of intimidation if not force, and to expose how many women have been attacked by men with whom they are acquainted. It is also reinforced by the "blaming the victim syndrome," which insists that the victim provoked the attack, much as the aggression of one state against another has been rationalized by the aggressor as the consequence of "provocation." Social scientists and lawyers have had equally difficult and similar problems in defining both rape and armed aggression.

Is wife beating a phenomenon restricted to some parts of the world? Studies show that in some parts of the world women are mutilated in a variety of sadistic ways, and they may also be beaten. In some places women live in lifelong physical pain or are tortured to death as a result of barbaric rituals. This is the case with ritual genital mutilations—excision and infibulation—still inflicted upon women throughout Africa today, and practiced in many parts of the world in the past. Immediate medical results of excision and infibulation include: hemorrhage, infections, shock, retention of urine, damage to adjacent tissues, coital difficulties, and infertility caused by chronic pelvic infections. In addition, we should consider the psychological maiming caused by this torture.

The World Health Organization has refused for many years to concern itself with the problem. When it was asked in 1958 to study the problem it took the position that such operations were based on "social and cultural backgrounds" and were outside its competence. Mary Daly (1979, p. 157) comments: "This basic attitude has not changed. There has been a conspiracy of silence." As many feminists have pointed out, hatred of the clitoris is almost universal, for this organ is strictly female, for women's pleasure. Thus it is by nature "impure" and the logical conclusion, acted out by tribes that practice excision and infibulation, is to "purify" women of the capacity for sexual pleasure by removing the clitoris. Again questions to be asked could be: How widespread is the practice of genital mutilation? Is it more widespread among the rich than among the poor? What characterizes the tribes that practice excision and infibulation? Are they more aggressive in other ways too? What characterizes a tribe like the Luo tribe in Kenya, which is one of the few tribes in that area that does *not* partake in the practice of genital mutilation? Are the Luos more peaceful in other respects too?

In India, feminists are fighting against the increased incidences of "dowry deaths." According to official figures, 332 cases of "accidental burning" were reported in New Delhi in 1982 as against 305 in 1981 (Kelkar, 1983). But according to various women's organizations an equal number of accidental burning cases go unreported. Many times this is because of the refusal of the police to register the cases. The dowry witch hunt has taken its heaviest toll in the middle-class urban areas, but the burning of women for more money and domestic goods in the form of dowry is quite widespread also in the slums and rural areas. Indian feminist researchers see the dowry witch hunts in India as stemming from women's subordination in the structure of material production, the organization of marriage and family and the sexual division of labor (Kelkar, 1983).

For the past few years in New Delhi and other major cities in the country, women's organizations and housewives have had sporadic demonstrations against the husbands, in-laws, lawyers, and police officers involved in the cases of women burning or killing by other means. At the same time feminist researchers have tried to uncover the extent of this violence. How widespread is it? Who participates in it and for what reasons? Is this type of violence connected to other types of violence on a micro-, meso-, or macrolevel?

> The women's protest through their studies and demonstrations has made this violent crime of women burning visible as a serious social problem. It has opened a whole new vista by calling attention to the oppression, conflict and violence hidden behind the portrait of love, support, and nurturance in the family. (Kelkar, 1983, p. 7)

Indian feminist researchers are critical of the family research most prevalent in Indian social science. This research deals mostly with the nuclearization or nonnuclearization of joint-family structures. But what about the complex power relations between gender, caste, and generation that underlie the family, the ideology, and structure of dependence and sexual division of labor that strengthen the patterns of inequality and the oppression of women and children? These are aspects which feminist researchers have to analyze.

To tie this cell to other cells one may ask: Is there more or less of this type of violence in periods of economic decline (which may easily lead to a type of structural violence) or in times of war and revolution (the other type of direct violence)?

Some studies (Bard, 1974; Steinmetz & Strauss, 1974) show, for example, that the shortage of resources in a family group increases the incidence of violence in the family; thus verbal and physical attacks on women and children are one of the symptoms of such a problem. According to Elise Boulding (1978) women receive more beatings in periods of high unemployment. In the same study Elise Boulding finds that women feel themselves especially menaced when the level of general violence increases, because of the strong psychological nexus between violence and rape.

In periods of *political violence,* war, or revolution, some women who have not been directly involved in the struggle are imprisoned and tortured only because they are wives, mothers, daughters, or sisters of the combatants. The Chilean researcher Ines Vargas (1983) points to the fact that with respect to women the use of torture has taken on sexual-pathological properties, with rape and violence directed toward sexual organs as very commonplace. The female physiological functions are used as torture tools in very sophisticated ways. Many different elements of social, psychological, and cultural order contribute to making these sexual abuses including rape into tools for dissolving and destroying the personality of the victims. One aspect of this problem is that the women who suffer such torture find it difficult to denounce these men, and even are ashamed and feel a sense of guilt. According to Ines Vargas religious and cultural factors limit the denunciation of rapists and sexual abuses because the victim and her family prefer not to disclose such atrocities. This may be part of the reason why this violence is not studied as much as it should be.

In periods of war women are not only tortured and slaughtered like men are, but it is common practice that they are raped. There are reports of gang rapes of Vietnamese women by American soldiers during the Vietnam war. The last soldier "making love to her" shot her afterwards (Brownmiller, 1975, p. 110). But usually rape is reported only when committed "by the other side." Such selective reporting stimulates and justifies retaliation in kind by "this side" (Daly, 1979, p. 362). News of sexual abuses and rape caused by "this side" is not usually included in All the News That's Fit to Print. Susan Brownmiller (1975) shows that selective reporting of rape has provided an ideological excuse for men to rape women "belonging" to other men. She also shows that since rape has frequently been a preclude to murder, it has conveniently been minimized in reporting of the allegedly more serious act. As Brownmiller (1975, p. 114 ff.) indicated, rape has been perpetrated everywhere, and always on all sides, of patriarchal wars. She states: "From prehistoric times to the present, I believe rape has played a critical function. It is nothing more or less than a conscious process of intimidation by which all men keep all women in a state of fear."

The American peace researcher Betty Reardon (1982, p. 45) comments on the fact that the male-dominated media are rather unwilling to report that women who were murdered have also been raped. She refers to the rape and later murder of four religious American women in El Salvador in December 1980. She claims that there was a virtual failure of most media to report that before they were murdered they were also raped. One who *did* report it was Mary Bader Papa in the *National Catholic Reporter* (here taken from Reardon, 1982), who wrote: "A special message was sent us by the rapists and murderers of the four American women. They wanted to make it clear that women who step out of their place will find no special protection behind the labels of 'nun or churchworker.' Or even 'American.'" Betty Reardon comments: "Rape is, indeed, a deliberate device to keep women in line."

If we were to look at all the unorganized, physical, direct violence going on in the world, we would probably find that women are victims of this violence more than men, at least if we include in this violence, what all radical feminists would, the so-called private violence going on in the homes. But more men than women are likely to be victims of some type of violence such as street fights and car "accidents."

In most cases the violence committed is committed by a male. Yet in some cases, as with the dowry burnings and killings in India, the male executer of the violence is helped by a woman, in that case often the bride's mother-in-law and in other cases, as with the infibulation practices in Africa, women are the executers of the violence (yet we may argue, as most radical feminists do, that these women do not have any choice, they are just fulfilling their task under patriarchal rule—as most soldiers do too).

We have seen that interesting data can be gathered about the extent of such violence, about who the victims and who the persecutors are, and about the connection of this type of violence with other types of violence.

Cell 2: Absence of Organized, Personal, Physical, and Direct Violence

We deal here with the question of war and a series of research questions of particular relevance for women could be asked. One is: How have women contributed to war through the education they have given their children? (I shall return to this point in the chapter on peace education.) Another is women's contribution to the maintenance of the military institution through their work as camp followers, army prostitutes, military wives, military secretaries, and regular soldiers. Cynthia Enloe (1983) has made an excellent study of this integration of women into the military institution.

It would be interesting to make a study of the basic perspectives motivating some women to go into the Army and some others to erect all-women peace camps. Both groups insist that they work for peace and try to abolish all wars. One could argue that both a conservative, that is, a biological deterministic approach, and a liberal feminist or Marxist feminist perspective could lead women to join men in the military, in violent fighting, and killing. With a biological deterministic perspective women, as well as men, will believe in the inborn aggressive nature of man, and even women may believe that the best way to tame that nature is through military force and "protection." Women viewing the world through this perspective may not join the Army themselves (believing that women "by nature" are milder and less aggressive and were meant to look after men and children, to care for them and make home a safe and cozy place for them to retreat to after the challenges in the male world), but they will believe in the necessity of a strong military defense, and they will want their husbands and sons to join the Army. They will not be regarded as "real men" by her if they don't. Women viewing the world from a liberal perspective will find that women should join the military in the name of equality both because "it is fair that women also carry the burdens and responsibilities when they want the rights" (as the argument goes) and because the military is a powerful institution and women should get to centers of power. Viewing the world from a Marxist perspective, women are also likely to join the military or revolutionary troops or guerrilla fighters along with the men because they believe that the revolutionary struggle must come first before the liberation of women may be achieved, and that they will prove themselves worthy of equal status with men through their brave fighting alongside them.

The struggle against war through peace marches, peace camps, and campaigns is most in line with radical feminist thinking where the insistence that the means are in line with the aims is very strong as is, also, the insistence that women should not copy the ways of men, should not get equal on men's terms, but should build up a new future and alternative structures.

Yet, far from all of the women in the peace campaigns and marches are radical feminists or at least would not call themselves so. In other places (Brock-Utne, 1981a, 1985a) I have tried to explain their commitment and looked at what characterizes their peace work. Other research questions that rightly belong to this cell are: Are there differences between the way women and men normally view questions concerning the military buildup, like the stationing of cruise missiles or military spending?

Opinion polls in many Western countries show that women are far more negative in their attitudes toward the increase in military expenditures and the deployment of new weapons than men are (Brock-Utne, 1982c). A higher percentage of Norwegian women than Norwegian men were, for instance, against plans for stationing weaponry for the U.S. Marines in the middle of Norway, thus making Norway even more of a base for U.S. warfare against Soviet Russia. While 54 percent of the Norwegian men sampled said they accepted these plans, only 29 percent of Norwegian women did.

A majority of the Dutch population was against the deployment of the new missiles. Research shows that within this majority, 10 percent more women were against nuclear weapons compared with the males of the Dutch population (van der Gast, 1982).

In earlier opinion polls concerning military questions there are more abstentions among women than among men (Brock-Utne, 1982). Now the previous abstainers among women are voting no to the continued arms race. Organizations like "Women for Peace" in which women undertake study-group activities and organize teachings have probably been instrumental in giving women enough self-confidence to rely on their own judgment about questions concerning peace and war.

Through opinion polls and statistics we find that many women have other attitudes toward military questions and military expenditures than men do and even that the gap between the sexes is widening. Another question, which also can be looked into empirically but through other and more time-consuming methods (qualitative interviewing) would be: *Why* is this so? Our own guess would be that the greater independence of women through their own earnings and economic independence will make them more independent of men in their thinking too. It would be interesting to see if women with high economic independence have other attitudes to military questions than do men in the same positions and with the same educational background or if they have other attitudes than do women who rely on their husbands for economical support. The answer to that question is not quite easy to predict. One could anticipate two possibilities: (1) that this group of economically independent women would be more independent than other women from the judgment of males and be more likely to voice their own antimilitary views, or (2) that they, on the contrary, through the higher education they have been given together with men and through socializing with men all day in the workplace will think more like men than do women who live more in a women's ghetto, are closer to their early upbringing, and use their time taking care of children. These are questions I shall return to in the chapter on peace education.

Other questions that could be asked here are questions about the effects on the lives of women of high military expenditures. Although it is now a well-documented fact that the arms race creates unemployment (see for instance, Thorsson, 1984, with further references), there is limited research showing *which sex* loses the most when money is used in the military instead of the civilian sector.

Some years ago one could often hear the argument that military spending is good for the economy and creates jobs. Marion Anderson (1982b) points out that if the U.S. government had spent $80 billion on any other number of things in one year in 1941 instead of spending it for military purposes it would have ended the Depression. The federal government could have carried out a vast scheme of replacing worn-out housing, run-down schools and decrepit hospitals, and it would have had the same effect of creating jobs and ending depression. But most Americans just observed that the war began, the Depression ended, and therefore assumed that military spending was good for the economy.

It is generally accepted that armaments and the arms race—apart from their inherent political harmfulness as agents of international tension, violence, and war—represent a socioeconomic burden on society in general, since arms production is by its very nature a socially unproductive pursuit (see Thee, 1983). Although it is usually included in the national product, it does not provide socially useful goods or services, neither has it any capacity to raise levels of consumption. An important feature of the arms industry is the fact that it is exceptionally capital-intensive. Investment costs per work-place are far higher in the arms industry than in the civilian sector of the economy. It is certainly true that the higher the investment in armaments, the lower the growth rate and the efficiency of the civilian sector. This is perceptible in both East and West (Dumas, 1981).

A recent study from the UN (Study Series 5, 1982) on the relationship between disarmament and development notes: "The job-creating differential between spending $1 billion on the military sector and the same amount on public service employment has been estimated to be roughly about 51,000 jobs in a major industrialized country like the United States."

The number of jobs directly or indirectly created by the investment of $1 billion in various sectors of the U.S. economy, as given in a Bureau of Labor Statistics document, "The Structure of the U.S. Economy in 1980 and 1985" (Washington n.d., p. 110), are as follows: military production: 76,000; machinery production: 86,000; administration: 87,000; transport: 92,000; construction: 100,000; health: 139,000; education: 187,000. This means that if $1 billion is spent to create jobs in the educational instead of the military sector there will be 111,000 more jobs created. This means that, contrary to what was earlier a popular belief, continuation of the arms race creates unemployment while disarmament and reallocation of money into the civilian sector would create more jobs and cut down on unemployment.

Both men and women suffer a net loss of jobs when military spending is high. The substantial job gains men have as military personnel is more than counterbalanced by their loss of industrial and governmental jobs. An interesting question here is: Which sex loses most work opportunities when military spending is high? How does high military spending affect women and men respectively? How does it change the balance between the sexes? Does it affect that balance negatively in the same way that developmental aid has done? Parallels could be drawn to studies of the effect of developmental aid on the lives of women, thus connecting various types of violence.

From the analysis done by Anderson (1982b) it clearly seems that women are losing more jobs in relation to men. Workers in services and in state and local government suffer the most in lost job opportunities when military spending is high. Women are 54 percent of service employees, including hotel and restaurant employees, including teachers, librarians, office workers, and social workers. American women's jobs are heavily concentrated in manufacturing, services, and local governments. These are the hardest-hit categories of the economy when military spending is high.

In her analysis Marion Anderson determined on a state-by-state basis how many fewer jobs for women there were when military spending was at the 1980 level of $135 billion. She found that there were over 1,895,000 fewer jobs for women in civilian industry, services, and state and local government because of the military budget. "These are the civilian jobs lost or never created (forgone) when people are heavily taxed to pay for the military and are unable to spend the money upon their own needs or upon the services provided by their state and local government." During this period 232,000 women were engaged in work on military contracts. When the 232,000 jobs generated from military contracts and the 382,000 jobs held by women in the armed forces in the United States were subtracted from the 1,895,000 jobs lost, the total net loss for women turned out to be 1,281,000 jobs. This means that every time the Pentagon's budget goes up $1 billion, 9,500 jobs disappear for American women.

Anderson's study shows how women lose job opportunities when money is spent in the military instead of the civilian sector of the same country. The 1,281,000 net job loss to women she claims to be a conservative estimate since it does not account for additional jobs when the laid-off teachers, office workers, and production workers buy less because they are out of work. It has been estimated that for each person laid off, at least one other job is affected. Most of the women who lose their jobs because of increased military budgets have entered the work force out of economic necessity; many of them are the sole supporters of their families.

Marion Anderson's study is small and exploratory. It should be followed up by other studies around the world. What does high military spending, apart from all other inherent bad effects, do to the relationship between the sexes in the workplace and at home?

Money used in the military sector could also have been used for food. In a pamphlet distributed to announce the first "National Women's Conference to Prevent Nuclear War"[1] (Capitol Hill, Washington, DC, September 12, 1984) Marian Wright Edelman, who is the President of the Children's Defense Fund, discusses United States' plans to build about 226 missiles at about $110,000,000 each. "For each missile we cancel, we could eliminate poverty in 101,000 female-headed families for a year." She further states that if the United States canceled the whole program, poverty for all children in the United States could be eliminated all over and there would still be enough left to send all female heads of low-income families to college for a year.

---

[1]This conference has been organized by women, for women, as a project of the Center for Defense Information in Washington. The advisory board includes among many others: Geraldine Ferraro, Helen Caldicott, Betty Goetz Lall, Marion Anderson, Eleanor Smeal, Marian Wright Edelman, and Gloria Steinem. Admiral Gene R. La Rocque is said to have been the initiator of the project. Like Ghandi he believes that women can save the world.

Military spending, which is highest in the industrialized countries in the northern half of the globe, could also have been used to overcome hunger and illness in developing countries. In the 1978 UN Special Session devoted to disarmament the Swedish disarmament expert and UnderSecretary of State, Inga Thorsson, used the annual yearbook on the *World's Military and Social Expenditures* by Ruth Leger Sivard to show what a redistribution of 5 percent of the world's military expenditures to meet the needs of children in developing countries could mean (Thorsson, 1978). For this sum, which would amount to $17.5 billion, one could save the lives of millions of children and prevent thousands of children from becoming blind by giving them and their pregnant mothers vitamins and a proper diet.

The question Inga Thorsson was asking here was: How could the lives of children and women in the developing countries be improved had some of the money now being used on weapons, mostly by the industrialized countries, been used to feed undernourished groups in the Third World? Through this question and the answer she gave to it she made a connection between organized direct and organized indirect violence. For political purposes such a connection is certainly warranted. The money *could* have been redistributed in the way she proposes if there was a political will to do it.

In the 1981 edition of *World Military and Social Expenditures* Ruth Leger Sivard (1981) comments: "No evidence more directly and starkly measures the impact of military expenditures on the social condition than the fact that the 550 billion dollars now spent in one year for arms and armies equals the entire income of 2 billion people living in the poorest countries. This is the bottom line on the world's military-social balance." When we know that everywhere where there is hunger and deprivation women and their children, especially the daughters, suffer the most, we see that women pay for the male priorities of this world with their lives. They pay even when there is no war by virtue of the fact that money that could have been used for food to maintain their lives and those of their children, for vitamins and medicines, is being used on arms and armies.

Comparisons like these are quite often made not only by women researchers like Ruth Leger Sivard, and women politicians like Inga Thorsson, but generally by people in the peace movement. In a recent newspaper article the peace researcher Tord Höivik (1985) warned against such comparisons, arguing along much the lines peace researchers do when they try to apply some stringent thinking to the various categories the peace concept may be divided up into, that the various cells are logically independent of each other, that is that it is possible to do away with structural violence and hunger and still retain a great military buildup and high military expenditures. It is also possible to do away with armaments and use the money for some other useless purpose (he mentioned speedboats and wine, which I do not happen to find useless) and still have starving masses.

Logical as his argument is, he does not say much more than that even if we had a disarmed world, we still might have to combat poverty and starvation and the unequal distribution of resources. But most people who compare military and social expenditures do not think that the world would automatically become a welfare state for all if we did away with armaments. But comparisons such as the ones made make us see the craziness of our world. And armaments are not only useless things like plastic toys and speedboats, they are instruments of murder which may destroy our whole civilization.

Cell 3: Absence of Unorganized, Indirect Violence Shortening the Life Span

Are there inequalities in the way vital resources are distributed within microstructures like the family which will be more threatening to the length of life for one or some of its members than for others?

An interesting Indian study, reported in the Indian feminist magazine *Manushi* (Horowitz & Kishwar, 1982), makes it clear that the traditional male-constructed economic indicators such as average household income, per-capita income, and per-capita food consumption, all fail to tell us who actually gets how much of what. They fail to look into essential questions such as:

1. How are economic resources distributed within the family and with what consequences?
2. Which family members have acquired greater decision-making powers over others?
3. Who within the family makes how much contribution to family income?
4. What is the labor contribution of each family member?
5. Are the contributions of each family member commensurate with the benefits he or she derives from membership in the family?

Looking into the internal distribution of money, of food, and of decision-making power within families one finds a steady pattern of discrimination of women which varies little from one class to another. The previously mentioned Indian study showed that those who decided whether the woman in the family would be available for paid work outside of the family were men; mostly the husband, sometimes sons or a father-in-law. This fact did not vary according to whether the woman belonged to a landowning family or to a landless agricultural family. The same study shows that even when the women worked for wages, very few of them seemed to have much of a say in how the bulk of the family's income would be spent nor were they allowed to participate in other important areas of family decision making. Some of them reported being subjected to severe physical violence in the family. The lives of the women were hedged in by crippling restrictions. This was especially true for women from the landholding families. They were even more restricted and powerless than the women in the landless families.

Of the millions of *refugees* and displaced persons who come under the mandate of the UN High Commissioner for Refugees women constitute a majority caseload in the adult refugee population. In some countries the breakdown on the basis of sex reveals that women and children refugees comprise as much as 90 percent (UN High Commissioner for Refugees, 1980). What is the situation for these women refugees and their children in comparison to the male refugees?

The High Commissioner for Refugees reports studies which show that even after adequate supplies of basic and supplementary food (earmarked for vulnerable groups) were available, women and children *continued* to suffer from malnutrition. It was observed that in such situations the patterns of distribution, both within the refugee camps and within the refugee family, reflected the discriminatory socioeconomic relations prevailing in the refugee groups.

The High Commissioner for Refugees deplores the fact that the final stage of food distribution *within the family* is difficult to observe or control. He notes that the widespread cultural practice of men eating first may result in major health problems for the other members of the family when food is scarce. We quote the High Commissioner's report: "Relief workers have become familiar with the sight of well-fed men alongside underfed and sickly women and children." He tells how in camps in Bangladesh for refugees from Burma, the distribution of supplementary food had to be completely reorganized to give direct benefit to gaunt women and malnourished children.

The report from the High Commissioner shows us that even when there were adequate food supplies and no organized, structural violence, women and children still got too little to eat due to discrimination on the microlevel and cultural habits. The structural violence here was an unorganized kind in the sense that it had not been organized through state policies, terms of trade, or multinationals. Yet, from a radical feminist perspective this type of violence can be seen as a manifestation of the institution of patriarchy and in that sense organized through culture and male-centered traditions.

But still, even though discrimination against women is widespread in families all over the world, it normally does not lead to a shorter life span for women than men (if one aggregates the numbers from the micro- to the macrolevel). The shorter life of men, especially in some industrialized countries, may stem from their life style and role as the economic provider of the family.

An interesting question for analysis here would be: How do family sex roles in one setting (for instance, in industrialized countries) shorten the life span of men and how do sex roles and customs in another setting (for instance, India, Pakistan) shorten the life span of women? A liberal feminist perspective with concepts like equality, no discrimination, and sex roles and norms would be useful in the analysis, together with the radical feminist concept of patriarchy.

Cell 4: Absence of Organized, Indirect Violence Shortening the Life Span

In this cell we have included both the economic structures built up within a country or between countries so that the life chances of some people are reduced and also the rape of nature through pollution and radiation also causing too-early deaths. This last phenomenon has been especially well analyzed by the Canadian researcher Rosalie Bertell (1985). In her book: *No Immediate Danger?* she tells how we already die from nuclear weapons even though they are not used in warfare. But the testing of them causes so much extra radioactivity that medical statistics from areas where the testing is going on (as, for instance, in the Pacific) show high increases in cancer, abortions, and still births. Women do not die in any greater number from this testing than men do, but women, because of their childbearing capacities, have some extra pains when the amount of abortions and stillbirths or defective babies increases. The rape of nature through science and technology has been the object of much writing and studying by feminists (for instance, Carson, 1964; Merchant, 1980), a point to which we shall return.

In Höivik's (1971) interesting study from Mexico the population studied was divided into socioeconomic groups but not by sex. But as I have demonstrated (Brock-Utne, 1985a, pp. 4–6) there is considerable evidence which shows that women and girls feel the pinch of food scarcity earlier and more frequently than their husbands and brothers do (Carloni, 1981). Where difficult choices have to be made about which child to feed, a boy is more likely to be fed than a girl. Field studies by the Indian Council of Medical Research showed that, in 1971, girls outnumbered boys four to three among children with kwashiorkor, a disease of severe malnutrition (Newland, 1979). Even more discouraging was the subsequent observation that among children who were hospitalized for kwashiorkor there were more boys than girls. Though girls were more likely to be suffering from the disease, boys were more likely to be taken to the hospital for treatment.

Giele and Smock (1977) report a mortality rate in Bangladesh for girls under age five that is 30 to 50 percent higher than that for boys in the same age group. The same researchers attributed higher death rates among girls admitted to a large university hospital in Africa to the girls' inferior nutritional state. More girls than boys died from routine infectious diseases such as measles, which seldom kill unless a child is weakened by malnutrition.

All over the world, more boys are born than girls. But in the developed countries so many more baby boys than baby girls die that the expectation of life at birth is higher among females. This is not so in some of the developing countries. In India, for instance, since 1901 the male population has always grown at a faster rate than the female population. According to official estimates, quoted in the "Report of the Committee on the Status of Women in India" (1974), the total population of India in 1974 was 301 million males and 280 million females. There were 21 million fewer females. According to the 1981 census there were 22.9 million fewer females than males in India.

The data from the Indian subcontinent (and we can find the same phenomenon of shorter life span for women in Pakistan) are not representative of the difference in life span between women and men on a world scale. In our part of the world infant mortality is higher for boys than for girls, and women live longer than men. The female sex seems, by nature, stronger than the male sex and is likely, if all other factors were equal, to live longer than the male sex.

The Norwegian sociologist Regi Enerstvedt has used the case of sex and gender for a thorough analysis of the interplay between biological and social factors in the human being. Through tables and data he shows that if we move backwards in time in a country like Norway women had a lower life expectancy than men, the opposite situation of today. The reasons for this he finds in the great risks that constant childbearing and child births posed to women. Having compared various societies and at various times he concludes that: "It seems that the human female is biologically better equipped than the human male" (Enerstvedt, 1979, p. 110). We should, according to Enerstvedt, expect women to live longer than men if other factors are equal, but probably not so much longer as in some industrialized countries. Using this purely quantitative measure, one could say that in those countries men are victims of that type of structural violence *more* than women. We are here dealing with societies where everyone has an adequate diet, where there is little lack of material resources but where men die from stress, heart diseases mostly, and from a wilder life style (car accidents, for instance).

Whether it is a better life to be able to use one's full potentialities up until age 70 and then die from a stroke or to have been kept in ignorance, secluded in the home but live until one is ninety (the last years with constant diseases), is another question and one that is again more difficult to measure.

Cell 5: Absence of Indirect, Unorganized Violence Reducing the Quality of Life

In this cell we are dealing with repression in microstructures leading to less freedom of choice and fulfillment. We could think of various problems that would rightly belong to this cell, for instance: To what degree are children allowed to voice their opinions and have real influence on important family matters? There are also several questions we could ask about the relationship between the sexes in the microstructures, questions which have to do with self-fulfillment and enjoyment of fundamental basic rights. I shall here look into two:

- the right to some spare time, leisure time, to develop oneself spiritually and bodily
- the right to be able to express oneself and be listened to without constant interruptions

Regarding the first of these rights, we have statistics from all over the world showing that women, especially those living with a man, have much less leisure time than men, less time to go into politics, to read or watch television, less time to engage in outdoor activities and especially organized sports, less time for games like bridge and chess. A study (Bergom-Larsson, 1979) from Sweden reveals that the leisure time for men, in families with children in which both spouses are gainfully employed, is two to three hours longer per day than for women.

All over the world, women are required to undertake unpaid housework, usually in the name of love. Norwegian statistics show that full-time housewives in Norway spend 5.4 hours each day on unpaid housework while wives who are full-time career women spend 3.8 hours per day on the same amount of work. This means that women are forced into a double shift. The Norwegian researcher Berit Ås (1981) names this double workload system the "double ghetto in which modern women are exploited both by employers and husbands." The same statistics already referred to (studies of the use of time, from the Norwegian Central Bureau of Statistics, 1972) show that husbands spend exactly the same amount of time—0.7 hours per day—on unpaid housework whether their wives are full-time housewives or full-time career women.

The work that men do has been organized into paid labor, while women's work has been kept invisible and unpaid. Indeed, unpaid work has been kept so invisible that full-time housewives raising four children and taking care of a big house without any help answer when they are asked if they are working: "No, I am not working. I am only at home." Yet they usually work longer hours than their husbands do; they have less leisure time, they have no vacation, no sick leave, no pension, and no salary. And they are brought up to do all this "for love."

In Upper Volta, for instance, the working hours of a sample of rural women exceed those of men by about 27 percent while men, on the average, have two more hours of leisure per day. The same is found in Botswana, where rural women appear to work 20 percent longer than men and have 20 percent less leisure (Buvinic, 1981). These studies show that as women in poor households enter the labor market, it is their *leisure time* rather than time spent in work at home that is reduced.

We could go on and on adding empirical studies showing similar patterns from all over the world: Women do most of the work and have the least leisure time, time for themselves. Official UN statistics from the UN Women's Decade Conference (the one in Copenhagen in 1980) show that women do two-thirds of the work in the world (paid and unpaid), receive 10 percent of the salaries and own 1 percent of the property. If the right to property should also be a human right, it is not a right granted women to a degree that it is granted (some) men. But we shall here look at one of the other liberal human rights: *The right to express oneself freely,* that means of course also the right to decide on the topics for discourse and the right to be listened to. A vast amount of studies by radical feminist researchers show that in mixed-sex conversations men talk two-thirds of the time, decide on the topic for conversation and are responsible for 90 percent of the interruptions (for an overview of such research see Spender, 1980; also, Ehrenreich, 1984; Vetterling-Braggin, 1981). In a thought-provoking article on the politics of talking in couples, called "Conversus Interruptus and Other Disorders," Barbara Ehrenreich (1984, p. 73) writes about what she sees as "a profound crisis in intersex conversation . . . which threatens not only the family, but also the casual affair, the illicit liaison, and possibly the entire institution of heterosexuality."

She sees what to the individual woman may seem to be her own, *individual* problem—unfortunate conversational mismatches—as a crisis of gender-wide proportions. When a woman speaks about something that is of great importance to her a man does not listen but has his thoughts on other things. He also does not let her speak long but interrupts her, normally changing the subject to whatever is on his mind and expecting *her* to listen. The American sociologist Pamela Fishman (cited in Ehrenreich, 1984) has done a series of studies in which she planted tape recorders in the homes of couples and recorded—later analyzed—a vast number of hours of mixed-sexed conversation. She found that topics introduced by men "succeeded" conversationally 96 percent of the time, while those introduced by women succeeded only 36 percent of the time and fell flat the rest of the time. More analysis along these lines is needed, not only of a quantitative but also of a qualitative type. What topics do women introduce in conversation when they fall flat? Which are the few topics that succeed in attracting the interest of males? Is this breakdown in inter-sex conversation found to the same degree in all social classes and in all societies? Is it experienced also by women working in typically male-dominated fields, women who like to talk about and have competence in fields which mostly attract men? Are younger men more likely to talk about personal matters than middle-aged men?

Barbara Ehrenreich sees the crisis in inter-sex conversation as so deep, analyzing both men's wish to dominate and their basic insecurity when it comes to talking about personal feelings and other "private" matters, that she recommends therapeutic centers to treat Male Conversational Dysfunction. Using some of the same sexist language men do in weapons research (we shall return to that point) she suggests categories like "Conversational Impotence" (total inability to get a subject off the ground), "Premature Ejaculation" (having the answer to everything before anyone else gets a chance to utter a sentence), "Conversus Interruptus," and so forth. It may even be necessary, in the extreme cases, to provide specially trained female Conversational Surrogates, she suggests. She holds that the conversational crisis will be solved only when women and men—not only women—together realize their common need for both social and *personal* change.

Analysis of discourse in all-male settings in comparison to in all-female settings show great differences in style (see Ehrenreich, 1984; Spender, 1980). In male settings discourse seems to be a sort of competitive sport in which points are scored and adversaries blocked with shoulder thrusts or tackled with sudden interruptions. In female settings discourse is of a more cooperative kind where turns are taken in both talking and listening. In consciousness-raising groups within the feminist movement women look at conversation as an act of collective creativity, the intimate sharing of personal experience, and the weaving of the personal into the general and political. As far as I can see this radical feminist analysis, based on a vast amount of empirical data and on a theory of patriarchy, should not be without interest for peace researchers who normally have looked at the right to speech as a liberal and human right granted (or usually denied) whole populations. From a feminist analysis, such an outlook is too limited and misses the point that even in societies where there is a public recognition of the right to free speech women are often not free to speak and especially not to be listened to.

Cell 6: Absence of Organized, Indirect Violence Reducing the Quality of Life

In this cell I have included the repressions in a country of free speech, the right to organize, form political parties and so on. We shall see that in this area also there are great differences between women and men.

In *capitalist* countries with so-called free flow of information, that flow is a lot freer for some people than for others. We have a vast number of studies demonstrating the male dominance of the media, how, for instance, the news items on television are picked out from a male's world and point of view, how men are interviewed when women could have answered even better. Women also have trouble getting their writings published, especially if they write from a feminist perspective. (See especially Spender, 1982, for documentation.) There are few feminist journals, analyzing the world from feminist perspectives. And in time of economic decline, these journals are among the first ones having to give in (the two most important feminist journals in Norway for instance have both died within the last five years).

This is true also in some so-called *socialist* countries where there is a general censorship on writing, publishing, and media expression. Through interviews Robin Morgan (1980) has had with some exiled Russian feminists in Vienna, we know how these women were treated when they tried to publish a feminist magazine in the Soviet Union, giving information on the actual conditions for women in that country in relation to abortion, contraceptives, living alone with a child, wife battering and so on. They were all thoughtful, educated women who wanted to reach out to other women, to share their experiences, offer sisterhood, and perhaps create a nucleus of a group to work for change in woman's lot. It is illegal for individuals to possess copying devices, so they had to type each copy of their journal individually: they produced ten. They were terrorized by KGB men who attacked the women and threatened to rape them. Then they were imprisoned, interrogated, and the four leaders finally exiled. Some of these women had spent time in the camps but their work cannot be published in Russia. Even dissident men reject feminism, calling it frivolous, the government considered it treason and claimed that the women had gotten feminist ideas from the West. Yet these Soviet women who produced this first feminist samizdat—underground publication—knew absolutely nothing about feminism in other parts of the world. They wrote and tried to distribute their journal because of their own hunger, and the hunger of other women they knew, for a voice.

In countries with censorship and repression women are repressed the same as men are. But women have to face yet another repression, even from repressed men, when they want to be able to write, speak, be listened to about the lot of women. Using a radical feminist analysis, we can say that patriarchy denies many women a voice, no matter under what economic system.

SUMMARY REMARKS

Before we look more closely into some of the texts on women and peace from the official UN Women's Decade conferences we shall make some summary remarks on our thinking and results so far. We have in this chapter discussed the peace concept and tried to place it within a peace research tradition. We have made the normal distinction between negative and positive peace, direct and indirect violence. We have introduced a division between unorganized and organized violence and in the category of indirect violence we have introduced a division between a type of violence which shortens the life span and one which reduces the quality of life, reduces the chances of self-fulfillment and enjoyment of liberal human rights. On the basis of this division six cells have been described and illustrated, two in the category negative peace (absence of personal, physical, and direct violence) and four in the category positive peace (absence of indirect violence). We have maintained that peace is a state where both negative and positive peace exist and where no violence can be found in any of the six cells we have outlined. According to this thinking we cannot say that there is peace in a society where human rights are violated or resources distributed so unevenly that some people die from malnourishment. We have also argued that our six cells are logically independent of each other though quite often some empirical relationships will exist. This logical independence means that there may be an absence of organized, personal, physical and direct violence (war) in a society and not be an absence of *unorganized*, personal, physical, and direct violence in that same society (for instance wife battering, rape)—in which case we would hold that peace does not exist. If one used a narrow definition of peace meaning solely the absence of war or armed conflict between states (or within a state) peace could logically exist in a state where there was both much personal violence such as rapes and unequal distribution of resources so that some people starve to death.

Over the past two to three decades the more maximalistic peace concept has gained ground both within the peace research community and in intergovernmental meetings dealing with peace. Through looking at some UN and UNESCO texts I have demonstrated (Brock-Utne, 1985a, pp. 2–4, and 1986b) that the narrow peace concept is politically outdated within the intergovernmental community and that peace now is taken to include both development and the enjoyment of basic human rights. We shall have to remember that the texts we have referred to are consensus texts where the different parts of the world have been able to get their main definition of peace to be part of the peace concept (the socialist countries stressing peace as the absence of war and as disarmament, the Western bloc stressing the enjoyment of human rights and fundamental freedoms and the Third World stressing development). But we can often find that in the same document where peace is defined in the broad, maximalistic sense in one paragraph, it can be taken to mean only the absence of war in another.

Concentrating on the narrow peace concept has some scholarly advantages as it limits the field under study. But in this chapter I have shown that such a limitation has scholarly disadvantages, too, as well as political ones.

I believe that both the peace movement and the peace research movement need a wide peace concept to tie together the various parts of the peace research movement in all parts of the world. When visiting the Women's Center for Development Studies in New Delhi, for instance, I found that our research interests were very similar because what *they* called development was included in my peace concept. Another advantage of using a wide peace concept is that it makes for an analysis of how different forms of violence are connected to, often caused by, other types of violence.

When I outlined my wide peace concept covering all the six cells I did this not only to show what peace researchers, according to my opinion or to feminist concerns, according to intergovernmental texts or other normative statements, *ought* to be concerned with; rather, because the wide peace concept also has *analytical* advantages. I have tried to point at some empirical connections between the various cells; many more could be found. Including the unorganized violence of both a direct and an indirect kind in the peace concept seems to me to be necessary to fully understand how organized violence comes about and is sustained. Maintaining, for instance, like Gandhi did that only women can save the world and abolish war necessitates a study of how women and women's thoughts are repressed in microstructures (my cell 5). When looking at imperialist economic structures (my cell 4), which lead to a shorter life span for people in the developing world, it would be an analytical mistake not to investigate the differential effects of malnourishment on men and women. If we find that women are more likely to suffer from malnourishment than men are, then the interplay between economic exploitation and cultural practices becomes important to study. For such a study a feminist perspective, especially one including a theory of patriarchy, becomes necessary.

Though the advantages of a wide peace concept to me clearly outnumber the disadvantages, some of the difficulties using this wide concept in research have to be mentioned too. First of all there is the obvious difficulty that stretching the intellectual boundaries of a concept may make it mean most anything and make it too unwieldy to serve as a precise concept for research. One leading peace researcher complains that: "Peace research has become what a black hole is in astronomy. There seems to be no social problem which in the final analysis does not have its legitimate place within peace research, and therefore is absorbed by the definitional processes in peace research" (Tromp, 1980, p. XXVII). To some extent the widening of the peace concept has been an inescapable result of the transition of peace research from being essentially North Atlantic in the sixties to having become more truly international in the seventies.

A way for peace researchers to deal with this wide peace concept has been to divide it up and concentrate individual research on a part of it. The danger here is that the connections between various types of violence are not analyzed. This may easily happen because hardly any peace researcher has an overview of the entire field and hardly any peace research institute has more than some parts of it represented. The Swedish peace researcher Håkan Wiberg laments: "To many peace researchers, it is a source of embarrassment that a field which prides itself on its transdisciplinarity should become so compartmentalized" (Wiberg, 1984, p. 183).

My own attempts here to get a peace concept fruitful to handle for a feminist analysis may have compartmentalized the field even further. I have also demonstrated that, for several of the cells, analysis from one of the feminist perspectives would be different than from one of the other. I have outlined six feminist perspectives in the first chapter and six peace categories in this. It is logically possible to apply any of the six feminist perspectives to any of the six peace categories, making for thirty-six variations. It is also possible to give examples of studies clearly belonging to one of the thirty-six variations and some such examples have been given. But, as I hope I have demonstrated, feminist perspectives are not meant to be just another theoretical construct that can be used to analyze research data, but can be perspective transforming, shedding new light on the field of peace research itself, making it more objective, if by objectivity is meant seeing more sides of reality, as well as the underside, as Elise Boulding (1976) has called the reality of women.

Peace researchers who have done research without a feminist perspective may ask themselves: What would this piece of research look like when viewed from a feminist perspective? Normally such a question will have clear consequences for the research under question. The rewriting of it to include, also, a feminist perspective will normally lead to a more complete picture, to better research. In such a way a feminist perspective may be perspective transforming. Some peace researchers may find it fruitful to use a feminist perspective on some parts of their research or to combine it with other perspectives. I am not a purist here. My main point is that a feminist perspective is important in peace research.

TWO GROUPS OF FEMINIST PEACE RESEARCHERS

I feel convinced that studies combining insights from peace research and feminist research will be challenging and provoke new thoughts, research themes, and actions. The meeting of minds between feminist scholars and peace scholars is likely to be fruitful. The examples so far have been thrilling (Burns, 1986; Easlea, 1983; Enloe, 1983; McLean, 1986; Merchant, 1980; Pietilä, 1985; Reardon, 1985; Roberts, 1983, 1984; Silverman, 1986). Feminist peace research is also a trend to which some of my works belong (Brock-Utne, 1985a, 1986a, 1986b, 1986c, 1987a, 1987b), including also the present analysis.

There are two groups of people who are able to bridge the two fields—either feminist scholars who will most often be women, entering the peace research community, or peace researchers, who will most often be men, entering feminist research. Since both of these groups are small and of recent origin, it would be worth a research study of its own to see how they are treated and what their possibilities of influencing the entering research field or the new hybrid—feminist peace research—are. My bet is that male peace researchers drawing on feminist insights will be better received within the feminist research community than feminist scholars drawing on insights gained through peace research. What would the reasons for such differential treatment be? I shall name three rather obvious ones:

1. *The higher status of males in patriarchy.* Males have higher status than women in our society and this fact is known by both women and men, researchers as well as lay people. Males and their words carry more status and weight than the words women utter—even though they may be identical words. Getting men into a female-dominated field *raises* the status of the field. Getting women into a male-dominated field *lowers* the status of the field. This is the reason why women are so eager to get more men into the kindergarten and nursing professions and quickly give them leading positions within these fields. This is also the reason why carpenters and plumbers do not want females in their occupations and see to it that they have difficulties getting a job or a promotion. We may also draw our examples from the male-dominated universities and take a look at staffing practices.
2. *The personal threat a feminist perspective may pose to men.* A feminist scholar entering the field of peace research is unlikely to feel her foundations shaken by perspectives within peace research. But she will find that the perspectives she brings with her and wants to use for her analysis may seem threatening to male peace researchers who have not been exposed to feminist ideas before or who have been exposed to them and do not like them. Frequently the reason for their dislike lies in the way they have organized their private lives combined with the feminist insistence that the private is political.
3. *The "rationality of caring" adhered to by feminist scholars.* A useful analytic concept developed in Norwegian feminist research is the concept of "caring rationality" (Sørensen, 1982; Tornes, 1981). The concept is used to analyze the way women behave in a workplace where they are present not only as waged workers collecting their salary, but also as caring human beings, caring for their family and for the personal well-being of their work-mates.

It is my hope that peace researchers will find their scholarship enriched as they start paying increased attention to questions raised from feminist perspectives on issues pertaining to peace. It has been my intention in this chapter to raise some such questions and to show some attempts at partial answers. The field of feminist peace research is in its very beginning and any analysis will mirror that fact. It is my hope that mine will carry this new field a small, maybe just a *tiny*, step forward.

THE DEVELOPMENT OF THE PEACE CONCEPT THROUGH THREE UN WOMEN'S DECADE CONFERENCES

We shall here pose the questions: How has the peace concept developed through the UN Women's Decade (1975–1985)? Has the feminist understanding of the necessity of including the effects of so-called private violence been reflected in the work of the UN on the peace concept? The documents I am going to use for my analysis are the three official final documents from the three world conferences arranged by the UN on equality, peace, and development for women: the plan of action (Mexico), programme of action (Copenhagen), and forward-looking strategies (Nairobi). (See also Brock-Utne, 1986b and Brock-Utne, 1988c.)

Plan of Action from Mexico

In the world *Plan of Action* from Mexico very little is said about peace at all. A feminist perspective on peace is not developed in the text. What is said about the content of the peace concept is found in paragraph 50, where we read:

> An essential condition for the maintenance and strengthening of peace is the promotion and protection of human rights for all in conditions of equity among and within nations . . .

This paragraph does not say very much and one would have to go to various preparatory texts from various states and amalgamated texts, so-called "mergers" in the UN language, to find out how the paragraph was developed. Most of the negotiations on the more sensitive paragraphs go on in closed meetings so we might not know anyhow. One guess would be that the so-called socialist bloc had wanted a paragraph explicitly dealing with peace (by them defined as the absence of war) and the others consented to this provided that the Western bloc got in their understanding of peace as the protection of human rights, and the Third World got their understanding of equity among nations.

Looking at this paragraph and comparing it to our six cells, it lacks our precision by not stating explicitly what is included in the peace concept, but rather stating that "an essential condition for the maintenance of peace is . . ." where, by peace, one easily thinks of the absence of war, in which case the rest of the sentence is logically incorrect according to our earlier arguments. If by peace here is meant the wider concept, development, equality, human rights are ingredients of that concept, so the sentence is rather meaningless and a straightforward definition of peace would have been much better. But the point in UN circles has not been to say something about the conditions for peace as they can be found through logical or empirical analysis. The point has been to create a peace concept where different groups of nations got their main concerns taken care of so that consensus could be reached on the definition of peace.

Programme of Action from Copenhagen

In the *Programme of Action* for the second half of the UN Women's Decade—the *Copenhagen* document—we find that the peace concept is explicitly dealt with only in paragraph 5, where it says:

> Without peace and stability there can be no development. Peace is thus a prerequisite to development. Moreover, peace will not be lasting without development and the elimination of inequalities and discrimination at all levels. Equality of participation in the development of friendly relations and co-operation among States will contribute to the strengthening of peace, to the development of women themselves and to equality of rights at all levels and in all spheres of life . . .

We find the same shortcomings in this text as in the Mexico text or even more so here because here it is clearer that peace is taken to mean absence of war, yet one claims that there can be no absence of war without development and equality. In this chapter I have given a lot of examples of societies where there is structural violence and inequality and no war.

Neither, in this paragraph, is there an acknowledgment of the gender-specific problems of women. It is maintained that the participation of women in the development of friendly relations among States will contribute to peace. Here peace is taken to mean absence of direct and collective violence between states (war). It does not mean the absence of direct personal violence against women in so-called peaceful time. But in the Copenhagen document we find other paragraphs dealing with violence against women. They are just not made part of the peace concept. We find for instance this insight in paragraph 11:

> . . . women have often been regarded and treated as inferior and unequal in their activities outside the domestic sphere and have suffered violations of their human rights. They have been given only limited access to resources and participation in all spheres of life, notably in decision making, and in many instances institutionalized inequality in the status of women and men has also resulted . . .

In contrast to the plan of action from Mexico, the Copenhagen document singles out women as a special group in relation to the violations of human rights. Paragraph 11 deals with the collective structural violence experienced by women—although these concepts are not used. We find another paragraph in the Copenhagen plan of action dealing with direct violence. Neither this paragraph is seen in relation to the peace concept. I here quote paragraphs 141 f:

> . . . policies and programmes aimed at the elimination of all forms of violence against women and children and the protection of women of all ages from the physical and mental abuse resulting from domestic violence, sexual assault, sexual exploitation and any other forms of abuse . . .

Forward-Looking Strategies from Nairobi

Of the Three documents analyzed it is only the Nairobi *Forward-Looking Strategies* for the advancement of women that sees the absence of both personal and collective, direct and structural violence against women as part of the peace concept. In paragraph 257 we find the following sentences:

> The questions of women and peace and the meaning of peace for women cannot be separated from the broader question of relationships between women and men in all spheres of life and in the family. Discriminatory practices and negative attitudes towards women should be eliminated and traditional gender norms changed to enhance women's participation in peace.

And in paragraph 258 we find a definition of peace that radical feminists have been arguing for. We find that there is no peace as long as women are being beaten, as long as so-called private violence exists in the home. It says here:

> Violence against women exists in various forms in everyday life in all societies. Women are being beaten, mutilated, burned, sexually abused and raped. Such violence is a major obstacle to the achievement of peace and the other objectives of the Decade and should be given special attention. . . . National machinery should be established in order to deal with the question of violence against women within the family and society . . .

The Nairobi document has acknowledged that there is no peace when there is domestic violence.

We can say that with the Nairobi document the feminist understanding of the necessity of including the absence of so-called private violence in the peace concept has been acknowledged by the UN and the intergovernmental community. It is the radical feminist perspective with its analysis of patriarchy which is reflected in this conceptual shift or "conquest" of the peace concept, as some may term it, but a conquest which I think will make for better understanding of the whole field of peace research.

4

Feminist Perspectives on Peace Education

WHAT IS PEACE EDUCATION FROM A FEMINIST PERSPECTIVE?

So far I have discussed and outlined various feminist perspectives. I have mentioned that I see a perspective combining thoughts from radical feminism and socialist feminism as especially useful. In an analysis of peace education this means making the radical feminist distinction between *power-over* and *power-to* a central distinction. It also means incorporating an analysis of patriarchy and an insistence on seeing private and personal experiences as political. It further means not only realizing the fundamental oppression of women everywhere but that this oppression varies according to class, race, and culture. Not *all* women are more oppressed than *all* men. But generally, women are more oppressed than men of their own race, caste, or class. These understandings, concepts, and elements of analysis will be central when I now start analyzing peace education from a feminist perspective. I devote three chapters to this analysis. In the first one I debate some theoretical issues within peace education. The second one deals with out-of-school influences, and the third one with the more formal education taught in schools. The reasons for devoting more time and space to the second of these chapters than to the third are both the fact that there is reason to believe that what children learn out of school has greater impact on their attitudes and behavior than what they learn in school, especially through the official curriculum, and the fact that peace education is normally talked and written about as something mostly going on within formal education.

WHAT IS PEACE EDUCATION?

In my discussion of the peace concept I maintained that peace is an essentially contested concept. So is peace education. It faces a lot of the same analytical problems as the peace concept does and also meets some additional ones. Peace education is a controversial concept and, as I shall show when discussing peace education as a subject to be introduced in schools, is regarded as political and even endangering the security of the country. This is especially the case with the rather recent subfield of peace education: disarmament education.

The whole field of peace education is extremely difficult to treat in a scholarly manner because the term is open to so many different political interpretations. For political reasons—to reach consensus on a definition of peace education to be used in the international community or in the official school curriculum guidelines—the term is intentionally made to be open to various interpretations and accommodate various viewpoints.

To come to grips with the concept for more analytical purposes there are essentially two ways to go:

- *Through an empirical approach* where we could study peace education programs around the world. What do they have in common—if anything at all? How do they vary? How do they relate to official guidelines for peace education nationally and internationally? Is there a gap between the peace education outlined in these guidelines—the norms for a peace education with an official stamp—and the type of peace education which in reality is going on in schools, kindergartens, homes, and in leisure activities? Using this empirical approach, studies would be made of peace education programs as carried out, and documents would be compared and analyzed.
- *Through a more theoretical approach* where we, through a discussion and analysis of the purpose for which we are going to use our definition, seek to justify our way of defining the concept. In this more theoretical approach discussions of the peace concept as well as of the education concept are necessary, as is a discussion of the juxtaposition of peace to education.

In this work my approach is the more theoretical one, even though an analysis of the development of the peace education concept in the UN Women's Decade conferences is also included here, an analysis belonging to the first of the two approaches.

One of the first questions that must be answered is the difficult question of the juxtaposition of peace to education. Education to me means the way children get socialized into our culture whether this socialization is intended or not intended by the adult society having direct or indirect responsibility for the education of the young.

When education is defined as an academic discipline, for instance in one of the newest Norwegian encyclopedias, it is defined as "the study of the socialization and training process taking place in society—first and foremost in the home and the school—but in principle in all the institutions of society" (Befring, 1980, p. 104—my translation). The academic discipline of education is a broad subject area integrating theory and educational practice and drawing on various other academic disciplines and professional outlooks. "Education is by its very nature an inter-disciplinary subject in demand of a variety of scientific approaches and research methods" (Befring, 1980, p. 104).

Most socialization processes can be divided into three:

- *The intentions, ideals, and ideologies* which exist more or less officially and have been formed by the socializing agents—governmental authorities, curriculum boards, parents, and commercial interests. Those formed by, for instance, governmental authorities are normally in written form and can be scrutinized and analyzed as any text. Parents normally have aims for the education of their children. These aims may be more or less explicit and well-founded. Through interviews with parents one may find out what their stated aims are. One could also interview advertising agencies, toy producers, fashion makers about their stated aims.
- *The institutions* in which the socialization processes take place, the home, kindergarten, peer group, leisure activities like sports, the entertainment industry with films, video, pop, rock, and fashion, the school with its official curriculum, its textbooks, exams, and teachers with their various qualifications and teaching methods.
- *The real practice* going on, as this practice is experienced by those subjected to the socialization process in the various institutions where the socializing is going on. Here we find the unintended consequences of officially claimed aims. Here we find the hidden curriculum, the hidden messages, the concrete day-to-day practice. Officially it may be forbidden to give grades in the first years of elementary school. Yet in some classes the teachers give the pupils, for instance, three minutes to make as many correct calculations as possible and then the class is ranked according to how many calculations each was able to do and the ranking list read aloud. This practice then teaches the pupils a lesson different from the one which was originally intended in the approved governmental plans. The ideals try to downplay competition, practice encourages and *promotes* competition.

Though it is more difficult to analyze practice than ideals, any analysis that does not take into account the discrepancy between ideals and practice misses what to me seems as the most important reflections to be made within the field of educational research. When education means the way children get socialized into our culture, whether that socialization is intended or unintended, why not use the word socialization instead of education? One may ask the question: Why coin the word education when socialization means about the same thing? The question, to make sense, would have to be put the other way around since education is the older and more commonly known of the two concepts. Though there are overlapping meanings between socialization and education the concepts also have different connotations and meanings, mostly related to the process/product dimension. While the term education may signify both the process and the product of education, socialization mostly signifies the process. When education is given the more limited definition of intended, formal schooling going on in institutions set up for such purposes with a prescribed educational curriculum and evaluation of the outcome of the education, then education may be seen as a more limited concept than socialization, as a subdivision of that concept.

There are some analytical advantages to limiting the concept of education to the study of the formal education going on in schools. The same applies here as in the discussion of the peace concept—that the wider the concept gets, the more difficult it is to handle analytically and the easier it is to say that the concept means everything and nothing. The reasons for widening a concept are often, as was seen in the discussion of the peace concept, political ones: the need to get national or international agreement on a definition has been more strongly felt than a need voiced by some researchers of having a precise and limited concept to work with. But in the case of the concept "education" the widening of it to include also informal education and the hidden curriculum of the school has also been a result of educational research drawing more and more attention to these areas, showing their greater importance for the social and intellectual growth of the learner than earlier believed, often much more important than the formal schooling itself. Many of these findings come from more recent and more critical studies within the academic field of education. One of these, the Study of Social Education at the University of Oslo, has had as one of its main points of departure from the more traditional academic study of education, a criticism of a concept of education limiting education to formal schooling. It was argued that the educational influences of the home environment, of children's reading habits, the reading of cartoons for instance, television viewing, of the leisure environment like sports and youth club activities may be much greater than educational influences of the formal educational institutions. So, in the case of the concept "education" educational researchers themselves have widened the concept, thereby making it more unwieldy and necessitating subdivisions of the concept. The wider the education concept gets, the more it will overlap with the socialization concept. Even though I use a wide education concept, I still see a point in retaining the socialization concept because of the process orientation of that concept along with its strong connotations of informal learnings.

EDUCATION *FOR* PEACE AND EDUCATION *ABOUT* PEACE

The above discussion of the education concept has implications also for my discussion of the peace education concept. A distinction can here be made between education *for* peace and education *about* peace. When we try to analyze more closely the difference between the more cognitive, fact-oriented, and formal approach to peace education found in the term education *about* peace and the broader approach found in the term education *for* peace, we discover that not only do the two prepositions differ in the two juxtapositions, but so does the seemingly same word "education." Depending on the preposition, education may mean the more limited, formal learning of facts, (schooling about) or the broader informal learning of attitudes (schooling for).

When peace education is taken to mean education *about* peace, the definitional problems are of a different kind and much easier to tackle than when peace education is also taken to include education *for* peace. But it follows from my discussion of the education concept that I favor a broad definition of education and therefore shall also deal with the broad kind of peace education called education *for* peace. I am aware of the fact that my task would analytically have been an easier one had I settled for the more limited education *about* peace concept. In that case, the peace concept would have been the key concept. What does a world look like where peace exists? Which ideals are realized in a peaceful society? Which types of idealized states exist in micro and macro settings where peace, as it has been defined, can be found? The peace education in such a context would deal with questions of this type as well as with what type of analysis can be made to answer such questions. In a way the content of such a peace education has already been outlined in the previous chapter, where the peace concept has been discussed and defined and the relevance of feminist perspectives has been pointed out.

But I have not been searching for a limited definition in order to make my analytic task easier. Too often in research that is what we do. We carry out research where the empirical instruments are abundant, methods easy, and concepts precise and narrow. We are reminded of the man who on a dark night was searching for his watch under a lamp-pole. A passer-by asked the man if that was where he had lost it. No, he answered, he thought he had lost it further up the street, but there it was too dark and too difficult to search.

It seems to me that peace education in the sense of education *about* peace can be found under the lamp-pole while peace education in the sense of education *for* peace has to be searched for where it is unwieldy and difficult to search. Yet it may be there that the more important peace education is located. If we think this is so, as I happen to, we shall have to live with some definitional headaches, a couple of which I outline in the following paragraphs.

Education *for* peace may mean such education or socialization that *results* in more peace in the world or that at least has as a result the greater likelihood that peace will be the existing condition than the case would have been without that education. The trouble with such a definition is that in order to evaluate this type of peace education, we must know much more about the conditions that make for peace and the educational effects of various types of socialization for peace than we do now. We may say that too much of the necessary knowledge to build up education for peace is in the dark.

Education *for* peace may also be defined as an education *aimed at* bringing about peace in the way I have defined that concept. The trouble with this definition lies with the verb *aimed at*. If peace education is any process which from the point of view of an international or national body or an individual educator is aimed at bringing about peace, these processes may be as varied as the educators. This way of defining peace education may open up a "free-for-all" definition of peace education where the only criterion to call something peace education is that the educator *believes* that it will bring about peace. And some educators may believe that a certain type of education may bring about peace while other educators may believe that it is exactly the opposite of the type of education that will bring about peace. The beliefs may be rooted in the educator's view of human nature as either inherently bad and aggressive, or as inherently good, or as capable of developing either good or bad traits. The opinions on what might be aimed at bringing about peace will also vary, from quite subjective views based solely on what the individual believes, to somewhat more at least intrasubjective views based on the opinions of more people, on research findings, and on conducted experiments.

Within the unwieldly field of education for peace we shall have to live with these definitional headaches, the one caused by the limited knowledge of conditions leading to peace and the effect of education on producing such conditions, the other by the difficulty of getting beyond subjective viewpoints of educators aimed at bringing about peace through educational influences. I am treating a field where guesses have to be made, where there is a high degree of uncertainty. It is important to realize this fact when dealing with the field of peace education. Yet it does not make the field inaccessible for analysis and research, neither does it set the field drastically apart from other fields having to do with human behavior. Even the economic researchers working in the Norwegian Central Bureau of Statistics have ceased to call their trend-prolongations prognosis and now call them guesses instead. But a guess can be more or less informed, more or less well-founded. All we can do within unwieldly fields dealing with human behavior is to make the best guesses we are able to at the moment and argue for these guesses until we, maybe through our own arguing and study, find reasons to discard the guess we have made and come up with one, which from what we now know, seems to be a better one. My discussion in the following is based on what we, so far as we can now see, seems to create peace the way I have defined it. I shall attempt to make the best informed guess of which I am now capable as to the type of socialization process and education most likely to bring about peace.

The division of peace education into various subfields like human rights education, disarmament education, and development education may be looked at as an attempt to make the unwieldy peace education field somewhat easier to handle analytically. Roughly speaking, those who place most emphasis on the structural violence part of the peace concept would also like to see development education as the most central part of peace education. In a previous paper I have tried to relate the concepts disarmament education, development education, and human rights education to each other and to peace education, which I have seen as the generic umbrella for all the different disciplines (Brock-Utne, 1981b, 1988b). Peace education is sometimes also taken to include education for world citizenship, education for international understanding, or global education. And a field like disarmament education is sometimes termed "nuclear age education" both in an attempt to limit the field and to make it less controversial.

PEACE EDUCATION AS A CONTROVERSIAL CONCEPT

When peace education is normally debated, for instance in newspapers or in Parliament, it is as a subject or part of a curriculum to be introduced in schools. *That* part of peace education termed development education or education for international understanding seems to be less controversial than the newly established field, disarmament education. (See Brock-Utne, 1981b, 1982f, 1982g.) When, after the UN Special Session for Disarmament in 1978, it was recommended in the final document that disarmament education be introduced in schools, this seemed to be a recommendation that social-democratic parties paid some lip-service to and tried partly to follow up on, while more conservative parties went against the recommendation.

In Norway, for instance, the conservative government insisted that a curriculum plan for the teaching of disarmament education in secondary schools, developed by a group put together by the social-democratic government (I was a member of that group), be totally reorganized to include defense and security policy and have a chapter on "NATO as a peace force." It was also sent to the Defense Department for final approval. Some people fear that disarmament education means teaching youngsters that our side should disarm, and this they see as threatening the security. The propaganda against unilateral disarmament—there is little against unilateral rearmament—has worked. Peace education for many people is equated with disarmament education and they are afraid that peace education in schools will make youngsters less likely to do their military service, to defend their countries, to do their duty. Since peace in the sense of nonwar is a word used often by the Soviets—*mir*—both in schools and in great gatherings, some people in the West feel that we give in to the Soviet Union (and the people there are inherently bad as the argument goes) by introducing peace studies in school. Also, in England, peace education has been looked at as a subversive activity. As in Norway the conservative government in Britain wants peace studies to focus on problems of deterrence and to teach the importance of a strong national security, while the Labor party endorses a broader concept of peace education that includes, among other topics, disarmament studies and studies of nonviolent conflict resolution (Hunter, 1984). This same type of debate can be found in West Germany between the social-democratic (SPD) and conservative (CDU) states when it comes to peace education in schools (Lutz, 1984).

Hanns-Fred Rathenow and Paul Smoker (1983) at the Richardson Institute for Conflict and Peace Research have conducted an interesting survey of the attitudes of local education authorities in the United Kingdom toward the teaching of peace studies in schools. They asked the authorities which of 17 topics should be included in peace studies. There were clear differences between the ways in which authorities and councils in labor-governed and those in conservative-governed communities answered. Labor councils were, for instance, more likely to answer the questionnaire than Conservative councils. Very few (14.6 percent) failed to respond in any way. In contrast 19 of the 52 Conservative councils (36.5 percent) failed to reply, either to the initial letter and questionnaire or to the subsequent reminder. A quarter of the Conservative councils replied with a negative letter, as compared to just one negative Labor letter. When it came to the rank order of topics to be included in peace studies there were also some interesting differences between Labor and Conservative authorities. According to Labor the most important topic to be studied in peace studies was the nuclear arms race and as second topic, international integration and conflict. The Conservatives ranked group conflicts as number one and aggressive tendencies in human nature as number two. The Labor authorities also gave a higher priority to the study of nonviolent action than did the Conservative councils.

RECENT DEVELOPMENTS IN PEACE EDUCATION

Professional educators interested in disarmament and peace issues have formed both local, national, and international networks for the professional development of peace education. The networks have been built up around organizations like "Teachers for Peace," "Educators for Social Responsibility," the U.S.-based COPRED (Consortium on Peace Research, Education and Development) and IPRA (the International Peace Research Association). A wealth of material has appeared, from the more didactic and classroom-oriented material which gives good advice to teachers (see, for instance, Reardon, 1988b; Carpenter, 1977), to the more theoretical which discusses the direction of this new field of study (see, for instance, Alexander, 1984).

If one wants to get an overview quickly of the development and current state of peace education in the United States (and partly in other parts of the English-speaking world) I would recommend a recent book by the American peace educator Betty Reardon (1988a). In her book *Comprehensive Peace Education* with the subtitle Educating for Global Responsibility, Betty Reardon (1988a) gives a well-informed overview of the evolution of peace education during the last 20 years. Her book is an attempt to define the field and look at the pedagogical purposes and the political goals of peace education. It is an attempt to answer the question of how education can be used to interrupt the cycle of ever-increasing violence in which we are now swept up.

As a person who has been in peace education for a number of years Betty Reardon is able to look back and analyze the perceptions and professional practices of peace educators since the second World War. She writes about three phases in the development of peace education: These are, in chronological order: the reform phase, dating from the end of World War II; the reconstructive phase, developed in the 1960s; and the transformational phase, which she sees as the phase currently evolving. The approach used in each phase is characterized by certain assumptions about the causes of war and about how education could help to create the conditions needed for peace. Each approach, according to Betty Reardon, embraces a different political goal, and therefore each pursues a somewhat different set of pedagogical objectives. The goal of the reform approach is to prevent war, while the reconstructive approach seeks to reconstruct international systems, abolish war, and achieve total disarmament. The transformational approach seeks a larger and more comprehensive goal: the rejection of all violence, not just arms races and war. The goal of the transformational approach is to make violence unacceptable, not only in interactions among individuals but also in interactions among nations. The changes sought are behavioral and institutional but also, and primarily, changes in thinking and in the formation of values. Betty Reardon announces that it is the transformational approach that, in her view, holds the most promise for the future of peace education (Reardon, 1988a, p. xi). This approach challenges some of the fundamental value assumptions of the present system and the very bases of the social order. And she also admits, "Most of the elements of what I now define as transformational peace education came into focus for me when I brought a feminist perspective to them . . . It is through feminism that I have gained my insights into wholeness and integrity. Feminism is, I believe, the most fully human current perspective on peace and peace education'' (Reardon, 1988a, p. 10). Using feminism the way she does she really means what I term radical feminism, a feminism bent not only on demanding half of the pie but on creating a new recipe for the pie, a new value system.

Betty Reardon's book has a very useful appendix describing significant works in the development of the Pedagogy of Peace (Reardon, 1988a, pp. 83–109). The works cited include journals in the field, books, pamphlets, and monographs. She gives a brief description of the contents of the works and points at the strengths and weaknesses of the works as she sees them.

Taking Gender into Account

My main point and the new insight I am trying to convey here is that no matter whether the field is called peace education or education for global understanding, whether it is subdivided into fields like disarmament education and even further into nuclear age education, a feminist perspective on the field is sorely lacking. The lack of such a perspective makes the whole field of peace education incomplete at the least. One may even say biased, that is, biased in favor of the male as norm. The fact that boys and girls are educated differently is normally a nonissue in peace education. It is my intention here to make a scientific point out of this fact. The whole field of peace education has, for the most part of its existence, been lacking an analysis of patriarchy. Even the fact that a peace education given to ''the young'' will be given to young *girls* and young *boys* is underscored. Even quite recent, extensive and well-referenced works on peace education treat children, the young, students, parents as genderless, and fail to acknowledge the fact that most education seems to be gender-specific, teaching girls one type of behavior and attitudes and boys another.

For instance, a very thorough German book on peace education by Hermann Röhrs (1983) is written to give advice to parents and teachers on how to conduct peace education without mentioning the fact that there are gender-specific learnings in our culture. Hermann Röhrs gives advice on how to teach peace to children in kindergarten, to their parents, and to teachers and pupils in various subjects. He uses the term ''parents'' (or rather ''Eltern'') when he describes a peace education project in a kindergarten when only mothers were interviewed. He stresses the importance of knowing how the ''parents'' educate their children before starting to work with peace education in the kindergarten. But he only asks the mothers, and he asks them about the education they give their ''children'' without making any distinction between the education they give their sons and the education they give their daughters. The fact that there are gender-specific learnings in our culture is now so well documented that it has to be taken as a point of departure in any educational setting, also in peace education. What is more, the gender-specific teaching of boys and girls is especially marked when it comes to the handling and expression of aggression and violence, domination and submission, cooperation and competition—all elements of acknowledged importance within peace education.

From this insistence on taking gender into account in peace education, it does not at all follow that I envision and make a claim for a gender-specific peace education as an ultimate goal of peace education. On the contrary, I envision a peace education of an androgynous kind, a unisex peace education built on some of the elements today found in the socialization of girls, doing away with other elements, and some of the elements today found in the socialization of boys, doing away with other elements. But such a peace education has to take as its point of departure that today there are few examples of androgynous socialization, that the socialization processes all around the world seem to be gender-specific with girls taught to be more relationship-oriented, trained in a caring rationality, and boys to a higher degree taught to be competitive and to accept the relative subordination of women. Focusing on gender as a form of social organization means a fundamental revision of all canons of knowledge to take account of a genderized world, even those areas of knowledge previously thought to be gender neutral.

Even though our aim may be a unisex education for peace we have to start it from the knowledge gained, mostly through women's studies, that education as it is now conducted both formally and informally, in the school, home, through the media or leisure activities is gender-specific even when officially proclaimed that it should not be. We also have to be aware of the fact that even if we should be able to carry through a gender-neutral or nonsexist education in one institution, for instance in formal schooling, other institutions like the family or the media may carry on their gender-specific socialization and thus counteract the efforts of the school.

Level of Information and the Readiness to Act on the Information

There seems to be no automatic correlation between the level of information about peace issues and the readiness to act to improve conditions in order to enhance the aim of world peace. In a Swedish UNESCO report in 1976, no connection whatsoever was found between the information level of the students and their attitudes toward important social questions. The study concludes that factual information may not change attitudes and modes of thinking if the conditions surrounding the learning situation do not change simultaneously (Samhällskunnskap och samhällssyn," 1976—"Knowledge of and Attitudes to Social Questions"). On the other hand, Stig Lindholm (1986), in an analysis he has made of a survey conducted in 1984 by the Peace Association of Stockholm's Gymnasium schools, interprets the results to mean that "generally, increased knowledge goes together with increased belief in one's own capacity to influence development" (Lindholm, 1986, p. 17). A warning may be in order here not to interpret a correlation as a causal correlation. We do not know if increased knowledge increases one's self-concept and belief in one's capacity to influence development or if those with stronger self-concepts and beliefs in influencing development will also be the ones who see to it that they acquire more information and increase their knowledge. We may also have found a spurious correlation merely indicating that the correlation may be due to a third factor, for instance the effect of higher social class, which may tend to develop both an appetite for learning and a belief that one may be likely to influence the course of events.

The seeming contradiction between the results of these two surveys may be explained by the ten-year lapse of time between them. But there may also be other factors involved like the age of the pupils, the wording of the questions, the teaching they had been exposed to, the gender composition of the subjects, and the teachers. In none of the surveys are the attitudes measured not only against information level but also against actual behavior. There is reason to believe that such correlations will be very low, as actual behavior does not depend only on attitudes held but also on what the person sees as realistic options for actions and on the relative strength of norms that are in conflict.

A comparison between information level and actual behavior would be more difficult to make than a comparison between information level and attitudes. The best method here would make use of observations over time and in-depth interviews with acquaintances of the respondents. One research method which may not be so reliable but would be useful and certainly less time-consuming would be to have respondents report on their peace-related activities such as being members of peace groups, participating in peace marches, subscribing to peace journals, listening to or giving peace talks, and to compare the extent of such activities to the information levels of the respondents. Such studies would be of great interest from the point of view of a further exploration of the relationship between factual knowledge, conveyed as information and attitude formation as well as changes in behavior—in short, further exploring the relationship between education *about* peace, *about* disarmament, *about* development, and education *for* peace, *for* disarmament, and *for* development.

FEMINIST PERSPECTIVES ON VARIOUS APPROACHES TO THE DEFINITION OF PEACE EDUCATION

A couple of the old-timers within the Peace Education Commission within the International Peace Research Association, Mario Borrelli and Magnus

Haavelsrud (1983) are currently undertaking a study of the development of the concept of peace education within the archipelago of peace research. So far they have covered the period 1945–64. Here they attempt to look at peace, violence, and peace education from three different approaches: the structural, dialectical, and the evolutionary. None of their approaches is outlined from a feminist perspective. They seem gender neutral. While summarizing these approaches here, I shall also try to show what they would look like had feminist perspectives been applied to them.

The Structural Approach

According to Borrelli and Haavelsrud (1983, pp. 5–10), in the *structural approach* peace is an absolute concept and education for peace is therefore not possible as long as violence is still present in the societal structure. "A society which is structurally violent cannot educate people for peace, because the socialization process to which education is directed is always orientated to perpetuate violence" (Borrelli and Haavelsrud, 1983, p. 6). A feminist analysis from this perspective (see, for instance, Brock-Utne, 1982b) shows how the teachers, classmates, and schoolbooks all contribute to make girls accept boys and men as their superiors, to be content with their secondary role. It does not give much hope for change, as it sees the structures as unchangeable. What is going on in the classroom is merely a manifestation of the strength of these structures.

The Dialectical Approach

In *the dialectical approach* education for peace is considered to be the social process through which lower social classes gain necessary power to control the productive process. This education aims at making people not only aware of the existence of the struggle between social classes, but conscious of the superiority of working classes inasmuch as they produce the resources and as such are masters of the power that derives from them. From a feminist perspective this approach could mean the social process through which girls gain necessary power to be in control. Some socialist feminists like Shulamith Firestone claim that women must be in control of the means of reproduction if they are to eliminate sexual classes. Radical feminists with their analysis of patriarchy and with concepts like "women's culture" try to show women that they in many ways are the superior sex working harder and longer than men, caring more for other beings, bearing and feeding children, and seldom resorting to violence.

The Evolutionary Approach

In the *evolutionary* approach the authors have differentiated between the five possibilities outlined below. (I have here summarized their viewpoints following their text closely and using their concepts.)

- When emphasis is given to *genetical capital*, peace and violence become the fruit of a delicate, biological manipulation of experts, and peace education will also deal with the effects of the physical environment on the person.

Here a parallel can be drawn to the conservative feminists—those adhering to a biological determinism. As mentioned when discussing this perspective, Laurel Holliday's suggestions for a less violent world are selective birth devices to see to it that the numbers of males are drastically reduced in the world, administering drugs to male babies, or marijuana later in life.

- When emphasis is given to *instinctual capital*, education for peace will be the psychoanalytic methodology used to orientate the instinct of death in the right direction for biological survival.

This emphasis can be retraced in works by feminist theorists combining a socialist feminist perspective with a psychoanalytical approach (Chodorow, 1978; Mitchell, 1974; Rubin, 1984) although they are not talking about the instinct of death in an old Freudian sense of an instinct to seek one's own death but more as an instinct of aggression or to cause the death of others. Building on these theorists Brian Easlea (1983) sees the arms race as part of a revenge on the side of men because they are unable to create life. Women have a life-giving power which men envy. But men can create death and come to nourish the thoughts of death and play with death.

- When emphasis is given to the *physical* environment as a determining factor in the development of human behavior, peace is identified with ecological balance and education for peace will become the same as environmental education.

Among feminist thinkers placing their main emphasis on the physical environment we find Carolyn Merchant (1980) and Rosalie Bertell (1985), the former analyzing the theory of a narrow and masculine science with penetration of nature as its aim, the latter showing the practical consequences of this science on the human organism, on animals and plants.

- When emphasis is given to *sociocultural* factors as determining factors in the development of human behavior, education for peace may take two paths: either it will be the practicing of a reconciliation of human behavior with the existing sociocultural factors or it can be a methodology for the change of behavior which will create non-aggressive sociocultural structures.

The first of these paths is advocated by educators believing strongly in dialogue, seeing open communication and dialogue as the solution to most problems. Within peace education they may be advocating what they term "symmetric peace education" (for a debate on symmetric peace education, see Pikas, 1983a, 1983b; Brock-Utne, 1983e, 1983f). Radical feminist thinkers who are used to analyzing patriarchal institutions will easily see that symmetrical communication in asymmetrical relationships will not necessarily do away with the asymmetry, it might perpetuate it.

There is probably no clear-cut answer to the question of the effects of increased formal symmetry in situations with real asymmetry. In some instances such formal symmetry may increase the existing asymmetry; in other cases it may decrease it. It is important to have studies that will aid people in deciding in which cases formal symmetry will increase and in which cases, decrease, a real and existing asymmetry.

It is also a question whether a dialogue can be really symmetrical (that is "herrschaftsfrei") in a situation where the one part holds power over or tries to dominate the other. Dialogue is not necessarily an instrument for social change. Between unequals it may mean an improvement of social relationships, learning to adjust to a situation of inequality and oppression. There may be oppressive relations one should *not* adjust to, dialogues which have to be broken. This education for peace may mean appeasement, pacification, learning to resign and be content with one's lot. It can be found in popular glossy magazines for women teaching them to please their husbands, understand him when he is tired, make his favorite dish, and dress nicely to make him happy.

While it is difficult to find any feminist thinkers advocating an education built on a reconciliation of human behavior with the existing sociocultural factors, we find many feminists advocating change in human behavior as part of a strategy to create nonaggressive sociocultural structures (Brock-Utne, 1985; Burns, 1985; Pietilä, 1985; Reardon, 1986; Stanford, 1983). All of these researchers share the belief that through the creation of other learning situations in school, during leisure time, and at home, it should be possible to also teach boys to relate, to care, to cooperate and share, and to also teach girls to stand up for their rights.

Borrelli and Haavelsrud (1983, p. 72) criticize this position in a footnote by saying that it is an ambivalent position "because human behaviour is considered to be at the same time cause and effect of socio-cultural factors." The feminist researchers I have referred to seem to be able to live with this ambivalence, recognizing that changes have to be made at different levels simultaneously, both in structures and in people. Rather than deploring this "ambivalence" I would look at the recognition of it as a strength. It means both avoiding the idealistic pitfall, thinking that if just the individual person is changed, the whole world changes *and* the stereotyped Marxist pitfall holding that if just structures change, people will change or that people cannot be changed unless the existing structures are torn down and reorganized.

- When emphasis is given to the combination of *ecological* factors coupled with *sociocultural* ones, peace remains the effect of a correct equilibrium between these variables and education for peace a balanced, well-geared composition of ecological education and behavioral development education.

This fifth position seems to be the one the authors prefer, having no critical comment to it. I would rather prefer the last part of their fourth position, as the fifth position says nothing about a change in behavior to create nonaggressive or nonviolent structures, though that of course may be assumed. Nonviolent structures to me are also structures that do not do violence to nature and the environment.

THE DEVELOPMENT OF THE PEACE EDUCATION CONCEPT THROUGH THREE UN WOMEN'S DECADE CONFERENCES

Women's interest in peace education could be analyzed in many different ways. We could look at who promotes peace education in politics, in schools, in the peace movements. I assume that we would find women in the forefront everywhere. And within IPRA, the commission with the largest proportion of women is the Peace Education Commission. Right from the start of WILPF women have been eager to promote not only peace research but also peace education. Therefore it strikes one as strange that there is no mention of the concept of peace education in the first two final documents stemming from the three UN Women's Decade conferences, the one in Mexico in 1975 and the one in Copenhagen in 1980. (See Brock-Utne, 1986b.)

Plan of Action from Mexico

In this *Plan of Action* from the first Women's Decade conference, held in Mexico in 1975, the term *peace education* does not exist. But one paragraph deals with education for global understanding. In paragraph 55 we read:

> Women and men should be encouraged to instill in their children the values of mutual respect and understanding for all nations and all peoples, racial equality, sexual equality, the right of every nation to self-determination and the desire to maintain international co-operation, peace and security in the world.

This paragraph seems to deal with peace education or education for international understanding in the home, not in school. There is no mention of the fact that women and men do not have the same opportunities to instill values in their children. Even though mothers spend more time with their children, especially when they are small, the children soon come to learn the relative inferiority of the mother in relation to the father and also how women are viewed and treated under patriarchy. As I have shown in the preceding chapter fathers seem to influence their children more than mothers do. Mothers are certainly placed in a dilemma when they are encouraged to instill in their children the values of sexual equality when they themselves are oppressed both in the family and in society at large.

Programme of Action from Copenhagen

Neither in the Copenhagen document is there any mention of the term *peace education* as such. But there are ingredients which are normally included within the term peace education in *some* of the paragraphs. In paragraph 167 we find the concept "education for non-violence" and in paragraph 185 there is an encouragement for human rights education. In paragraph 167 one of the objectives of education and training is:

> to take into consideration in educational programmes and methodologies the special perspective of education for non-violence, mainly with regard to relationships between women and men.

And in paragraph 168 the term "education against violence" is used. What the paragraphs say is that men and women should be trained not to use violence against each other. The gender-neutral form in which paragraphs 167 and 168 are put does not mention the fact that in the case of violence in the relationships between women and men, men are usually the aggressors, the actors, and women the victims. But, as I have shown in the third chapter, this fact has been stressed elsewhere in the Copenhagen plan (§ 11 and § 141 f) and could well have been applied to the thinking about education for nonviolence. One could assume that this education is more sorely needed for men than for women.

The violence described in paragraphs 167 and 168 seems to be of a direct kind and at the microlevel, a personal kind of violence. One of the priority areas for action within the educational sector mentioned in the Copenhagen plan is to:

> Develop programmes at the secondary, tertiary and adult education levels to encourage a basic understanding of human rights, including the Declaration of Human Rights and other relevant instruments. Such courses should stress the fundamental importance of the elimination of discrimination on the basis of race and sex. (paragraph 185)

We may say that this paragraph contains a feminist perspective albeit a liberal one since it sees the elimination of sex discrimination of such fundamental importance. Even though the elimination of sex discrimination is important from any feminist perspective, from a radical feminist perspective it is not the *most* fundamental. Radical feminists are not as concerned about getting a bigger or more equal share of the pie as they are in changing the basic recipe of the pie. Also, sometimes discrimination on the basis of race and sex may be used to favor underprivileged groups. Affirmative actions are in a way discriminatory acts on the basis of race and sex, yet may be defended as temporary measures used to gain the aim of greater equality. The present Norwegian government is unlikely to have consisted of almost half women had not the Labor Party adopted an affirmative action plan in its statutes insisting that at least 40 percent of any committee had to be women. This affirmative action plan was first put forward by the women's movement within the Party.

While the Mexico document deals more with an education *for* peace (without using the concept), the Copenhagen document with its emphasis on educational programs deals more with an education *about* peace, about nonviolence, disarmament, and human rights (without using the term education about peace).

Another paragraph legitimizing the provision of more formal peace education, in this case especially to women, is paragraph 76:

> Women of the entire world should participate in the broadest way in the struggle to strengthen international peace and security . . . High priority should be given to providing training and educational opportunities at all levels. These might include university or college courses, lectures on international affairs, panel discussions, conferences, seminar and other educational activities.

But the paragraph says nothing about the inclusion of a feminist perspective in the lectures on international affairs. Women may just become trained in mainstream thinking and learn little about the peace activities of women through ages. If women learn to conduct disarmament negotiations the same way men do, there is no reason to believe that the negotiations will be more successful than they have been so far.

Forward-Looking Strategies from Nairobi

In the *Nairobi* document the term *peace education* is used several times. When we look at all three documents resulting from the three UN Women's Decade conferences there is no doubt that peace education as a distinct area of concern for educators and policy planners has first been introduced in the Nairobi document. Here we also find a distinction between the nonformal education *for* peace and *for* disarmament and the more formal education *about* or *on* peace. Paragraph 255 says that:

> Peace education should be established for all members of society, particularly children and young people. Values, such as tolerance, racial and sexual equality, respect for and understanding of others, and good-neighbourliness should be developed, promoted and strengthened.

The following paragraph stresses that peace education

> should be part of all formal and informal educational processes as well as of communications, information and mass-media systems.

Paragraph 272 as well as paragraphs 274 and 263 deal with the role of women in peace education. In paragraph 263 we read that:

> Women's participation in the World Disarmament Campaign and their contribution to education for disarmament should be supported.

And in paragraph 272:

> Governments, non-governmental organizations, women's groups and the mass media should encourage women to engage in efforts to promote education for peace in the family, neighbourhood and community. Special attention should be given to the contribution of women's grass-roots organizations. The multiple skills and talents of women artists, journalists, writers, educators and civic leaders can contribute to promoting ideas of peace if encouraged, facilitated and supported.

Paragraphs 273 and 274 both deal with the content of peace education, the first of them dealing with what should be discouraged in children's environment in order to give them a peace education and the second one dealing with what should be *encouraged* and included in peace education. In paragraph 273 we read that:

> suitable concrete action should be taken to discourage the provision of children and young persons with games and publications and other media promoting the notion of favouring war, aggression, cruelty, excessive desire for power and other forms of violence, within the broad processes of the preparation of society for life in peace.

The genderless words "children" and "young persons" do not draw any attention to the fact that boys and girls are educated very differently in all societies and that the games favoring aggression and violence are aimed at the boys and played by the boys. One may maintain that this fact must not necessarily be mentioned in a peace education paragraph as one may assume that it will form an important part of a further study of how to implement such a paragraph. But a quick survey of the available peace education literature will assure us that such an assumption is incorrect. In fact when I was given the assignment by UNESCO in 1981 to write an expert paper on the role of mothers in the education of the young for peace, it took me quite a while to realize that I could not treat "the young" as a genderless group, yet this was the way they were treated in the peace education literature I came across. It would have been an advantage, as far as I see it, if the above-mentioned paragraph had mentioned something about the necessity of looking more closely at the gender role socialization in relation to peace education.

In paragraph 274 governments, educational institutions, professional associations and nongovernmental organizations are asked to cooperate to develop high-quality programs, books, and materials on peace education:

> Women should take an active part in the preparation of those materials, which should include case studies of peaceful settlements of disputes, non-violent movements and passive resistance and the recognition of peaceseeking individuals.

We have to turn to paragraph 344 to find that the role of women in promoting peace should constitute an important element in peace education. Here international machineries that promote and support education for peace are asked to

> co-ordinate their efforts and include the role of women in promoting peace in their curricula.

It says further that:

> Particular attention should be paid to the Declaration on the Participation of Women in Promoting International Peace and Co-operation adopted by the General Assembly in 1982. The University of Peace should play a leading role in this regard.

The final document from Nairobi signifies a big leap forward in feminist understanding as governments are encouraged to make the role of women in promoting peace part of the curriculum for a peace education. Often the role of women in peace making has been made invisible in books dealing with peace initiatives and peace heroes.

CAN PEACE COME ABOUT THROUGH PEACE EDUCATION?

I have already pointed to the fact that there are contradictory results of studies analyzing the connection between information level and attitudes. What about an education which is likely to bring about changes in attitudes in individuals? Would such individuals with peaceful attitudes also work for peace at a macrolevel? Would a whole nation built up of peaceful, nonaggressive individuals be more likely than other nations to refrain from using violence in international disputes and, at the same time, work for a more even distribution of resources? Or would such a nation show friendship toward each other and be able to solve conflicts among each other nonviolently and constructively but show outward hostility and favor the use of violence between nations? It is difficult to claim a priori that peaceful attitudes among individuals will aggregate on to meso- and macrolevels. In peace education this is normally assumed, even though the claim is little discussed. One may maintain that it seems likely that a nation built up of peace-full individuals would also behave peacefully internationally and that those who find such a connection unlikely must be the ones who have to prove and argue for their thesis. The empirical studies we have, which throw some light on this relationship, are not conclusive. If we look at some standard anthropological works like Berndt (1962) or Montagu (1978) we find descriptions of societies in which intergroup aggression is high but in which intragroup aggression is low, as among a number of New Guinea peoples. There are other societies in which both inter- and intragroup aggression is low, as among the Toda of Southern India, and societies where both inter- and intragroup aggression by some researchers has been held to be nonexistent as in the case of the Tasaday of Mindanao in the Philippines (Montagu, 1978; Nance, 1975).

Ashley Montagu (1978) in his book on learning nonaggression defines aggression as "behavior designed to inflict pain or injury on others." This definition is used quite often in aggression research especially by anthropologists studying aggressive behavior in natural environments. The definition has the advantage that it is comparatively easy to measure and observe behavior directly. One difficulty with the definition is the expression "designed to" which adds a subjective element to the definition. It is, according to this definition, not enough to register behavior—the motives for the behavior must also be known. But who is going to judge those motives? There could be at least three judges: the actor, the victim, and a researcher. The actor may maintain that the behavior in question was not "designed to inflict pain or injury" though the victim was actually injured and also claimed that the behavior was designed to injure him. It is also possible that the actor may maintain that a certain behavior was designed to inflict pain or injury, yet the victim may not have been aware of this at all. The actor may, for instance, intentionally have broken a vase which was very precious to the person he wanted to cause pain to, yet that person may think this was an accident, not done to harm him. We may illustrate our point through the following fourfold table:

	Behavior designed to inflict pain/ injury	Behavior *not* designed to inflict pain/ injury
Injury and felt pain	1	2
No injury and no felt pain	3	4

All the four cells can easily be filled with illustrative examples. An operational definition would include all examples in cell 1 and 2 as acts of aggression since the outcomes, not the motives, would be the important thing. Montagu's definition would leave out examples in cell 2 and 4, including those in 1 and 3. An attempt to make Montagu's definition more operational would be to limit a study of aggression to phenomena which will be included in cell 1 where the actor and a researcher are the judges of the motives for the behavior while the victim and a researcher are the judges of the outcome of the behavior. Even here there will be subjective elements when we touch on the borderline phenomena of felt pain; some may feel something as painful which others would not, something may be regarded as an injury in some cultures and not in others. Of course there are incidences of physical injury which are clear cases of injury everywhere while other behavior might be regarded as injury in one culture but not in another. Is it at all possible to arrive at a culture-free definition of aggression? Such a definition would be necessary for making cross-cultural comparisons.

We see that even when we, like Montagu, concentrate on behavior when we define aggression, we run into problems of subjectivity. These problems multiply when we, like many aggression researchers from the field of psychology, claim that aggression is not primarily behavior, acts, but also and sometimes *only* an emotion. This definitional discussion may be looked at as the result of some conceptual confusion where the concept is discussed as a question of reality, that is, "What *is* aggression?" rather than as a question of what are the most fruitful definitions for a particular piece of research.

When aggression is defined as behavior and not as emotions a vast amount of psychological research on aggression will fall outside the definition and will not be regarded as aggression research. In psychotherapeutic research aggression has primarily been looked at as an emotion. The Finnish aggression researcher Kirsti Lagerspetz (1981, 1983) at the aggression research unit at Åbo University makes a strong claim for including also the emotional side of aggression in a definition of that concept.

Though one may maintain that focusing both on behavior and on emotion is to deal with levels of different ontological natures, it is still possible to have definitions of aggression including both behavior and emotion, which was also shown in my further elaboration of Montagu. His definition is not as strictly behavioristic as it may seem at first.

This definitional discussion among psychologists and anthropologists regarding the concept of aggression also has relevance for peace researchers and peace educators. If aggression is defined as behavior, wars of any kind must be looked at as aggression. But those involved in the planning and execution of wars are often guided by feelings other than aggressive feelings toward the "enemy." Kirsti Lagerspetz (1983, p. 232) claims that mammals other than humans do not kill others of their own kind without aroused aggressive feelings. In human beings this is quite different. Human beings may kill each other without having aggressive feelings toward each other. They may do so out of a sense of loyalty and duty or a fear of being labeled a coward or a lesser man. Kirsti Lagerspetz claims that the scientists developing nuclear weapons in Los Alamos were not especially aggressive beings. They were not guided by a sense of aggression but one of ambition, sometimes even intellectual curiosity. They were driven by oneupmanship, by a wish to be the first, the most advanced, the leading scientists of the world. Some of them may even have been driven by a fear of retaliation, should they have second thoughts about the project.

It is possible to commit aggressive acts without possessing aggressive feelings and it is also possible to have aggressive feelings and not commit aggressive acts. In modern wars feelings of aggression are probably less pronounced than feelings of fear—fear of the enemy, fear of one's superiors, fear of being labeled a coward. Soldiers in battle do not seem to be motivated to kill or injure from any hate of the enemy but rather from a sense of self-protection or a protection of their buddies in the small military unit of which they are a part. Modern wars further seem to require some amount of strategic planning and thinking, a sense of loyalty and duty, obedient behavior and cooperation, the willingness to sacrifice, even one's own life.

I agree with Kirsti Lagerspetz that a discussion of aggression has to take into account aggression both as behavior and as an emotion. But the distinction raises further questions. Even though there may be little correlation between emotions and acts of aggression when a person acts on behalf of, or commanded by, his country there may be a stronger correlation between emotions and aggressive acts if a person just acts on behalf of himself. If this is so, it may be possible that a person who commits aggressive acts out of aggressive emotions on an individual level may be directed by other emotions when it comes to aggressive acts on a national and international level and go against those. It is also possible that a person who advocates aggressive acts on a national scale—from, for instance, a feeling of fear, loyalty, obedience—will refrain from aggressive behavior on an individual level in peacetime (not war) because he holds few aggressive emotions.

Kirsti Lagerspetz's work on the relationship between human aggression and war has consequences for peace education also from a feminist perspective. If people waging wars and being engaged in wars are not primarily driven by feelings of aggression but rather by feelings of loyalty, obedience, fear, and are eager to cooperate and even sacrifice themselves, there may be elements in the upbringing of girls which may predispose for war as much, maybe even more, than elements in the upbringing of boys.

Other works on the causes of aggressive behavior seem to indicate that in order to understand such behavior one also has to understand causes for inhibition. Dan Olweus has, through his research, tried to understand the personalities of aggressive Swedish school boys, ages 12 to 16, the so-called bullies, who subject other boys of the same age, the so-called whipping boys, to physical and/or mental violence and oppression for longer periods of time. He has found (Olweus, 1969, 1978) that the bullies may be said to be characterized by an aggressive personality pattern with a tendency to react aggressively in many different situations, with weak controls or inhibitions against aggressive tendencies and with a positive attitude to violence. In his doctoral thesis where 44 boys from Stockholm, aged 12–14 years, were examined he found the personality pattern of the bullies to correspond to a combination of high habitual aggressive tendencies and predominantly low habitual aggression inhibitory tendencies (Olweus, 1969). Olweus has centered his aggression research on boys. In his doctoral dissertation he gives this reason for concentrating on boys: "Previous investigations and theoretical considerations suggest that development in the sphere of aggressive motivation is partly different for boys and for girls and consequently it was deemed suitable to confine at least an initial phase of research to only one sex. Boys were chosen because there are more empirical data with boys as subjects" (Olweus, 1969, p. 28). His argument strikes me as peculiar. The fact that there are more empirical studies with boys as subjects might lead one to the opposite conclusion of the one he reaches; having so little empirical data with girls as subjects, there is a stronger need to get such data on girls than on boys. Also, since the development of aggressive behavior seems to be different for girls and boys, it may be interesting to look at the difference.

In his later studies he has also concentrated on boys, using girls only to evaluate the bullies and the whipping boys. In a book called *Aggression in Schools* which more correctly ought to have been called *Aggressive Boys in Schools* Olweus (1978) reports five separate studies. The first one involved all the boys in the sixth grade at Solna, 299 in all. The second one involved 113 sixth-grade boys from three schools in the central and southern areas of Stockholm. Participants in the third investigation were 142 boys from 12 sixth-grade classes distributed over six schools in east, central, and southern Stockholm. The fourth and fifth investigations used boys from Solna. The fourth involved 217 boys in the sixth grade, and the fifth involved 215 boys from the eighth grade. On the basis of the results obtained, Olweus finds it natural to assume that the attacking and harassment of weaker boys gives rise to feelings of superiority in the bullies and also provides them with a certain prestige, at least among *some* of their peers. Their aggressive behavior cannot be interpreted as some kind of defensive reaction in response to frequent attacks or provocations from other boys since Olweus found that the bullies were not attacked or teased by their peers more often than boys in general. The bullies enjoyed almost average popularity among the boys and more than average popularity among the girls. He has not commented on this latter fact though it strikes me as extremely interesting and suggests that the role of the girls, even though they are less aggressive than the boys, may not be as innocent as one would think. The role of cheerleader giving prestige to competitive and aggressive boys is a role that may influence the behavior of boys to a high degree.

When it comes to the whipping boys, Olweus makes a distinction between the passive whipping boys (and they are the great majority of whipping boys) and the provocative whipping boys. The passive whipping boys had very low values on the peer-rated dimensions "Tease," "Start Fights" and "Verbal Protest" (even when the provocative whipping boys were included, the mean values for the whipping boy group were lower than those for the control boys). There was no connection between the extent of being the target of other boys' attacks and a boy's own aggressive behavior. The whipping boys were found to be generally anxious, to have a high sensitivity, and to lack assertiveness, aggressivity, and toughness. A typical whipping boy is one "who does not retaliate when he is attacked, who becomes afraid and perhaps cries, who is unwilling or unable to ward off attacks by even fairly harmless antagonists. Generally, he disapproves of taking part in rough games with the other boys of the class" (Olweus, 1978, p. 142).

For a boy with bullying tendencies the potential whipping boy is an ideal target as he does not dare retaliate. The bully usually wants to have others join him, and he soon induces his closest friends to pick on the whipping boy. Many boys are afraid of reducing their own status by being together with the whipping boy. Olweus tries to explain why more "neutral" boys now and then harass the whipping boy by looking at the following mechanisms: (1) social contagion, (2) weakening of the control of inhibitions against aggressive tendencies, (3) distribution of responsibility, and (4) cognitive changes.

But *some* boys are not susceptible to the mechanisms mentioned above and do not take part in the harassment of the whipping boys. Olweus points at some factors that may explain why these well-adjusted boys do not contribute to the harassment of whipping boys: (1) These boys are relatively secure, confident, independent, well liked by their peers, and they probably find little satisfaction in defeating the whipping boy; (2) They have rather weak habitual aggressive tendencies; (3) They have strong controls over aggressive tendencies; and (4) They have a negative attitude toward violence. "In other words, they have an internal system of norms that would probably lead to self-criticism and guilt feelings if they went along with attacking a rather defenseless whipping boy" (Olweus, 1978, p. 147).

The difficult questions for peace educators must be: How do we avoid the development of bullies and whipping boys, and how do we promote the development of well-adjusted boys? In many ways the whipping boys have traits that one might have liked to have seen developed in boys, such as sensitivity and lack of aggressiveness and toughness. A challenging task for further studies would be to come up with thoughts on how such traits can be developed in a boy without his becoming the target of harassment and ridicule.

The studies by Olweus also point to the necessity of analyzing factors that raise or lower the threshold of inhibition, if one wants to understand aggressive behavior. Some such factors which are likely to lower the threshold of inhibition will be discussed in the following pages, among them the desensitizing process which may result from the frequent viewing of televised violence. Other inhibition-lowering factors have already been alluded to in my discussion of aggressive behavior committed by people not feeling aggressive but being under command, as during war. Someone else has taken over the responsibility for the aggressive acts being committed. Several studies, among them Milgram (1975), have shown that when someone acts under the pressure from authority, even under a low pressure, he or she may inflict pain, like electrical shocks, on innocent victims. In some of the experiments he conducted, some people were asked to be part of learning experiments concerning the effects of punishment on learning performance. Some people were asked to be teachers, some pupils who were to solve some mathematical problems. The ones chosen as teachers were really the subjects in this study, while the "pupils" were actors and part of the experiment.

The teachers were instructed to give the "pupils" electrical shocks when they made mistakes, and each time they were told by the leader of the experiment how much to increase the shock. The teachers could see the victim through a glass wall and see how he was suffering (in reality the "pupils" were not given any shocks at all, but this the teachers did not know). The pupil started showing discomfort when the teacher "gave" him a 75 voltage shock, started complaining at 120, asked to have the experiment stopped at a voltage of 150. When the voltage of the shocks was further increased, the "pupil" showed all the signs of a person being tortured. The teacher was now caught in a serious conflict between obeying the orders of the leader of the experiment or identifying with the pain of the "pupil." Every time the teacher hesitated before administering a stronger electric shock to the pupil, the leader of the experiment would encourage him to go on. One might think that only sadists would continue giving stronger shocks when they saw that the victim was in great pain. But Milgram (1975), through his experiments, showed that that is not the case. Almost two thirds of the teachers obeyed the leader of the experiment even when they saw that the victim was in great pain. The teachers Milgram has used for his experiments have come from all walks of life. They have been workers, clerks, regular teachers, intellectuals. Most of his subjects have been men, but in one case he made the experiment with 40 women as subjects. He did not find any difference between the male and the female subjects. He tries to explain this finding by suggesting that there may be two contradictory forces influencing women—on the one hand their empathy and caring—on the other hand their strong tendency to obey authority.

The strong inclination to obey orders and to let someone else, someone in authority, take the responsibility for one's acts may also explain atrocities like the medical "experiments" conducted by Nazi doctors, the gassing of the Jews, and the massacre at My Lai.

When we move from the micro- to the macrolevel in our discussion on aggression and start talking about aggression between states, we shall there find that in international law the discussion and definition of aggression is highly positivistic and empiricist, as it is a certain *behavior* that is defined normatively and forbidden. These international texts, UN texts mostly, do not make any attempt at describing the intentions or emotions of those committing or being victims of aggressive acts.

Attitude Formation and Social Behavior

There seems to exist a certain relationship between attitude formation and social behavior (see for instance, the doctoral thesis of Eva Nordland, 1948). Years ago Margaret Mead (1935) was the first anthropologist to inquire into the aggressiveness in nonliterate societies. In her well-known book *Sex and Temperament in Three Primitive Societies*, she pointed to the fact that the child who received a great deal of attention and whose every need was promptly met, as among the New Guinea Mountain Arapesh, became a gentle, cooperative, unaggressive adult. On the other hand, the child who received perfunctory, intermittent attention, as among the New Guinea Mundugumor, became a selfish, uncooperative, aggressive adult. Later anthropological research among nonliterate and literate peoples has mostly confirmed a relationship between child-rearing practices and later personality development, though there are also studies which seem to indicate that the relationship is not so clear cut.

In an article called "Small Peace" presented by Paul Smoker (1981) he refers to studies by Fabbro (1978) of peaceful societies. These societies varied considerably when it came to child-rearing practices, from the more permissive ones to the more authoritarian and punitive ones. David Fabbro (1978) has made an analysis of the following seven societies which he termed peaceful: the Semai of Malaya, the Siriono of eastern Bolivia, the Mbuti Pygmies of the Ituru Forest, the Kung Bushmen of the Kalahari Desert, the Copper Eskimo of Northern Canada, the Hutterites of North America, and the Islanders of Tristan da Cunha. In the first five of these societies child-rearing practices are characterized as permissive with little or no physical punishment and a great deal of encouragement and warmth. The child-rearing practices of the Hutterites and the Tristans are, however, characterized as authoritarian. The premise of child development is that they are expected to behave badly because they have not yet learned to cope with their carnal desires. Children are severely punished. Punishment is usually physical, arbitrary, and inconsistent and, from the child's point of view, often unpredictable. One may conclude from Fabbro's studies that there may be low correlation between child-rearing practices and the peacefulness of societies. The definition of peaceful in Fabbro's work is, however, a rather limited one. The societies he has selected as "peaceful" have to meet the following five criteria:

1. The society has no wars fought on its territory.
2. The society is not involved in any external wars.
3. There are no civil wars or internal collective violence.
4. There is no standing military-police organization.
5. There is little or no interpersonal physical violence.

When it comes to the fifth criteria the Hutterites and Tristans really do not satisfy this one, as there is considerable physical violence committed by parents and directed toward children. Among the Hutterites there is also considerable violence between children. Among several of the so-called peaceful societies there is considerable violence between husband and wife, mostly wife beating as among the Tristans, the Copper Eskimos, and the Mbuti Pygmies. Other "peaceful" societies practice infanticide. This is, according to Fabbro, the case with the Kung Bushmen, and the Copper Eskimos. Several of the societies are sexist. This is especially the case with the Hutterites, where according to their ideology God is at the top, then men who preside over women, who together control children, all of whom dominate nature. Women do not participate in deciding colony affairs either by voting or by holding leadership positions. Sexism exists in a blatant form where women are believed to be intellectually and physically inferior to men. In such a society, according to my discussion of the peace concept, there is structural violence, and I would not describe the society as peaceful. Smoker (1981) however argues that such a society may not necessarily be experienced as structurally violent by those who live in it and take part in its sociocultural totality. Here he is, as far as I see it, mixing up two levels of analysis. The one is the more objective or structural level based on a certain set of agreed-upon criteria, criteria which often are based on human rights concepts, on justice, and equality; the other one is the more subjective level of experience. A woman who is economically dependent on her husband, lets him make all important decisions and obeys him with pleasure may not feel oppressed. But from more objective criteria she is oppressed and the day she, for some reason, does not want to obey him anymore she will also feel the oppression.

It is likely that a closer connection between the peacefulness of a society and its child-rearing practices would have been found if peaceful had been given a broader definition, more like peace has been defined in my Chapter 3. Then a peaceful society would have to be a society where there was also absence of structural violence and gross inequalities. In a more than fifty-year-old book the American anthropologist Ruth Benedict (1934) describes the Zuni who are part of the Pueblo Indian culture of the southwestern United States. Their members, at least in 1934, lived much as their forefathers did. (I know little about the Zunis today.) Ruth Benedict writes that the Zunis try to share evenly and equalize rewards. Even in contests of skill like their foot races, if a man wins habitually he is debarred from running. They are interested in a game that a number can play with even chances, and an outstanding runner spoils the game. They will have none of him, she tells (Benedict, 1934, p. 90).

In a book edited by Ashley Montagu (1978) on learning nonaggression, he asks the question: Why are aggression and violence totally nonexistent in some cultures? Through a series of anthropological studies described in the book he gives this answer, summarizing the studies: "The answer lies in childrearing, particularly in the treatment of infants . . . In each nonaggressive society, infants' basic needs are continuously satisfied without obstacle, and young children learn without punishment to cope with angers, fears and hostilities" (from the cover of his book). In the introduction to his book he describes the Tasaday of Mindanao in the Philippines—a society in which both inter- and intragroup aggression are nonexistent. Aggression is here defined as "behavior designed to inflict pain or injury on others." John Nance (1975), a journalist who spent some 73 days over a period of three years visiting with them, found the Tasaday to be "inspiring emblems of social peace and harmony, of simply love. Their love was, everywhere—for each other, for their forest, for us—for life. They are altogether a loving people. They have no weapons, and no apparent aggressive impulses" (Nance, 1975, p. 447). Yet classic aggressive behavior between toddlers could be seen among the Tasaday, arguing over a stick or slapping at each other. The key question for Nance was how the Tasaday managed aggression in their children so that they grew to be loving adults. He concluded that the answer would appear to be that from an early age the Tasaday reward cooperative behavior and discourage aggressive conduct, while setting models in themselves for their children to imitate.

Drawing parallels from such studies to our own west-European society we may ask: To what extent do we reward cooperative behavior and discourage aggressive conduct in our children? Are there indications that cooperative behavior is rewarded less in boys than in girls, that aggressive conduct is encouraged more in boys than in girls? And, drawing on Kirsti Lagerspetz's research, we may further ask: What role does aggression as an emotion play compared to other feelings in people advocating doctrines of strength, first strike, rearmament, and limited nuclear war?

We may also look at the models our youngsters have to imitate. And they do not, like the Tasaday, find grown-up models only in the nearest grown-ups communicating with them but also, sometimes even more so, in adults presented on television, in advertising, in magazines. How are adult males portrayed here? What models do they set for young boys to imitate and what do they teach young girls?

I agree with Montagu in the conclusion he draws after having studied aggressive behavior in many societies: "Human beings can learn virtually anything. Among other things, they can learn to be virtually wholly unaggressive . . . Whatever humanity's potentialities for aggression may be, and we know that such potentialities exist, it is clear that expression will largely depend upon the environmental stimulation they receive" (Montagu, 1978, p. 6).

In the introduction to a book called *Violence and the Brain* by the two medical doctors Vernon Mark and Frank Ervin (1970), William Sweet, who is a professor of neurosurgery at Harvard Medical School, states that his two colleagues, the authors of the book, do not accept "the theories of those sociologists, anthropologists, economists, and psychologists who have proposed that man is an innately fighting, murderous species incessantly warring over territory, women, food and drink" (Mark and Ervin, 1970, p. viii). It is interesting to note that he seems to equate "man" with the male species of the human being since he sees him warring over women. Mark and Ervin, who in their book present a convincing case for the role of the physician in treating at least some violent individuals, those whose unacceptable behavior is partially the result of focal brain disease, do not believe that human beings are born violent or have violent instincts. After a discussion of such a view they conclude that in a well-ordered brain the mechanisms of violence may be there but they need never be out of control. Similarly, in well-ordered hands there is no danger that matches will be used for arson. "After all, keeping matches in the home does not imply that the homeowner is a pyromaniac" (Mark and Ervin, 1970, p. 32).

If this is so, and I find this likely, there is reason to be optimisitic when it comes to the possible effects of a peace education. For if we understand the conditions that produce aggressive behavior, there is some hope that by changing those conditions, we may be able to control both its development and expression. Today we know, for instance, that by far the larger proportion of child batterers were themselves battered or neglected as children (Kempe and Helfer, 1968). We know that those who have been emotionally deprived are likely to turn into aggressive adults and that those who have been adequately loved as children are likely to develop into loving, unaggressive adults (Montagu, 1975).

It would appear that while potentialities for aggression exist in all human beings at birth, such potentialities will remain nothing more unless they are organized by experience to function as aggressive behavior. Aggressive behavior is no more innately determined, it seems, than the behavior we call speech. We are born with the potential to learn to speak any language. A black child born from African parents and adopted by Norwegians at birth will learn to speak Norwegian like a Norwegian and will not know Swahili unless she is taught that language later on.

In the truly peaceful cultures mentioned, both men and women are non-aggressive. In a book review Elise Boulding (1986b, pp. 552–554) maintains that the question of a viable peace culture calls for an examination of a whole range of minority cultures in the world and does not necessarily present itself as women's versus men's cultures. She mentions the spirit camps of the native peoples of Alask, which are both recreating and transmitting a strong traditional peace culture to a younger generation as a case in point. The question I am asking here is whether we in our culture, through our gender-specific socialization patterns, educate girls more into a peace culture than we do boys? Would our societies be more peaceful if boys were given the type of education now given girls? Is the nurturant behavior that can be found in many women and makes up much of what has been called "the woman's culture" primarily a desirable outcome of an intentional socialization process or might it also be the product of women's victimization and powerlessness? If this is the case, the entire nurturant culture of women may in fact be a pathological result of women's oppression. If we speculate along these lines, we should also try to outline what a nonpathological culture looks like.

One may see from my discussion here that I find that the social learning paradigm is the one with the most to offer when it comes to explaining aggressive behavior in human beings. This I find holds true also when we consider the frustration-aggression school of thought where it is maintained that aggressive conduct is the result of frustration. But every element of thought in the aggression-frustration hypothesis, when further analyzed, also seems to depend on social learning. We learn what is frustrating and under which conditions aggressive acts seem legitimate or not at all permissible. We further learn what types of aggressive behavior are *possible* to expose and which ones are then judged to be the legitimate ones, where the limits go.

After a thorough examination of the frustration-aggression theory Bandura (1959, 1973, 1977) has concluded that on no point is this theory better able to explain aggressive behavior than social learning theory. He finds that frustration is most likely to provoke aggression in people who have learned to respond to aversive treatment with aggressive attitudes and actions. He also finds that: "A culture can produce highly aggressive people, while keeping frustration at a low level, by valuing aggressive accomplishments, furnishing successful aggressive models and ensuring that aggressive actions secure rewarding effects'' (Bandura, 1973, p. 59).

But attaching such importance to learning as Bandura and also I do may indicate that we underscore the importance of the material base of society, of the economic and political structures that have been built up. Is it at all possible to make changes in these structures through the education given to individuals? Is it not the other way around—that one must first make changes in the economic conditions and political structures of society before new attitudes can be formed and reeducation take place?

I see changes in the material bases and economic conditions as quite central for learning changes to take place. I have found in my own research that people change attitudes more easily by being put in new situations than by being told what to do (Brock-Utne, 1981). Similarly Bandura (1973, p. 67) holds that in predicting the occurrence of aggression, one should be more concerned with predisposing *conditions* than with predisposed *individuals*. Given that aggressive modes of conduct have been learned, *social circumstances* largely determine whether and when they will be performed.

If people, for some reason, are made to change their behavior, this frequently leads to a change of attitudes. From the theories we have of cognitive dissonance this is also to be expected. People tend to harmonize attitude with behavior. This mechanism has been used by churches, political parties, and totalitarian institutions for a long time. The Norwegian philosopher Jon Elster (1979) refers to Blaise Pascal's reasoning about how one comes to believe after one has been intellectually convinced that it is necessary to believe. Initially there is no reason for believing, only a reason for *making* yourself believe. The causal efficacy of a belief might constitute a reason for precommitting oneself to the belief, in the sense of setting up a series of actions that will have the predictable result of coming to believe. Elster holds that in Pascal's argument these actions can be described as ''going through the motions'' (Elster, 1979, p. 48), acting as if one believes in order to generate the real thing. Behaving as if one believes, one may, according to this argument, after some time start believing.

Political conditions, structures, whole societies, and corporations are man-made, created and run by people holding certain attitudes and having been socialized in a certain manner. It is likely that the attitude these people hold will impact on the way structures are built and institutions are run. We shall have to work to change both economic structures and the values and attitudes of people in those structures.

I am also aware of the fact that collective actors cannot be treated as if they were individuals or governed by leading individuals. Theoretically and even empirically a group of individuals displaying no aggressive behavior on an individual level can still plan and execute a collective aggression such as war. The same person may behave differently in one type of collective than she does in another type. As Håkan Wiberg (1981b, p. 142) has pointed out when individuals appear as representatives of their groups, their behavior is often more strongly colored by the explicit or implicit expectations of the group than by their own intentions and personalities.

The warnings concerning the validity of analogies between levels are relevant and have to be taken seriously. Nations are not small groups and do not have the same social dynamics, nor does the international system.

When discussing peace education within the formal educational system I deplore the lack of interdisciplinary studies at the universities and the compartmentalized type of knowledge taught. The social sciences also seem to contribute toward this compartmentalization when political science concentrates on the macro level, sociology on the group level, and psychology on the individual level. Theories and studies trying to combine insights arrived at on different analytical levels seem to be necessary. Feminist researchers are constantly trying to develop such theories and insights. A fascinating attempt has been made by the Danish psychologist Eva Ethelberg (1983, 1985) analyzing the existence of patriarchy and the general oppression of women at the macrolevel, male dominance at the group level, and various personality strategies used at the individual level to meet this male dominance. She tries to show how patriarchy takes on different forms at different levels and how personality strategies at the individual level mostly just help girls and boys to acquire their proper place within patriarchy. She finds that the patriarchal structure of society is decisisve when it comes to inculcating femininity—the acceptance of playing a serving and secondary role—in girls and masculinity in boys. She criticizes most theories, including recent feminist theories, for jumping from the macro- to the microlevel without looking at what is going on at the meso- or group level. She finds that it is at the mesolevel, between people within the same group, the same family, between spouses, that male dominance is most pronounced and has the greatest consequences for personality development. She shows that an analysis taking us directly from oppressive structures on a macrolevel via mothers to "the inner enemies" that are self-oppression and women's own inclination to refrain from an independent development makes an unscientific jump which renders the analysis incomplete. She maintains that the self-oppression of women cannot be understood unless one also analyzes how they are treated by fathers, brothers, husbands, and lovers. Here the concept of relative oppression which I discussed in the chapter on feminist theories is of importance (see especially Haavind, 1982).

The warnings about analytical jumps have to be kept in mind, especially about not leaving out the mesolevel. I see the likelihood of there being some connection between the various levels of analysis as greater than the likelihood of there being no connection. But I see the assumption that changes at one level will automatically lead to changes at other levels as naive. I find the traditional Marxist assumption that if the economic structures and basis are changed and the workers own the means of production, the oppression of women will cease as just as naive as the claim that if we just become better people individually and do not slap each other, there will be no more war. I believe that changes both in the economic structures and in the values which are transmitted through the socialization process are necessary to create a more peaceful world. I also find that we have enough empirical studies and examples—Adolf Hitler being a good case in point (see especially Miller, 1980)—to warrant the conclusion that there is some connection between child-rearing practices, the way the young are socialized into our culture, and their later personality development. This means also the likelihood of youngsters growing up to work for equity and justice and refraining from the use of violence.

Following Eva Ethelberg's insistence on the importance of the mesolevel in social analysis I shall look at how young girls and boys are socialized in some of the most important socializing institutions of our society. In this chapter I also look at the nonformal institutions of the family and of leisure, here with a focus on the socializing effects of the media and of the institution of organized sports. This is done from a feminist perspective focusing on gender-specific socialization and relating it to the concept of patriarchy, seeing the personal as political and differentiating between power-over and power-to. Using this perspective I attempt to answer the question: Do we give girls more of a peace education than we give boys, making them more inclined to work for social equity and less inclined to use violence at any societal level? This may look so from a first glance, and I have maintained so elsewhere (Brock-Utne, 1984) since girls normally are the ones taught to care for offspring and personal relations while boys are allowed to show aggressive behavior, are given war toys and taught to fight for their country. Would we be socializing the young more for peace if they were all given the education now given to girls?

5

Feminist Perspectives on Peace Education in the Nonformal Sector

PEACE EDUCATION WITHIN THE FAMILY INSTITUTION

The Role of Mothers

The German philosopher Nietzsche is widely cited for the words: "Man should be trained for war and woman for the recreation of the warrior" (Nietzsche, 1885).

The American philosopher and associate professor of theology, Mary Daly (1979), in her book *Gyn/Ecology* on the metaethics of radical feminism, claims that Nietzsche was right not only in the obvious sense that the war State requires mothers to produce sons to become soldiers. His statement is also true on the deeper psychic level: the psychic sapping of women in patriarchy functions continually to re-create its warriors. She claims that the State of Patriarchy is the State of War, in which periods of recuperation from and preparation for battle are euphemistically called "peace." As long as the State of Patriarchy continues to exist, women will go on re-creating warriors. In a patriarchal society men have placed themselves at the top of a hierarchy with women and children at the bottom. Women are exploited, victimized, and oppressed. In the above-quoted work (*Thus Spoke Zarathustra*) Nietzsche (1885) gives men the following advice: "Are you meeting a woman? Do not forget the whip." In a partriarchal society women are mutilated and physically abused, and with the same argument which Nietzsche used: women are to learn who their masters are, they are to learn "their proper place." Their proper place is not in the Senate, not in the government nor in the leading positions of big newspapers or transnational companies.

They find their proper place in doing unpaid household chores or taking care of children, and children are to be brought up to reproduce the patriarchal society. What else can mothers do, when they themselves are part of this society? Sometimes women are so totally oppressed as to have internalized the value system and beliefs of the oppressor, even concerning their own worth. It is not an uncommon experience of women working in the Crisis Centers for battered women in the Western industrialized world that battered wives blame themselves, claiming that they have deserved the whipping, beating, torture their husbands have subjected them to.

How is it possible for a mother to teach her daughter that she has as much value as her brother—when the mother herself does not believe so, and has much less value than her husband? How is it possible for her to teach her daughter to stand up for her rights, to be self-assertive, to change the world—when she is so oppressed herself that she is unable to envisage any other world? And how is it possible for a mother to let her son grow up in a noncompetitive way—when she believes men must be trained to become winners? How is it possible for her to let her little son be weak and allow him to cry and show emotions—when she believes men have to be strong and tough?

These questions resemble the question asked Virginia Woolf by an educated man who wanted her opinion on how war could be prevented, how to put an end to all wars. Her answers to him in *Three Guineas* (Woolf, 1938) also resemble the answers I am trying to give here, though in a different form. In short, the answer is that if women are to help men prevent war they have to be liberated themselves, and accordingly also have to fight for their own liberation. Not for equality on men's premises, but for liberation from capitalist (both private and state) *and* patriarchal structures. They have to fight to better their own conditions as women and as mothers.

In the Western world the classic picture that comes to mind when one speaks of "the family" consists of a male wage earner, a female homemaker-mother, and one or more (usually two) dependent children. Yet even in the United States this pattern actually accounted for only 16 percent of all households in 1977. In Norway in 1984 it accounted for only 10 percent of all households. Kathleen Newland (1979) claims that the twin myths of the nuclear family, with its male breadwinner and female housekeeper/child-raiser, and the extended family, which cares for its disadvantaged or dispossessed members through all adversity, have nearly blinded planners to the problems of the woman looking after herself and, most likely, raising children on her own. In the realm of middle-class attitudes and government policies, the women-headed household hardly exists; and when it does command attention it is viewed as an aberration, the product of a disaster.

But woman-headed households can no longer be considered exceptional in countries rich or poor. In most countries such households comprise a substantial minority and their number is constantly growing. According to Buvinic and Youssef (1978) one quarter of all Venezuelan families are headed by women; In the United States, the figure was 15 percent in 1982 and growing very rapidly; in Indonesia the figure given is 23 percent in 1978; and in parts of Kenya the proportion of households with female heads reaches 40 percent. In most of the countries of the Commonwealth Caribbean, at least one family in three is headed by a woman. (The figures are taken from Morgan, 1984.)

The picture that emerges of mothers all over the world is a complex and varied one. But all over the world mothers have one thing in common: they are exploited by male-dominated society. Most societies in the world are sexist societies though the degree and form of sexism varies. We talk of sexism when the sex roles assigned to men and women function in such a way as to assure the power of one sex over the other.

Sexism, like racism, is a belief system rooted in a world view that assigns varying levels of worth to different groups of human beings. The worth assigned is based upon innate characteristics such as skin color or sexual characteristics. Sexism, just as racism, is an attitude held by individuals but it can also pervade whole institutions. Institutions can be built up in a sexist way, to the constant detriment of one sex, and people may hold sexist attitudes. Logically it is possible that institutions can function in a sexist way without people in them holding sexist attitudes and vice versa. Empirically there will often exist a relationship so that the more sexist an institution is, the more people holding sexist attitudes one will find there.

As with racism, the assigned social worth under sexism also serves as a rationale for assigning less valued functions to those accorded the lower social worth. Betty Reardon (1981) maintains that in a form of circular reasoning typical of such belief systems, the assertion is made that men do more socially valuable work; therefore, such work is assigned to them because they are more socially valuable. Women are held to be inferior to men and have no legitimate claim to authority. Fulfillment of their social roles fixed by this "natural inferiority" requires submission to the exercise of authority. The socialization of women is distinctly different from that of men, and the more sexist the society, the more distinct is that difference. If women are raising children on their own, their households belong to the poorest in the world. They must make do with shockingly low incomes. They are exploited by employers and frequently receive little child support from the fathers of their children. They have to work long hours. If they are living together with a man, they are usually exploited by him in addition to being exploited by the employer if they are gainfully employed.

It is not easy in such a situation to try to change the world through peace education. Elena Gianini Belotti (1973) tells the story that when a son is born in Luciana, a mug of water is poured down from a window. The running water is seen to symbolize the boy running down the street and into the world. When a daughter is born some drops of water are splashed on the fireplace, symbolizing that a new citizen is born who is going to find her place within the house, near the fireplace.

Mothers know well enough the disadvantages that daughters inherit: low status, low earning power, lack of autonomy, long working hours, exploitation. If they are married, they know that their husbands usually prefer sons, especially the first born has to be a son. To be the father of a son adds to the husband's self-image of being masculine. These combined factors produce in mothers the cruelest misogyny of all: son preference. To be received into the world with a sign of disappointment is not a happy beginning for any child: but it is the fate of many girls. The natural ratio is about 105 boys to 100 girls born. In parts of North Africa and India, according to Newland (1979), parents' choice would be to have anywhere from three to six sons for every daughter. The desire for sons is usually explained in practical terms: economic contribution, support in old age, and continuity of the family line.

It seems likely that son preference will be especially strong in cultures where dowry is practiced, as in great parts of Asia and parts of the Middle East and less strong in cultures where a bride price is paid to the bride's parents, as in great parts of Africa. Newland (1979) claims that son preference serves as a kind of barometer of women's overall status in society, except that it registers changes in the social climate *after* they occur rather than before. The very mild degree of son preference found in Thailand can be seen as one manifestation of the relatively egalitarian nature of Thai society. Newland (1979) reports that in Korea, by contrast, customs and economics combine to generate a preference for sons that is among the strongest and most persistent found anywhere. A woman's status is closely tied to her ability to produce sons.

The strong son preference in Korea may have something to do with the nonegalitarian nature of Confucian culture which we also find in Vietnam, China, and in its own variety in Japan.

Nancy Williamson (1978) describes the disturbing development of techniques for intervening in conception or gestation so that parents can choose the sex of a child. Some of the preliminary results are chilling. A clinic in Singapore treated over one thousand women in a sex preselection experiment carried out in the mid-seventies; over 90 percent of the women wanted boys. The Chinese have experimented with an early sex-determination technique that permits selective abortion early in pregnancy; in the first trial, of thirty women who chose to have abortions, twenty-nine aborted females. In India private clinics which perform a sex-determination test by amniocentesis followed by an abortion if it is a female fetus, are thriving (Hoskins & Holmes, 1984; Roggencamp, 1984). The rapid development of new reproductive technologies including easy and cheap sex-determination techniques (both prior to and after conception) makes it highly likely that the specific abortion of female fetuses will be practiced even more widely. Such developments are often explained by saying that they will help "control" the population explosion. Yet the grave problem of rapid population growth should not be dealt with by selectively preventing the birth of girls. Doing so would be a capitulation to sexism at its most brutal.

It is also interesting that even though methods which enable parents to choose the sex of their child have been known for more than 20 years, they have been put to relatively little commercial use. One guess may be that many states have a common interest in keeping such methods from being publicly known and widely practiced, because this would mean the selective birth of sons, at least in a first generation. This again would mean a society 20 years from now with a great surplus of 20-year-old men. This would lead to great social problems, though it might also lead to a heightened value for young girls who would be a scarce commodity.

Feminist Mothers of Sons

Is there any reason to believe that committed feminists educate their sons in any different way than more traditional mothers do? This is the research question I am currently trying to throw some light on in a three-year project using qualitative interviews with feminist and nonfeminist mothers of sons (Brock-Utne, 1987b). One might assume that there would be a difference, but the empirical studies we have so far do not all together substantiate such a finding and point in different directions. (For a review of such research see Brock-Utne, 1987b.) For instance, a study by Lindsy van Gelder and Carrie Carmichael (1975) revealed that of the 40 feminist mothers interviewed, more than a third had never thought about giving their sons a nonsexist education, a socialization in line with that of a nonsexist man according to the ideals voiced in the feminist movement. Most of the rest felt at best ambivalent about the mother-son experience and at worst powerless to prevent their sons from growing up into male chauvinists. The only two mothers interviewed who judged their sons to be feminists were the two most committed and articulate feminists. The others, who also adhered to feminist ideas and also participated in the women's movement, were eager to educate their daughters to become strong, independent feminists but were afraid of influencing their sons, afraid that the boys, through a nonsexist education, would not turn into men. Lindsy van Gelder and Carrie Carmichael, themselves mothers of daughters, felt that the mothers they interviewed who all defined themselves as feminists, assumed that the typical male personality was the ideal and that it was "exclusively up to us, the mothers of girls, to equalize things by making our daughters more 'active' or 'masculine'" (Gelder & Carmichael, 1975, p. 53). They heard a lot about the joys of buying football helmets for little girls but when they asked the mothers what they were doing to make their sons less typical males, they either drew a blank or an antihomosexual response. In one of the interviews in my current project *Sons* one of the feminist mothers tells that when her son wanted a real doll for his birthday and she gave him one, her mother-in-law called her and asked her if she wanted to turn the boy into a homosexual. Homophobia seems to be pronounced. But it seems contradictory that mothers who believe that their child-rearing practices may create a homosexual boy (such an assumption seems very doubtful) do not believe that they may succeed in creating a nonsexist man. And some of the ones Gelder and Carmichael interviewed did not even want to. One of them said: "If I had the powers to make a child into a liberated non-male-chauvinist, I don't know whether I would do it. You cannot alienate the child from his culture" (p. 53). Gelder and Carmichael conclude that it looks like feminists are only willing to expend their energies liberating girl children. They seem to have one on-stage behavior when they in the women's movement criticize male chauvinists and another off-stage behavior when they educate their own sons at home. The researchers try to explain this discrepancy by suggesting that even feminists secretly believe "real" men are rough, tough, male chauvinists.

There might be other ways to explain this discrepancy also. So far it has been status-giving for a woman to have a son. If he also carries her name he may throw some pride on her. But if he does not have an important career but stays at home with the children for some years, he may not only be looked down upon by his male surroundings, but he will not throw light on his mother. Even feminist mothers may feel that a son should be able to fulfill the wishes the mother had for her own career, but which were thwarted because of the restraints of her sex role. As Adrienne Rich (1977, p. 193) expresses it: "I wanted to give birth to myself as a male." Feminists may want their children to succeed in careers whether they are boys or girls. This may also be the reason why women who rail against male privilege in their own lives are happy to capitalize on it where their boy children are concerned. If their sons have an edge in life because they're males some of the mothers Gelder and Carmichael interviewed concluded, "Well, yes it may not be fair, but that's life, and we all want our children to succeed, right?" (p. 53). These mothers, it seems to me, are defining "succeed" within a very traditional patriarchal framework, meaning get ahead of others within the paid labor market.

Having met many remarks like the above-mentioned the two researchers conclude pessimistically: "As the mothers of daughters, we began to feel that when our children reach womanhood in the early 1990s they will be confronted with a new generation of perfectly preserved 1969 males" (p. 53). Their findings were not at all in accordance with what they had expected to find. They had expected to find that feminist mothers would see it as a great challenge to try to educate a nonsexist man, a man corresponding to the professed ideals of a man accepted by the women's movement. They had expected that the feminist mothers of sons would run into problems trying to educate a nonviolent, nonaggressive, caring boy who would share evenly in the unpaid housework and child care with a future wife. But they did not expect them not to want to change male socialization.

The expectations that the two researchers had were met some years later when Judy Klemesrud (1979) interviewed some well-known and articulate feminist mothers of sons. Some of them were professional university teachers having specialized in sex role socialization. Some were also married to men who had officially proclaimed their solidarity with the women's movement. These mothers had very consciously socialized their sons along the ideals for male socialization adhered to in the women's movement.

My own research project *Sons* will continue until 1989 and the results will be written up in 1988 and 1989. We are first interviewing the mothers, then the fathers—not of the same sons though. So far we have interviewed the feminist mothers and are in the process of interviewing the more traditional mothers. We have just been able to analyze about half of the interviews made with the feminist mothers (Brock-Utne, 1987b). The trend in these interviews is that the mothers have other ideals for the upbringing of their sons than the traditional male ideals. They both want their sons to share more of the housework than boys normally do, want them to be able to talk about feelings and emotions, do not want them to display macho behavior. They seem to succeed better when it comes to having the sons take responsibility for house chores than when it comes to directing their sons away from playing with war toys and reading crime and sex magazines. From our interviews it does not seem as if they strive so hard when it comes to this latter part of socialization. The reason for this may be their own ambivalence about the male role and their fear of alienating their son from his male surroundings (what he does in the house no one sees while his refusal to participate in war games cannot go unnoticed). Another interpretation may be that the feminists we have interviewed who all have a career and identify themselves with the women's liberation movement may adhere more to a liberal feminist theory of equality where concepts like no discrimination, sharing and parity, equality with men, are important than to a radical feminist theory proclaiming to change the values of this society.

In a fascinating article about the cultural forces that push us toward war Charlene Spretnak (1983) tries to answer the question whether there is any evidence to indicate that the new generation of sons in the United States is being raised without the age-old macho glorification of doing "a man's duty" in a war. She tells about the Vietnam veterans who again and again express the unshaken opinion that most of the Vietnam protesters (who were primarily middle class) were simply afraid "to be a man" and go to war. She presumes that this view is passed on from father to son. She does not reflect upon the role the mothers play in the socialization of boys but probably finds that mothers either foster the same values as the fathers do or are not able to counteract the influence of the father. She mentions the recent boom in the sales of war toys as an indication.

The relationship between mothers and daughters is far more complicated than the mother-son relationship, right from the start. Of course it is easier to let a child have its way, to show it a lot of attention, than to restrict the child the way mothers often do with girls. Mothers report that from a young age they have many more conflicts with daughters than with sons (Belotti, 1973; Brunet & Lezine, 1966). They usually attribute this to the "more difficult character" of their daughter. At the same time the mothers admit that they bring up their girls more strictly than their boys. Belotti (1973) reports that those girls who are in for the most trouble with their mothers are those who are born with a high activity rate and have mothers who are rigid and place great value on tidiness, stability, and neatness. A Korean proverb states: A daughter lets you down twice; once when she is born and then again the day she gets married. In many parts of the world the father's ownership of his wife and children is symbolized by the fact that the whole family uses the father's family name/surname. The name is given to the son forever for him to pass on to a future wife and children. But the daughter keeps her father's name only until the day she gets married and is given her husband's name (the name of his father) as a token of her new identity as a member of her husband's family.[1]

Daughters are taught to be less demanding than sons. They are taught to help their mothers with unpaid housework and child care from the time they are very young. They are taught not to show signs of outward aggression, which often means that the aggression is turned inward—against themselves. In short: daughters are taught to be feminine. Being feminine here means behaving and acting in a way that suits men. A feminine girl never tries to surpass a boy. She is happy to be *the second sex*—Simone de Beauvoir's world-famous term.

So the girl is taught to be submissive, let her brothers have the best part, like the fathers have theirs. And she is taught to look neat, to care for her appearance. Mothers start to toilet train their daughters earlier than they do their sons, and they restrict their daughters' thumb sucking more severely. Teeth located in awkward positions may lower the market value of a girl. A pretty appearance is important to someone who is going to be looked at as an object.

In the glossy magazines young girls read in the Western world this indoctrination is continued. The important thing for a girl is to get married. To trap the right man, she must be good-looking and gentle. In countries where

---

[1]Feminists increasingly refuse to change their name on marriage. Some British feminists have replaced their surname with the first name of a girl-friend, for instance, Elizabeth Sarah (Spender, 1980).

divorce is common, women have to go on taking care of their appearance the rest of their lives: they must try to "stay young" so that their husbands will not desert them for younger and prettier women.

In the winter of 1973 a factory in my area arranged a ski contest for girls and boys ages 8 to 12. Winners of the girls' contests each received a cosmetics kit. Winners of the boy's contests received a shotgun. The lesson that the girls were given was that their task was to have an attractive appearance. The boys were taught that they were expected to defend themselves even to the point of killing.

Jeanne Martin Cisse (1975), ambassador to the United Nations from Guinea, writes that a characteristic feature of traditional African education was the initiation system, which served primarily to develop in boys a sense of honor and of the duty to serve their country, while cultivating their lofty feeling of superiority over girls, who were taught what was necessary to equip them to fulfill their functions as women in charge of family life. In her own words:

> Women were educated in this way for family life in order, first and foremost, to serve men to whom they owed complete obedience. They had to show submissiveness to their husbands, fathers, and brothers, so that education was a form of alienation and a means of ensuring the subordination of woman to man. This education was given by the older women who decided that all the girls in the clan would be required, on reaching a certain age, to undergo a period of special training to harden them and teach them to bear the lot which was and had to be theirs. Such conditioning was intended to improve what were held to be the qualities of wife and mother in the African woman and, at the same time, to strengthen her inculcated feeling of inferiority, thus justifying the Maninka proverb which says that a woman's devotion and unconditional submission to men will make her worthy of giving birth to a hero.

All over the world females tend to be more nurturant than males (Hutt, 1972). Little girls are more attentive to their younger brothers and sisters. Pope and Whiting (1973) found in a large cross-cultural study of children aged three to eleven that during the ages seven to eleven girls emerged strongly as the more helpful sex.

In a country like Norway, time studies show that at the age of 15 the girls spend an average of 1 hour 26 minutes per day doing unpaid housework at home, while boys in the same age group spend on the average 16 minutes. At the age of 15 both girls and boys in Norway are attending the nine-year compulsory school and living at home (Time Studies, Norwegian Central Bureau of Statistics, 1972). This means that already at this age the boys have more time at their own disposal, time they can use to watch TV, or can spend on competitive sports, on experimenting with their science kits, or earning some extra money by doing occasional paid work.

Belotti (1973) tells from her studies in Italian kindergartens how small girls are trained and expected to wait on the boys, lay the table for them, put the boys' toys away when they have played with them. The teacher may ask all the children to tidy up: the boys won't do it, and she lets them get away with it. ("Boys will be boys.") Then she asks the girls—who are usually already putting away their own toys—to put away the toys the boys have been playing with as well. The girls seldom protest: they have seen their mother clear up their father's things, clean and tidy up his clothes, cook his dinner, and have it ready on time. The kindergarten teacher, instead of intervening and making the boys tidy up, loads all the work on the girls. She will not do the work herself: that would lower her prestige, but she has the girls do it. And she gets away with such sexist behavior. If she had asked black boys to serve white boys and to clear up their mess and tidy up their toys, she would have been accused of racism. But she is doing exactly the same thing: just that she is asking girls and not black boys. Her rationale is similar to a racist one: she is asking individuals who are considered to be of less worth to serve those considered to be of higher worth. There is a striking parallel between racism and sexism, both of which comprise such a big part of our culture that most people do not even recognize them.

Girls—and later mothers—are considered to be of less worth than boys—and later fathers. Girls are helpful, they wait on their brothers, yet they are oppressed by them. But there is one situation in which young boys also are expected to wait on others, to be oppressed. That is when and if they are soldiers.

The "Ideal Mother" and the "Ideal Soldier"

There certainly are some interesting similarities between the ideal mother and the ideal soldier, although mothers do not normally see this. And it is precisely because they are so exploited and oppressed themselves that they do not see how the patriarchal state also exploits their sons as soldiers and creates the patriarchal mind within them.

Both mothers and soldiers are exploited by patriarchy, both asked to take orders from men who have more power and a higher status than they, and both are asked to sacrifice their lives for others who are judged more important. "Not to reason why," just to accept the system is a virtue. The American peace researcher Betty Reardon (1985) maintains that what the soldier has done for the nation or the warrior for the tribe through centuries of doing what was expected of him, woman has done for the family. Woman has been trained to sublimate her own needs to the service of others. Soldiers and mothers have days dedicated in their honor. These are days on which society offers thanks for their sacrifices by, in Reardon's (1981) words: "reminding them that for such they were born and by such they will continue to be identified and find meaning; for war and domesticity are in the natural order of things, as are the fixed roles of soldiers and mothers in that order."

The military chain of command is conceptually close to the patriarchal family, both being essentially hierarchical organizations. In both institutions, obedience is a virtue and disobedience severely punished. Obedience to authority is the cornerstone of an effective military machine and the fundamental principle of the patriarchal family.

Namelessness is also a common trait of mothers and soldiers. Although a mother sacrifices her life for her children, the children will usually be known by their father's name. Their mother is forgotten in the history books, as most women are. Most soldiers who sacrifice their lives are also nameless. The grave of the unknown soldier under l'Arc de Triomphe in Paris has become a symbol of the nameless soldiers killed on the battlefield. In history books we read about Alexander the Great and the battles he won. Bertold Brecht has asked: Did he win them all by himself? Was he quite alone? Did he not even have a cook with him?

Though the similarities between the "ideal" mother and the "ideal" soldier are striking, there are also distinct differences in their training. Both are asked to sacrifice themselves, both trained to be obedient and submissive; but mothers give life and seek to protect the life they have given, while soldiers are trained to be prepared to take life.

George Gilder (1973) writes of training in Marine Corps boot camp: "From the moment one arrives, the drill instructors begin a torrent of misogynistic and antiindividualist abuse. The good things are manly and collective; the despicable are feminine and individual. Virtually every sentence, every description, every lesson embodies this sexual duality, and the female anatomy provides a rich metaphor for every degradation. When you want to create a solidarity group of male killers, that is what you do, you kill the woman in them. That is the lesson of the Marines. And it works."

Thus the behavior which many fathers and also some mothers think sex-appropriate for the little boy is carried to extremes in the training of the soldier. He must be tough, strong, never weak or troubled by soft feelings for the "enemy." And a mother who has trained her son to care for other human beings, to be emotional and warm and has had him play with dolls rather than guns may see much of her education destroyed by the military training her son is forced to go through.

An interesting question for research would be: What are the mothers of conscientious objectors like and what are mothers of career soldiers like? What are the differences between these groups in social attitudes, in the way they have raised their sons, in their feminist consciousness, in their working conditions, social class, and prospects for life?

I have not been able to find many studies that would throw some light on this research question. I would expect that there would be a class difference between these two groups of mothers, that the mothers of military sons would come mainly from the working class while the class background of mothers of conscientious objectors may vary according to the reasons the son has given for objecting to do military service. If these reasons are of a fundamental religious nature, the mothers might well belong to low income groups. If they are of a more ethical or political nature, the mothers will, I assume, have a more middle-class and intellectual background. An interesting study of the perspectives of mothers who encourage their sons to join the military has been made by Linda Rennie Forcey (1984). Out of a large group of such mothers she has selected four who were representative when it came to social background variables and conducted more intensive interviewing with them. Even though four subjects are too few to generalize from, questions raised through the intensive interviewing are of great value and would be interesting to follow up on with more quantitative measures.

Linda Rennie Forcey (1984) characterizes the four mothers as "tired, frustrated and otherwise overwhelmed" (p. 477). The women want their sons to have self-discipline, maturity, training, and skills, a free education and a secure job. It is their perception that there is no place else for them to turn but the military. There is good reason for feminists to listen to what these mothers say, not merely to castigate them. The study to me raises some interesting questions about the mothering of sons, maternal responsibility, and the significance of class in women's experience. Linda Rennie Forcey (1984, p. 478) states that the interviews she has had with the mothers "provoke old questions about the very structure of a society in which the preparation for war appears to be the easy way to provide for the well-being of our young males—much easier than attempting to go through the painful process of reconstructing a social and economic system for peace." If we listen to the four mothers Forcey has interviewed intensively, we can understand how they can be lulled into forgetting the purpose of the military—to prepare for and wage war. Each of these mothers felt strongly that there was no place else for their sons to go. The women themselves and their husbands had low incomes or were out of work, they were exploited and frustrated, wanted to feel assured that their sons got an education and an income. Given the circumstances these mothers are in, it is difficult to blame them for encouraging their sons to join the military. When the attitudes of these mothers are analyzed from a socialist feminist perspective, which I see as the most fruitful in this case taking economic conditions and class into account, their wishes are understandable and the blame shifted from individual mothers to the economic structures of a capitalist society. The radical feminist analysis of patriarchy is also important to an understanding of how a group of leading men exploit both women and other men—often the sons of these women. Women are expected to give birth to sons and are praised for doing so but then are not given the resources, financial and emotional, to give these sons the education they might have wanted for them. The responsibility of mothering sons is awesome, especially when this responsibility is assigned to primarily one person—the mother. This is often so even if the mother is living together with the father of the son—he is often absent, if not physically, then emotionally.

In the study by Forcey we learn about the motives and perspectives of some mothers who encourage their sons to choose a military career. We do not learn about the perspectives and motives of fathers who wish the same type of careers for their sons. There is reason to believe that their motives are of a different kind, that they are more occupied with ideas of their sons' becoming "real men," that they do their duty to the country, are courageous, and give honor to their country and regiment. The mothers do not mention such motives. They are more concerned with the welfare of their sons, that they get an education and are assured of a job and income. There are both theoretical works (Chodorow, 1978; Gilligan, 1982) and empirical studies (Gilligan, 1982; Zur, Morrison, & Zaretsky, 1985) supporting such a view. Gilligan's model of moral development and Chodorow's theory of psychosexual development both suggest that women's concerns and moral reasoning are defined in terms of interpersonal relationships, while men's morality is abstract and legalistic. A study of gender differences in attitudes toward war has been made, applying Gilligan's theory (Zur, Morrison, and Zaretsky, 1985). This study found that:

1. Men are more prone than women to justify war according to rational and legal criteria.
2. Women find it more difficult than men to accept, condone, or justify any acts of violence, killing, and destruction during war.
3. Men more than women accept stereotypical sex roles during war, for instance, men as warriors and protectors and women as caretakers.
4. Women will support war, at least as enthusiastically as men, when an appeal is made based on empathy for oppressed and vulnerable human beings, or an emphasis is placed on group cohesion and intensification of interpersonal relationships in the community during war.

This exploratory study made of 200 college students in the United States raises some interesting questions for further analysis: Are previous studies of attitudes toward war, showing that women are more against war than men, made up of items that appeal to men's set of moral concerns, that is, legalistic abstract justifications of violence against some impersonal well-defined other, while the attitude scales are devoid of items that would reveal the nature of the appeal of war to women?

It is difficult on the basis of existing studies to do more than raise these questions. But I see it as important that the questions are raised here as they pertain to the main question I want to throw light on: Do we educate boys for war and girls for peace?

Socialization into Violence and Aggression

In our type of society being masculine is practically synonymous with being aggressive—aggression here used in the way I have earlier defined it, as "behavior designed to inflict pain or injury on others." A survey conducted for the United States National Commission on the Causes and Prevention of Violence revealed that 70 percent of over one thousand respondents agreed with the statement: "When a boy is growing up it is very important for him to have a few fistfights" (Stark & McEvoy, 1970).

When my youngest son who, like my eldest son, Karsten, has never been given war toys and has been taught not to fight, was five years old he had a hard time in a kindergarten. He exhibited behavior at home that I had never seen in him before. He started beating us although he had never been beaten by us. And he cried more than before. I had the feeling he was not happy in the new kindergarten. When I called one of the teachers she said: "We were just about to call you about Gunnar. You must teach him how to fight. Because he does not know how to fight and does not want to fight, all the others want to fight with him. And then he cries and they call him a sissy and fight him more. You must teach him how to fight or the situation will get worse when he starts school." I replied that it was not my responsibility to teach my son to fight. On the contrary, it was her responsibility to teach the other children *not* to fight. It was her responsibility to intervene in fights, stop them, and help children to solve their conflicts through nonviolent means. It was difficult to teach her from my position as a mother. I asked her if she would have given us the same advice had Gunnar been a girl. She admitted that when she wanted to change his behavior it was precisely because he was a boy and not a girl.

From toddler age, boys engage in angry outbursts roughly twice as often as girls and are much more likely to attempt physical injury of their target. They grab toys, attack other children, and ignore requests from parents and peers. They quarrel with more children more often, and are more aggressive generally in all areas of behavior than girls. Corinne Hutt (1972) has made extensive studies of the social behavior of preschool children. She concludes "Boys are twice as aggressive as girls (aggression here including verbal aggression) but even more interesting is the fact that it is predominantly boys toward whom this aggression is directed." The boys manage to irritate each other enough for aggression to be the outcome twice as often as it is with girls. The sex difference in aggression is in evidence in all age groups that have been studied. Thomas Detre et al. (1974) found that there are approximately twice as many aggressive boys throughout the school grades as girls and three times as many aggressive boys in kindergarten as girls.

Some researchers maintain that the greater aggressiveness of boys and men may be partly biologically determined. I shall return to this discussion. But as educators we can only do something about the environment surrounding the child. When we compare these findings showing the greater aggressiveness of boys, to the lesson Gunnar's kindergarten teacher tried to teach him and us, his parents, we see that aggressiveness is encouraged in boys. She admitted that she would not have encouraged him to fight had he been a girl.

In the case of a girl physically attacking another girl she would probably have stopped the attacking girl verbally, the way she ought to have done with the boy attacking Gunnar.

If boys are encouraged to be violent and aggressive from infancy and onward it is not strange that researchers into aggression seem to agree with Arnold Buss (1971) in his conclusion: "Human aggression is a problem for men, not women. It is men who wage wars, engage in bitter competition, fight each other individually, and maintain vendettas lasting for years or even decades . . . Status as a male is to be achieved by being aggressive, and masculinity is perhaps the most basic aspect of a man's identity."

But it is also important to keep in mind the distinction between aggressive behavior and aggressive feelings. Not all of those who show aggressive behavior have aggressive feelings and people who engage in aggressive behavior on a macroscale because they are commanded to do so may not exhibit aggressive behavior on the interpersonal level. As mentioned when the similarities between women and soldiers were discussed, there may be qualifications other than aggression going into the makeup of a good soldier—for instance, loyalty, obedience, dependence on others, suggestibility—all qualifications which girls get in their socialization, maybe even more so than boys. It is also necessary to keep in mind the critical points that were raised in the study by Zur, Morrison, and Zaretsky (1985), previously referred to—that women *may* support wars though for other reasons than men do.

There are numerous studies from all over the world showing that boys are more likely to engage in aggressive behavior than girls are. For instance, a study conducted by Jacklin and Maccoby (1978) of *play patterns* of American preschool children playing with children of the same sex and with children of the opposite sex showed that boy-boy pairs were more likely to engage in a tug of war over a toy than girl-girl or boy-girl pairs. While both boys and girls were somewhat more likely to cry or retreat toward their mothers (who were quietly seated in the room) when playing with a boy partner, girls were particularly affected by a male partner and tended to retreat or stand quietly watching the boy play with the toys. Girls with female partners rarely exhibited such behavior. Apparently even very young boys do something that makes their partners wary. Jacklin and Maccoby state that they do not know what this "something" is.

Another American study referred to by Maccoby (1980) and conducted in 1977 by DiPietro of same-sex preschool children who were allowed to play freely in a room with a trampoline, a beach ball and a big Bobo doll (a child-size inflated toy with weighted feet) showed that some of the girls' groups developed a distinctive pattern of interaction that was almost never shown by boys. They organized their play by making rules. If one girl insisted on going first or taking a longer turn than the others, her partners would react by invoking the rules and arguing, rather than by using force.

This behavior the children may very well have learned from their parents. Sandora Kronsberg (1981) has shown experimentally that parents intervene physically when a child is a boy and verbally when the child is a girl.

DiPietro found little sex difference in level of physical activity. The girls jumped on the trampoline and moved quickly with the beach ball like the boys did, but they seldom engaged in roughhousing. The girls seldom tried to hit each other with the beach ball or push or play tug of war—things the boys did quite frequently (usually accompanying the activity with shouts of glee or excited laughter). The friendly rough-and-tumble of boys' play is sometimes hard to distinguish from more serious encounters with mutual intent to hurt, and roughhousing can turn into aggression quite quickly. Both types of interaction are typical in boys' groups in the Western world, but not in girls' groups.

These results have recently been confirmed in a Norwegian study of kindergarten children, five to seven years old. Tone Reithaug (1983) collected data from periods of free play where the children were allowed to choose their own activities. She found that the girls would gather in the doll corner and the boys in the building and construction corner. She then looked at the interaction between the groups and found that the interaction between the boys in the construction corner was highly competitive. They competed in building the nicest plows, the nicest trains. In the dolls' corner where mostly girls gathered, there was role play without competition. She also found that the boys shouted and called for attention much more than the girls and that more than 80 percent of the threats uttered during the free-play period were threats from boys.

Eric Erikson (1951) worked with 150 boys and 150 girls, ages ten, eleven, and twelve, over a two-year period. Among other things Erikson gave them the task "of constructing a scene on a table which they would find exciting as a set for an imaginary motion picture." After they had constructed the setting they were asked to tell the plot of the movie they were imagining. Erikson found that the girls' scenes were expressly peaceful while the boys, through the scenes they created, showed that they were already confirmed in their interest in violence.

The greater aggressiveness of boys seems such a universal feature that some parents take this aggressiveness as a biological fact. Aggressive behavior on the part of their son just shows them that their son is "normal," is a "real boy."

They are little aware of the fact that their own expectations have been working like self-fulfilling prophecies, or that the attitudes and expectations their little son is met with from his immediate surroundings, especially from his father, may determine whether his aggressive dispositions will cause him to commit acts of violence, become a delinquent, or whether he will use them in a nonviolent fight to better the conditions of others.

A huge number of studies have been conducted on the question of sex differences and, specifically, on the question of different levels of aggression between women and men. Many of them are tainted by conventional assumptions about male and female roles (thus revealing an unquestioned amount of sexism). In others the researchers do not question the methods they use and believe that counting, measuring, and collecting data will reveal "the" link (rather than provide an answer to the specific question they have asked). Despite these problems inherent in scientific work (endocrinological as well as behavioral), I shall proceed to discuss some of the research on aggression.

Maccoby and Jacklin (1974) have compiled a most extensive survey of research data on sex differences. They consulted more than 1,400 scientific works. The sex differences found were divided into three parts: (a) myths, (b) poorly substantiated findings, and (c) well-established findings. Within group (c) we find the greater aggressiveness of boys. This greater aggressiveness on the part of boys seems to show up at the age of two years, but not before. Maccoby and Jacklin suggest that boys may be biologically more prepared than girls to learn to become aggressive. If this is so, all it means is that it may be somewhat more difficult to channel a son's aggressive drives into a worthwhile and challenging activity than a daughter's.

Researchers do not agree on the question of whether differences in the brain or in the inner secretions of men and women make men more predisposed toward aggression. Lars Jalmert (1979) maintains that most researchers working in this field have had a very hard time defining aggression, or have not defined it at all.

This also seems to be the case in the extensive psychobiological work of Laurel Holliday (1978) on *The Violent Sex*. Sometimes she equates aggression with physical violence, sometimes with verbal assertion. When she started studying psychobiological differences between males and females she also started asking the question why males are so different from females. "I wanted to know why, for example, sex is the most reliable predictor of how violent a person will be in all cultures, races, and classes in recorded history. And why are 90% of all violent crimes committed by men? Why are males the violent sex? Because Daddy encouraged them to be tough and play with guns, because teacher said they were stronger and faster than girls and didn't cry, because Mommy took their dolls?" (Holliday, 1978, p. 11).

After extensive reviewing of studies showing how fathers treat their sons, how the rod spoils the boy, how media violence affects the male child, she still reaches the conclusion that there is an inborn disposition toward greater aggressiveness, here defined as a tendency to use physical violence, in the male of the species.

She holds that the greater aggressivity of boys must be rooted in biological differences because: "It is nearly inconceivable, otherwise, (1) that 600 cultures would have chosen arbitrarily to have men do battle while women keep house, (2) that "boys will be boys" even when they are too young to have been "socialized" to any great extent, and (3) that not only humans have adopted this pattern, but nearly all mammal species as well" (Holliday, 1978, p. 27). When it comes to her argument number three, there is all reason to caution about analogies from other mammal species to humans, apart from the fact that there certainly *are* animal species in which the female is the most aggressive. When it comes to her argument number two, that is the crucial argument because if she is incorrect here, then argument number one does not hold water. If there is reason to believe that boys will not be boys unless they are socialized into it from the earliest age, then the reason why men tend to do battle while women keep house may be that that is the way they have been socialized. The reasons for this socialization might originally have been practical ones like the necessity for women to stay near the house while breast-feeding. I have here and elsewhere (Brock-Utne, 1985a) compiled so many studies showing the differential treatment of boys and girls from the very earliest age, especially when it comes to inhibiting or allowing their aggressive responses, that I see little reason to use biology to explain the differences. Even if there exists a greater predisposition for aggressive behavior among boys, we shall have to go to social factors to explain why *some* boys develop these predispositions and others do not and also why some *girls* develop aggressive behavior.

Holliday uses analogies from mammals other than human beings quite frequently without having argued for the case that such analogies can be drawn. Taking examples from animals, she claims that the relation between the male sex organs and aggression has been obvious to animal breeders for centuries: castration has been used to tame aggressive bulls for at least 5,000 years. Only in the last two or three decades, however, have scientists technologically corroborated folk knowledge and shown that throughout phylogeny, androgens, the male sex hormones, are prime facilitators of aggression. Holliday here speaks of "prime facilitators," which is not the same as prime *causes*. One could think of situational factors that may lead partly to increased hormonal production and partly to aggressive behavior and that these factors are related through a syndrome more than the one being the cause of the other.

From her studies she concludes that male aggressiveness (whether in mice, monkeys, or humans) is connected with the level of androgen circulating in the bloodstream. She does not doubt that environment and conditioning influence an individual's propensity for aggression, but "the fact remains that the male of the species does not begin life with a propensity for peacefulness anywhere near that of the female, and equalization, in most cases, requires social inhibition of the male's inborn biological proclivities" (Holliday, 1978, p. 28).

Laurel Holliday argues convincingly that androgen levels are correlated with physical aggressiveness. Alcoholics have androgen levels five to ten times higher than normal men. The reasons for this are not clear, but alcoholism causes severe liver damage which in turn causes an increase in androgen levels. Normally the liver inactivates much of the androgen in the bloodstream, but a severely damaged liver is unable to perform this function; thus androgen levels rise precipitously. There is a strong correlation between violent crime and the use of alcohol. A four-year study in Philadelphia found, for example, that alcohol was involved in 70 percent of all physical assault murders and 50 percent of all murders (Wolfgang & Strohm, 1956). From this study we do not know whether it is alcoholism per se that is strongly correlated to violent crimes or the immediate consumption of alcohol. There are two separate questions involved here:

1. What is the relationship between the immediate consumption of alcohol and the probability of someone engaging in violent behavior, for instance through a reduction in the level of inhibition?
2. How is alcoholism related to aggressivity? Are intoxicated alcoholics more violent than intoxicated nonalcoholics?

In other words: Is it the use of alcohol or alcoholism that will best explain aggressive behavior and what is their relative role?

It is easy to agree with Laurel Holliday when she advises men who want to decrease their aggressiveness to cut down on alcohol. It is not so easy to follow her when she makes a case *for* the smoking of marijuana. But she is able to show that marijuana has been found to decrease men's potential for aggressive behavior as well as plasma testosterone levels. It has been suggested that the active ingredient in marijuana, THC, has a chemical structure very similar to estrogen and that it works as an antiandrogen in men who are heavy marijuana smokers. Laurel Holliday claims that there are clear indications that marijuana may be a valuable "herbal remedy" for aggressiveness.

Laurel Holliday points not only to the androgen levels in males but also to the structure and function of the brain and the work of the Y chromosome to explain the greater aggressiveness in males. If we assume that males really are born with greater dispositions for violence, if we think their biological makeup predisposes them for aggressiveness (which of course cannot be "proven"), what should be the consequences of such insight? I can see three obvious answers:

1. *To limit the number of male children.* Laurel Holliday claims that the most important step we as individuals can take to reduce the harmful effects of masculine psychobiological programming is to have fewer male children. In Appendix One of her book she gives what she calls complete directions on how to have a girl. Her directions are based on a woman's knowing the

exact timing of ovulation. She is also taught how she is going to know the time of her monthly ovulation.

I would be afraid of recommending such a practice. If a mother is able to choose to have a girl, she is also able to choose to have a boy. I have already mentioned how mothers normally prefer sons, maybe mostly to satisfy the wishes of their husbands. I am afraid that, given the position of women in society today, the practice of choosing the sex of an infant would work to the detriment of the female sex. I cherish more another of Laurel Holliday's recommendations: Try to look for a father for your children who belongs to the least aggressive of males. There seems to be much truth in the saying: "Like father, like son."

Yet such a recommendation is loaded with problems. First of all, while it has been demonstrated in animals, for instance in rats and mice, that it is possible selectively to breed samples who are more or less aggressive, no such experiments have, to my knowledge, been made on human beings. Second: How is one able to judge "who belongs to the least aggressive of males"? Low manifest aggressivity may be low latent aggressivity and a low level of inhibition, but it could also be high latent aggressivity counteracted by a high level of habitual inhibition. We may have great difficulties judging whether a person who exhibits low manifest aggressivity also is low on latent aggressivity.

2. *Have women rule the world.* The greater aggressiveness of males is sometimes used to explain why men hold leading positions. There is reason to ask if this trait should not make them unqualified to occupy such positions? I have already mentioned that the great peace activist Mahatma Gandhi believed that women were the only ones who could save the world. The peace researcher Johan Galtung has voiced similar beliefs in women. But if the greater aggressiveness of men is used to explain why men hold leading positions, this explanation may also be used when we look at leaders within the group of men and within the group of women. This may mean that the women who tend to get into leading positions will be the most aggressive women. One may of course hold that these women are still less aggressive than the most aggressive men even though they are more aggressive than most men. It may be necessary to look at the whole process of selecting people for leading positions. Does the selection process itself favor more aggressive personalities? Buckminster Fuller, Lionel Tiger, Lyall Watson, and many other men who have given thought to the problem of male aggression have concluded that the only hope might be to turn the world over to women. The U.S. Admiral Gene R. La Rocque, the Director of the Center for Defense Information in Washington, DC, asked the women members of CDI's Board and the wives of the men on the Board to join together and develop a women's project to prevent nuclear war. The first National Women's Conference to Prevent Nuclear War was the outcome; September

12th, 1984, Washington, DC. Admiral Gene La Rocque stated in a pamphlet to announce the conference that his generation had failed to stop the arms race. "But it's really the men who have failed. Now it's up to the women, and I believe they can do it."

Lionel Tiger and Robin Fox (1971) make this prediction in their book *The Imperial Animal*: " . . . a simple prediction. So long as the use of nuclear weapons could be banned for one year, if all the menial and mighty military posts of the world were taken over by women, there would be no war." Elisabeth Gould Davis (1971) related how Buckminster Fuller, on a television broadcast in 1968, shocked his studio audience when he suggested that society might be saved by restoring women to their age-old leadership in government while men confine themselves to gadgetry and games.

Laurel Holliday (1978, p. 171) tells about the Iroquois Indians who say that they have long recognized that there is a basic difference in the propensity of men and women for aggression, and for that reason gave the women the sole right to declare war of their nation against another. The ancestors of the people and the elders today still recognize that the men are too likely to lead their nation away from peace, and thus that authority must remain vested in women alone.

3. *Make men change*. The third consequence of the insight that men's biological makeup predisposes them for violence and aggression would be to counteract these predispositions either through clinical surgery and/or medication or through changes in the social and educational environment of boys. Though I feel rather hesitant about the first of these two roads to change I shall briefly mention some of the insights here. It has for instance been known for some time that castration decreases criminal practices (Hawke, 1950; LeMaire, 1956).

It has also been known that boys whose mothers were given estrogen during the critical period of gestation (the eighth week of pregnancy) are programmed to be less aggressive and less dominant than males who have no hormonal interference in utero. Dr. Richard Green (1974) studied the behavioral effects of this after having given pregnant diabetic women estrogen in an attempt to reduce fetal mortality. They assessed the male offspring of these women at age six and age sixteen and found that at both ages they showed less assertiveness, aggressiveness, and rough-and-tumble play when compared to normal controls and to sons of diabetic mothers who were not exposed to high levels of estrogen. In this case, the evidence is strong that the estrogen interfered with the process of fetal androgenization and had a dramatic effect on the boys' subsequent behavior. I have already mentioned that marijuana decreases a male's androgen production while alcohol increases it. But I am not going to recommend here either castration of men, hormonal interference in utero, or the smoking of marijuana.

It is again important to emphasize that the correlation between aggression and androgens is just a correlation and not necessarily a causal link. Most of the evidence would seem to indicate that high androgen causes high aggression, yet sometimes social influences can cause a change in androgen levels. Maccoby and Jacklin (1974) summarize this:

> . . . hormone levels constitute an open system. At the present state of our knowledge, it would appear that a high testosterone level can be both a cause and a result of aggressive behavior.

This seems to imply that there is a likelihood of a chain reaction between androgen level and aggression, higher androgen level—higher aggression, and so on. And it means that it is important to look at the social and educational environment we give our boys and whether it encourages aggression and violence or cooperation and caring. What sort of toys are our young boys given? What kind of entertainment do they receive on TV? What are they encouraged to read and watch? What games are they encouraged to participate in? Is the education and upbringing we give them likely to counteract their aggressive dispositions or are we, on the contrary, encouraging them and thereby increasing androgen level?

Before I go into the socialization we give boys and girls through the toys given them, the games they are encouraged to engage in, and the television shows they watch I shall look at the role fathers play in the socialization of children.

The Role of Fathers

Evidence suggests that fathers are generally more concerned than mothers that their boys and girls shall develop distinct sex roles (Goodenough, 1957; Lynn, 1976; Sears, Maccoby & Levin, 1957).

In a recent American experiment (referred to by Maccoby, 1980) boys were given "feminine" sets of toys to play with while girls were given "masculine" sets of toys to play with. The feminine set included a dollhouse with furniture, a large stove with pots and pans, and women's dress-up outfits consisting of dresses, hats, purses, shoes, and a mirror. The masculine set included an army game with soldiers and war vehicles, a highway tollbooth with cars, and cowboy outfits including hats, guns, holsters, and bandanas. The boys were asked to play with the feminine toys the way girls usually did. The girls were asked to play with the masculine toys the way boys normally did. Once each child began to play, the child's mother, father and a same-sex playmate were ushered into the room. It was quite clear from this study that it was the fathers who were most concerned about the sex-appropriateness of their children's play. Furthermore, fathers reacted more negatively to their sons' than to their daughters' sex-inappropriate play. Mothers' negative reactions to sons were not affected by the type of toy the child was playing with.

With daughters, mothers showed slightly more disapproval for cross-sex play. As to same-sex playmates, girls seemed to have no objection to other girls playing with boys' toys. Boys, on the other hand, did put extra negative pressure on other boys when they saw them engage in girls' activities. It seems that the sex-typing pressure exerted by peers is especially strong among boys (see, for instance, Maccoby, 1980).

This experiment is referred to without the researchers' passing any judgment on the educational value of the toys per se. What do the so-called masculine toys tell the children about the world? What is their educational message? And what do the so-called feminine toys teach children? Each set of toys teaches a lesson. As I have said before, the feminine set is meant to educate girls to take care of a house and children—activities which *all* human beings should engage in. The masculine set is meant to teach boys to kill other people—activities *no* human being should be engaged in. In this perspective, the results we have referred to become really alarming. Both fathers and peers press the boys into "sex-appropriate" play. When mothers do not do this—might the reason be that they find toys labeled girls' toys as more appropriate for both sexes? And when they object to their daughters sex-inappropriate play might that be because they themselves do not like war toys?

The most striking fact about research on the role of fathers in the education of the young is the scarcity of it. Cohen and Campos (1974) point out that there exists more research on the role of toys for the child's development than on the role of the father. It has been assumed that mothers are more important for the early development of the child: accordingly, little research has been done on fathers. The scant research that was carried out prior to the last ten years dealt mostly with the relationship father–son, especially the effect of father absence on the sex role development of the son. Studies in this area have indicated the tendency for boys to become either more feminine or to overcompensate their masculinity when the father is absent (Jalmert, 1979).

The overwhelming part of the research conducted during the last ten years on fathers and children shows that despite the little time they actively spend with their children, fathers play a greater role in the sex-stereotyping of children than do mothers. Thygesen (1971), Jalmert (1979), and Lamb (1978) found that as boys grow older, they gradually come to prefer their father to their mother. Some girls come to prefer their fathers as they grow older, some still prefer their mother, and some like both parents equally well. A very likely interpretation of these findings is that, with growing awareness, children come to realize the higher status of males in society and wish such a status for themselves. Lamb also seeks another explanation by studying the type of contact that fathers have with children. He found that although the fathers spent much less time with their children, the time they spent was mostly taken up with pleasure and joy. Furthermore, mothers and fathers touched their children for very different reasons. Mothers mostly touched the children in relation to ordinary caretaking: to dress or undress them, to feed them, to keep them away from objects and places. Fathers touched their children mostly to play with them. When their sons were two years old, fathers would engage in games of roughhousing with them and have friendly fights with them. They actively stimulated their sons in the direction of the typical male.

Other studies from the United States show that fathers spend much more time with their sons than with their daughters: fathers spend twice as much time with one-year-old sons as with one-year-old daughters (Lamb & Lamb, 1976; Lamb, 1977, 1981). It is important to note that mothers do not withdraw from sons nor step up their interaction with daughters in a complementary fashion (Lamb & Lamb, 1976). As the children grow older, middle-class fathers in the United States buy electrical trains for their sons and themselves to play with; they teach their sons to ski, jump, or play football. Even though fathers spend little time with their children, the time they spend is mostly used for play activities and mostly for their sons. And even though fathers in these studies spent very little time with their daughters, their effect on their daughters' sex-typed behavior seemed to be considerable.

In a study (Mussen & Rutherford, 1963) of actual efforts of parents to enhance sex-role behavior in first-grade children, the feminine-oriented girls had fathers who actively encouraged them to engage in sex-typical behaviors. These fathers were also more "masculine" on a questionnaire (sex role preference) than fathers of girls who were low in feminine orientation. In this study no comparable findings were obtained for fathers and sons.

Bronfenbrenner (1958), reanalyzing data originally compiled by Lansky (1956), found that adolescent boys with few masculine preferences had fathers who played a traditionally feminine role in the family.

It has been found that the more aggressive a father is, the more aggressive a son he will produce. Butcher (1969), for example, reports that the fathers of juvenile delinquents who were notably aggressive had high aggression scores on personality tests. Thomas Detre et al. (1974) has found that an antisocial attitude on the part of a *father* is the single best predictor that a boy will become violent later in life. Swedish researchers (referred to by Liljestrøm et al., 1976) have tried to identify common characteristics of men whom they viewed as "good" fathers, in the sense that they cared a lot for their children, respected their emerging personalities, and tried to understand the children on their own premises. These fathers had one characteristic in common: they all had spent more time with children than fathers normally do. The tragic part about this study is that the reason *why* the fathers had spent much more time with the children was not that they had volunteered to. Various circumstances, like unemployment or a sick wife, had brought them into this situation. In some cases they had been left alone with the children, either because the mother had died or they had been divorced and the father awarded custody of the children (a practice becoming more frequent in Scandinavia). Liljestrøm et al. (1976) mention that no matter what the original reason for the father's greater contact with his children, the result was that he became "a good father."

While I have mostly used a social learning theory, acknowledging also that biology may play a part, in my attempt to show how aggression, competition, and oppression of women are fostered in boys, socialist feminists who use a gynocentric psychoanalytic theory tend to locate the reproduction of male dominance and misogyny in women's mothering (Chodorow, 1978; Dinnerstein, 1977).

These theorists claim that the development of male devaluation of everything that is regarded as feminine rests ultimately on the fact that the male child, in breaking with his primary mother identification, must define himself as "not feminine" in order to be masculine. In this process, he develops hostilities toward and negative evaluations of women. He also develops stringent notions of what it means to be a male and what it means to be a female. The males' need to feel superior to females is an effort to reinforce their masculine identity (Johnson, 1977). Women, on the other hand, have no need to differentiate themselves from the femininity of the mother in order to achieve a sex identity and hence do not have the psychological motive for hostility to males, for dominating males, for oppressive behavior. These gynocentric psychologists claim that if the nearly universal patterns of women being the primary nurturers of both male and female infants were altered, this dynamic might be broken. If males shared equally with females in child care, males could "identify" with a male figure in a maternal role and thus feel securely masculine, which would in turn eliminate the male motive to dominate and oppress women and look down on anything feminine.

While I certainly feel that it is important that the father share equally in the nurturing of small children, I do not see this as a solution to male dominance in society as long as mothers and fathers are not equal to each other in marriage and in heterosexual relationships. If father takes more care of the children but leaves all the dishwashing, cooking, cleaning, and tidying up to mother, she will still be oppressed and the daughter and son will learn that mother does the dull things and father the exciting things. Fathers are unlikely to teach their children cooperation and sharing if they themselves compete in the workplace, want to earn more than their wives, and do not share household duties. It seems to be necessary that women who are living with the fathers of their children have to press these men to change their family role.

Numerous researchers have found that the more severely a child is *punished,* the more likely he or she is to become an aggressive juvenile delinquent. The more violence a child experiences at the hands of her or his parents, the more violent that child is likely to be to others as an adult. The parents who beat a child provide a living example of how to use force to accomplish one's ends. Extensive research has shown that physical punishment is one of the five major factors associated with the development of delinquency in young boys (Glueck & Glueck, 1950). Holliday (1978, p. 100) in her book *The Violent Sex* mentions research which shows that men who have been convicted of murder were physically punished in childhood twice as often as their brothers who had not committed murder. Some of them had almost been beaten to death.

Boys are punished more often and more severely than girls. Murray Strauss (1974) has found that boys are punished roughly twice as often as girls. Maccoby and Jacklin (1974) point out that fathers react more severely than mothers to their boys' aggressiveness and are more likely to physically punish a son for aggressive misbehavior than a daughter who does exactly the same thing. Boys are much more likely to be punished by their fathers than by their mothers. Laurel Holliday (1978) reports a survey conducted for the National Commission on the Cause and Prevention of Violence showing that almost twice as many low-education parents as high-education parents reported spanking their children frequently. According to Laurel Holliday (1978) there seems to be a predictable ratio between educational and income levels and violence toward children—as income goes up physical punishment goes down. There may be several explanations for this phenomenon. One is that the lack of space and resources leads to aggression. Another may be that people with more education have learned more about the harmful effects of spanking children. This might, in some instances, prevent them from physically abusing their children or at least make them ashamed enough not to *report* such behavior. But it is extremely important to stress the fact that some ethnic groups, though poor, rarely or never punish children. Some American Indian tribes, for example, never use physical force on their children, while child abuse is high among American blacks and Puerto Ricans (Gil, 1973).

Steinmetz and Strauss (1974) in their book *Violence in the Family* state, on the basis of several studies, that a physically punished child is more likely to be a harsh and violent parent and so to perpetuate violence down through the generations.

Holliday (1978, p. 102) reports a study by Drs. Leopold Bellak and Maxine Antell (1974) testing a hypothesis that Germans as children may be more subject to physical violence than children from some other European cultures. They studied parent-child interaction on German playgrounds as compared to Danish and Italian playgrounds. Their results here indicate clearly that German adults are significantly more aggressive toward German children, and German children toward other children, than are either the

Italians or the Danes. Laurel Holliday comments: "Though they do not claim that the parent abusiveness is *the* cause of German aggressiveness, their work strongly suggests that we take a long look at how we in this country punish children."

EDUCATION THROUGH CHOICE OF TOYS

Most parents provide different socialization experiences for their daughters and their sons at the same time that sex-typical toddler behaviors are emerging. Parents tend to buy their sons more transportation toys, sports equipment, and military toys while they buy their daughters dolls, stuffed animals, and domestic toys (Rheingold & Cook, 1975). The toys parents buy or make for their child form an important part of the child's immediate surroundings. All toys are educational and convey messages to children. Some toys are used for fighting, some for caring. Some encourage imitative play and the learning of existing social roles and others encourage the child to explore new directions.

Toy shops in most places around the world will generally have one section with toys for girls and one section with toys for boys. In the section with toys for girls, we find all sort of objects designed to educate the small girl for her role as homemaker: pots and pans, miniature stoves, and refrigerators; for her role as mother: dolls in all shapes; and for her role as object for men's sexual interest: cosmetic kits and haircurlers. In the section with toys for boys we find objects designed to train the small boy for jobs that carry prestige and are decisive for our way of living. Here are science kits of all kinds, buses and trucks, cars and trains. And we find big collections of war toys—from bows and arrows, to rifles, guns, machine-guns, revolvers, and even small uniforms. The choice of toys is made for the child long before she or he can make any personal choice. By the time the child is able to do that, he or she is usually conditioned into "choosing" the sex-appropriate toy.

Even the mobiles that are often put in the newborn baby's bedroom, frequently above the crib, are sex-typed. Mobiles for infant girls contain small dolls, angels, and flowers. Boats, cars, and cannons are for infant boys.

Elena Belotti (1973) tells from her many observations of preschool children how boys and girls are pressed into playing with sex-appropriate toys. A two-year-old boy asked his mother if she could buy him a small broom. The answer was no, that was not a toy for a boy. Boys who want to have a doll with them when they go to sleep are given a teddy bear: boys may cuddle with doll-like figures in the shape of animals but never in the shape of a baby or a real doll! When children were left on their own and believed that they had no observers, however, Belotti found that boys were eager to play with dolls, and girls with cars or anything that would move.

If toys are to form a part of peace education instead of being partly education for war, we must do away with war toys and also with the sex-labeling of toys. Both sexes ought to be able to play with dolls, to train themselves to take care of children and a home. Both sexes ought to be able to play with movable objects like buses and trains and, when somewhat older, to experiment with science kits.

On entering the GDR (German Democratic Republic—East Germany) through East Berlin some years ago I was asked by the customs clearance whether I brought with me any war toys. It was strictly forbidden to import war toys into the GDR. Being so much an opposer of war toys, I was rather perplexed at this question. I thought: maybe war toys are forbidden in the GDR. While studying in this country and deliberately visiting toy shops and day-care centers for children I noticed that this was not the case. Though the selection of such toys in comparison to other toys seemed to be smaller than in the Western world, it still existed. When I asked why I had not been allowed to bring war toys into the Republic, I was given the answer that they did not want NATO war-toys imported. Their boys should be taught to play with toys that copy the military equipment from the countries belonging to the Warsaw Treaty!

In both Norway and Sweden there have been successful campaigns against the production and sale of war toys; in both countries these campaigns have been started by women. And in both countries the women in the social-democratic parties have been supported by youth groups within the parties and have managed to get political acceptance for a line of severe import restrictions on such toys. Women are still working to have such toys done away with completely. It was mothers who organized and picketed Nabisco in 1971 to have them withdraw the kits of torture toys they had produced for boys (Holliday, 1978, p. 159). In 1971, the Aurora Toy Company introduced a new line of toys for boys—torture toys. There were eight different kits. A typical one included a seminude female who was to be strapped to the platform of a guillotine with a razor-sharp pendulum over her throat. The mothers who organized against these toys succeeded in having them withdrawn from the market. It was no accident that it was mothers, not fathers, who felt compelled to protect their children from such a glorification of violence.

The toys produced for our boys are certainly not of a kind intended to decrease aggressive dispositions. And we know that fathers (Green, 1976) and peers, especially other boys, are extremely negative toward boys who practice opposite-sex play behavior such as nurturance play with dolls. Such behavior in boys is actively discouraged.

I have, so far, not come across any studies which clearly show that aggressive behavior is caused by the use of war toys. Such studies, though interesting, may be difficult to conduct and especially to draw conclusions from.

Correlations may easily be spurious correlations. Children playing much with war toys may be more aggressive than other children not because of the war toys per se, but maybe because of the socioeconomic conditions surrounding the children or because they may have parents who do not care about the cultural influences, such as toys, that their children are subjected to. Also, there may be differences between habitual use of war toys and sporadic use. Some of the same questions that I asked in connection with alcoholism and the use of alcohol may be asked here too. Is it the habitual play with war toys that causes aggressive behavior? Is such behavior likely to occur also in a child who normally does not play with such toys if that child plays with them on a certain occasion? Is there reason to believe that boys become more aggressive when playing with war toys than girls do if they play as much and with the same toys as boys do?

A priori, it seems likely that there is a causal effect between playing with war toys and aggressive behavior, but it seems hard *a priori* to predict how strong such a link would be. It seems likely that we shall find some of the same links between the use of war toys and aggressive behavior that we find between the viewing of television violence and aggressive behavior. Also, in the latter case, many studies are difficult to interpret, especially when it comes to assessing causal relations.

THE ROLE OF TELEVISION IN PEACE EDUCATION

What are the effects of televised violence on children? Are there any indications that the watching of television affects girls and boys differently?

There have been a vast number of studies conducted on the effects of viewing violence on television. Even though most studies seem to conclude that there exists some relationship between the viewing of some types of violence and the acting out of some types of aggressive behavior, occasionally we may read newspaper headlines saying that no such relationship has been found. It seems to be rather necessary here to look at who has sponsored the study and what economic interests are behind it. Has it been commissioned by groups having an economic interest in a particular outcome of the research—in, for instance, trivializing the effects of televised violence? In such cases there is all reason to be skeptical to the results reported; there are large economic interests behind the mass media corporations.

Commercial television companies are interested in selling advertising time at as high a price as possible. They will get the best price for commercials broadcast during programs with high viewer ratings. If these programs happen to be the ones with a high incidence of violence, the television companies are interested in sponsoring research that trivializes the harmful effects of media violence.

Two British researchers, H. J. Eysenck and D. K. B. Nias (1978), have made a thorough analysis of the available international research data on the effects of watching violence on television. In their book *Sex, Violence and the Media* they conclude that it has been shown beyond any doubt that watching violence on television causes real-life violence. They argue against those who claim that there is no decisive evidence for the view that the media affect human conduct or that the evidence is contradictory. "As we shall see, the evidence is not really contradictory, except in the sense that a good study, properly planned, executed and analyzed, may be contradicted by a bad study, carelessly planned, badly executed and improperly analysed" (Eysenck and Nias, 1978, p. 11).

These researchers carefully analyze the results from the two U.S. national commissions on violence. The first one was appointed by Lyndon B. Johnson after the murders of John and Robert Kennedy and Martin Luther King. The commission made a thorough survey of the available research on the effects of violence on television and concluded that the overwhelming majority of this research showed that violence on television has negative effects on the viewers, especially on children. But they qualified their conclusion by also mentioning that it seemed as if the viewing of televised violence was an additional factor which contributed to real-life violence, but not the main cause of it. They made a long series of recommendations to reduce the amount of violence showed on television. These recommendations were not followed up on, partly because the second national commission had already started its work. This commission had been initiated by the Senate. It, too, was asked to make a survey of previous research on televised violence, but it was, in addition, asked to conduct new empirical studies in the area. Sixty researchers were engaged in working on 23 different projects. Their reports filled five big volumes and were summarized by the commission in a sixth one. It is interesting to note here how the second commission was composed and also how its reports were treated. After a list of prospective commission members had been drawn up, this list was put before the biggest American television companies who suggested that seven of the most critical researchers be deleted from the list. This was done. In the final selection of thirteen commission members, five had close personal connections to the largest television companies.

The researchers working on the 23 different projects sponsored by the second commission were asked to give an educated guess to the best of their knowledge about the relationship between watching violence on television and engaging in real-life violence. Seventy percent declared that TV violence leads to increased aggressivity; none held that TV violence was without effects; 30 percent held that it was too difficult to know which types of televised violence lead to which effects, so they declined to answer the question. The research reports were in a technical language and difficult to read for nonresearchers.

Those members of the commission who were affiliated with the large television companies did whatever they could to water down the conclusions of the research reports. Yet the commission drew conclusions such as "Violence depicted on TV can immediately or shortly thereafter induce mimicking or copying by children" and that "under certain circumstances TV violence can instigate an increase in aggressive acts." There were also more general conclusions such as noting that "data while not wholly consistent or conclusive do indicate that a modest relationship exists between the viewing of violence and aggressive behavior" (Eysenck & Nias, 1978, p. 84).

Some of these conclusions leaked out to the press a week before the final report from the commission was published. But the press concentrated only on the reservations and qualifications in the conclusions drawn. The *New York Times* ran the following headlines: "TV violence of no harm for youngsters." The communication researcher Gunnar Garbo comments: "First the conclusions from the researchers have been watered down whereupon they are also reported in a skewed form by the press" (Garbo, 1984, p. 40—my translation). The U.S. Surgeon General, Jesse Steinfeld, tried later in a speech before the U.S. Senate Committee on Communications to counteract the skewed version of the conclusion from the report. Dr. Steinfeld expressed his views as follows (according to Eysenck & Nias, 1978, p. 89): "The overwhelming consensus and the unanimous Scientific Advisory Committee's report indicates that TV violence, indeed, does have an adverse effect on certain members of our society. . . . While the Committee report is carefully phrased and qualified in language acceptable to social scientists, it is clear to me that the causal relationship between televised violence and antisocial behavior is sufficient to warrant appropriate and immediate remedial action."

This speech got little publicity. The first press version was the one quoted and the general impression remained that the second commission had weakened the conclusion from the first commission by saying that TV violence was not dangerous after all. Commercial television companies, as well as the commercial press, profit from the assumed effects of advertising on people's behavior. They have an economic interest in showing that advertising influences people's behavior; if not, they would not get advertising time sold. The fact that the advertising industry is paying billions of dollars for media messages indicates that the assumption is correct: Profit-making corporations would not have used their resources in this way if they had not discovered that their beamed messages influence viewer behavior. But at the same time, TV companies have an interest in showing that the practice is not likely to be influenced by fiction or news programs which tell them that they had better prepare for violence. If it was generally understood that media violence has such negative effects, then the showing of it might be met with increased political resistance. It seems extremely unlikely that advertising influences people's behavior while violence on TV does not. Either both advertising and violence influence behavior or neither one does. Even without research showing that media violence seems to increase violent behavior among heavy viewers, the likelihood that such a causal relationship exists seems greatest. Certainly the companies that spend billions of dollars on advertising do not only *assume* that advertising has an effect, but have substantial experience for this.

Even though independent researchers may favor the conclusion that televised violence is connected to violent behavior, they have no economic interests tied to such a conclusion. There is probably no researcher without some personal bias when it comes to the result of her or his research. The personal bias has to be checked and balanced through counter-arguments and counter-hypothesis. This is all the more difficult if the bias is supported through large economic interests.

The two British researchers Eysenck and Nias (1978), who are not affiliated with commercial television companies but are doing independent research at the Institute of Psychiatry at the University of London, have presented data showing that there is all reason to believe that "people who view a lot of violence tend to become more aggressive" (Eysenck and Nias, 1978, p. 123). After a thorough scientific examination of the available evidence, they conclude: "It can no longer be said that the evidence is ambiguous, or too contradictory to allow any conclusions to be drawn; the evidence is remarkably consistent, and congruent in its major aspects" (Eysenck and Nias, 1978, p. 275).

Laurel Holliday (1978, p. 108) claims that of all the situational factors known to increase aggressiveness, it appears that the viewing of television violence is one of the most potent. Most researchers are usually reluctant to say that one thing causes another; they usually say: "There is a strong correlation between" and point out that the strong correlation does not say anything about the causal relationship. But the case is so strong on television violence that a prominent and highly respected researcher, Dr. Robert M. Liebert, has stated: "It seems to me that it has been shown beyond the reasonable shadow of a doubt that watching television produces antisocial attitudes and behavior that would not otherwise occur among entirely normal children" (Liebert, 1974, p. 99). Similarly, Leonard Eron concludes from his ten-year extensive study of TV and violence that ". . . the most plausible interpretation of these data was that early viewing of violent television caused later aggression" (Eron et al., 1974, p. 412). But this direct positive relationship between violence of preferred programs and later aggression was true only for boys! Strangely enough, television violence, which has been found to be a major contributor to boys' aggressive behavior, does not seem to influence girls.

There may be several explanations for this. Laurel Holliday (1978, p. 104) mentions some: (1) girls are socialized away from aggression, and thus prefer less violent TV to begin with, (2) female characters are not as violent as male characters on TV and are therefore not as potent role models for aggression, and (3) females are often victims of male violence on TV and little girls identify with their pain. One explanation may also be that girls watch less TV than boys because they have to do so much more unpaid housework than their brothers do.

The Finnish aggression researcher Kirsti Lagerspetz (1982a) refers to a whole series of studies on televised violence and aggression in children (see especially the longitudinal study by Lefkowitz et al., 1977) including Finnish studies which she has conducted (Lagerspetz, 1982b) and reaches the same conclusion: The aggressivity of girls does not correlate with the viewing of televised violence, or if there is a correlation, it is much weaker than for boys. She tries to explain this finding by referring to the fact that girls are socialized not to show aggressive behavior or to try to solve conflicts through violence. There may, however, also be other explanations that have more to do with the content of what is shown on television. Such a hypothesis is supported by research which Kirsti Lagerspetz (1982b) herself refers to.

She refers to a large international project on televised violence in which she participated that concluded the number of violent females on American television has increased in recent years. This study has also found an increase in the correlation between aggression and TV viewing in American girls as compared to earlier findings. This finding points in the direction of Laurel Holliday's hypothesis number two as an explanation for the fact that earlier studies have shown no or only a weak correlation between aggressivity in girls and the viewing of televised violence. The reason for this *may* have been that there were few violent models for girls to model, females who were rewarded for their violent behavior. If this is the reason for the weak correlation that has previously been found between aggressivity in girls and the viewing of televised violence, it means that girls can also learn violence through television and that that medium is strong enough to counteract other socializing influences girls receive to keep them away from aggressive behavior.

Recent research on the question of media violence as the cause of aggression has been carried out along three main lines. One school works with the "arousal hypothesis," which holds that exciting media content (erotic, violent, humorous and so forth) can increase aggression if it is an appropriate response. The second major school works with the "disinhibition" hypothesis. It holds that television violence, especially if it is rewarded, weakens the inhibitions of the viewer against engaging in similar behavior and by implication increases his readiness to engage in interpersonal aggression. The third school bases its thinking on a social learning theory. It holds that ways of behavior are learned by observation not only of real performance but also of media-fed performance. Television violence may lead to the acquisition of aggressive responses that are imitated in appropriate situations in real life. These three schools are complementary and not exclusive.

Eysenck and Nias (1978) belong to the second major school. They have shown that the natural inhibitions against violence are grossly reduced in children if they have the feeling that their surroundings accept violence. Children get desensitized to the use of violence. Eysenck and Nias use the process of desensitization as their main explanation of the fact that watching and reading about violence may lead to real-life violence. It is a common method within behavioral therapy to desensitize people who have irrational phobias against certain things. Take a person who has an irrational phobia against spiders. Any kind of innocent spider. She or he starts screaming at the sight of a spider and goes all day long in a nervous state lest a spider should appear. This leads to nightmares about spiders so that the person is nervous to go to sleep. Behavioral therapists will try to treat this irrational fright by slowly desensitizing the patient toward spiders. They will talk to him or her in pleasant surroundings and try to talk a little bit about spiders. Then they will show the patient a small picture of a spider. When the patient feels safe and can talk about spiders the therapist will let them see one through a window. The next time he will walk in the garden and they will look at a spider from far off. In this manner the patient will slowly be desensitized in regard to spiders. Parents often use the same method to have their child overcome a fright about water and the sea. The parents play with the child near the water and gradually closer and closer to the water.

But this method of desensitization can also be used to promote negative aims. Eysenck and Nias maintain that if the population of the planet Mars wanted to find a method to brutalize the population of the earth they could not have thought of anything better than to invent a media system that would slowly desensitize humanity toward using violence against each other. If one wants to reduce inhibitions against the use of violence and allow for the violent person to come forward, one should—to follow the principles of desensitization—start by letting people watch violence in a safe and cozy atmosphere in their own homes. Through a gradual process of becoming accustomed to and accepting more and more violence some of the viewers will have lost their inhibitions against the use of violence in a given real-life situation. The daily doses of media violence have effect. Watching a lot of violence on television makes people insensitive to violence.

In their book *Violence as Communication* the Dutch researchers Alex P. Schmid and Janny de Graaf (1982) have a chapter on unlearning inhibitions against the use of violence. Here they remind us that an act of violence consists of two things: the act of aggression and the act of suffering from the consequences of the aggression. In violence portrayals in the media, emphasis is placed on the first aspect while the second is largely neglected. This is done for two reasons. The first is that the aftermath of violence is long while the act of violence is short. A shooting, a stabbing, a car accident takes only seconds to depict while the suffering of the victim and of her or his nearest family cannot be covered adequately given the time constraints which govern media programming. The second reason for this imbalance between aggression and suffering is that showing the agony of the victim is unaesthetic and upsetting to the audience. Schmid and de Graaf tell that some years ago a British commercial television station tried to broadcast a realistic crime series (*Big Breadwinner Hog*) in which pain and wounds and suffering were portrayed in true detail. This produced such a public outcry that the series had to be discontinued after one sequence. The viewers wanted to see people shot and killed, hanged and torn to pieces, but not how they suffered. The net effect of this imbalance seems to be that the television watcher cannot develop much sympathy for the victim. This is reinforced by the fact that in fictional crime series the people who have to suffer most are usually "bad guys" who "deserve" death and injury.

From an early age children get accustomed to violence without simultaneously learning what its consequences are. Television comic series, for instance, may depict how a "good guy" smashes a person with a rock, whereupon the victim reinflates like a balloon in the next scene to regain her or his original form. The humorous connotations of such scenes may ultimately not have the effect of harmlessness but facilitate the acceptance of violence as normal, inconsequential, and legitimate.

To say that much of TV violence is fictional does not excuse it. The public's ability to distinguish between real and fictional television material is limited. Schmid and de Graaf (1982) tell about a fictional series, *Marcus Welby, M.D.*, in which the leading character in the play is a physician. The actor received, during the first five years of the program, no less than 250,000 letters from the public, mostly with requests for medical advice.

Schmid and de Graaf show also that when real-life violence is shown on television—for instance in the news—the same thing happens: the act of aggression is shown but not the consequences of the act. We are led to believe that violence is excitement and not primarily suffering and pain.

Kenneth Moyer (1974) who, according to Laurel Holliday (1978), has probably written more than anyone else about the physiological correlates of aggressive behavior, reports that the neural systems involved in violence are sensitized and aroused by *competitive sports*. Goldstein and Arms (1971) did a study to determine what effect competitive sports have on aggressive behavior. They found that hostility significantly increased in persons who had just viewed a football game. However, they found no increase in hostility in people who had observed a gymnastic exhibition. They point out that intense competition can lead to catastrophic consequences. But the fact that they found that hostility among the spectators was especially aroused when people watched football games may indicate that it is not merely the intensity of the competition which explains violence in spectators, but also the degree to which the competitive sport is a more individualistic sport like running or a more collective sport like ball games, a sport where players have little physical contact, as in tennis, or more physical contact, as in football or boxing.

European-style football, or soccer, is undoubtedly the sport most affected by violence, occurring around a sport, even if it is not the roughest team sport. (American football and ice hockey are rougher.) It is, nevertheless, the sport that is by far the most seriously threatened by spectator excesses. Thousands and thousands of spectators have been killed or seriously injured while watching football matches. The deadliest match so far was the match between Peru and Argentina in Lima in 1964. Here more than 300 people were killed (350 according to Council of Europe statistics quoted by UNESCO, 126 EX/14, 1987; 320 according to Elimane Fall, 1987; and 301 according to Vaclav Pletanek, 1987) and more than 500 people seriously injured (this estimate is given in the quoted statistics from the Council of Europe and Pletanek, 1987 while Fall, 1987, has an estimate of more than one thousand injured). In the match between Rio de la Plata and Boca Juniors in Buenos Aires in 1968 more than 70 spectators were killed (72 according to the Council of Europe; 73 according to Pletanek, 1987; and 80 according to Fall) and more than 110 seriously injured (113 according to the Council of Europe; 150 according to Fall, 1987; and more than 200 according to Pletanek, 1987). A more recent tragedy happened at Heysel stadium in Bruxelles in the final game of the European football cup, the one between Juventus from Torino, Italy, and Liverpool, United Kingdom. Here 38 were killed and more than 200 injured.

Several explanations for the fact that football is the sport most threatened by spectator excesses have been given. Among these are economic difficulties affecting the communities from which the majority of spectators are drawn, the process whereby supporters identify with the players, the particularly high number of confrontations, the popularity of football matches and their tendencies to draw great masses of people, and the density of the masses.

In an analysis of violence in sports, all of these explanations are mentioned yet the conclusion is drawn that there is to date no clear answer to explain the excessive violence on the part of spectators at these football matches (UNESCO, 126 EX/14, 1987). None of the studies I have come across on violence in football gives statistics divided by sex. Yet we know that the overwhelming majority of those watching football, and of those who are killed as spectators at football matches, are boys and men. And all the players are men, at least in the well-known matches where spectators have been killed. The studies do not analyze competitive sport from a feminist perspective or attempt to connect such sport to male role socialization with its emphasis on competition, group identification, and channeling of emotions into aggressive outlets. The football field is a field where "men are men." Should feminists try to analyze what is happening in many competitive sports and advocate a change in them, or should they join in? The opinions are divided and may depend on whether one adheres to a more liberal or more radical feminist perspective.

SPORTS AND GAMES: POWER-OVER OR POWER-TO?

The radical feminist power concepts differentiating between power as dominance, power-over, and power as competence, power-to, may be important in an analysis of the contribution of games and more collective sports to peace education. Even though most games and sports contain elements of both competition and cooperation at the same time, the activities may be more or less competitive. Sometimes a game that is normally a competitive game can be changed into a more cooperative one by changing the structure of the game, some of the rules. Do we in research literature find that girls more than boys tend to favor cooperation rather than competition in games and sports?

Erikson (1951) in his study of ten- to twelve-year-olds found that the female child was interested in including others in her world and acting in relation to them—not in competition. The goal of oneupmanship, essential to aggression, he found to be less strong in female children. He found the male child to be less integrated with his environment and less sensitive to external cues, such as other people's faces. He was *acting upon*, rather than *in relation to*. And Erikson sees this as the beginning of a lifelong pattern of establishing separateness and oneupmanship rather than affiliation and cooperation with others.

In another cross-cultural study, which compared Anglo-American and Mexican children, five- through nine-year-olds were offered opportunities to make choices that would give them more rewards than their partners, equal rewards with their partners, or smaller rewards than their partners. Girls in both cultures and at all ages studied were more likely to try to equalize the rewards. Boys not only chose more for themselves but also made choices that reduced the partner's reward—even when this action did not yield more for the child himself (Knight & Kagan, 1977).

The fights that erupt in boys' groups are often related to forming and maintaining dominance hierarchies. In a cross-cultural study, Whiting and Whiting (1973, 1975) found that in five out of six societies in different parts ıe world, boys showed more egoistic dominance than girls. Edwards and iting (1977) also report higher male rates of such egoistic behaviors in five out of six African villages. In the same study, sex differences in the quality of the African children's social interaction were found, differences rather similar to what DiPietro (1977) found in American children: Boys more often competed, assaulted, teased, showed off to one another; girls more often offered help and affection to one another and more often used social commands, for example: "let's do . . ." "you do this, I'll do that." In other words, girls appeared to be setting up an agreed-upon procedure for social activity.

The games and sports of boys seem to be invariably more competitive than those the girls play. Nina Schjerve Pedersen (1980) conducted a study on the integration of the Norwegian Girl Scouts and Boy Scouts into the same troops. They had already belonged to the same scout association but to separate troops with separate leaders and also different games and sports. Nina, who was one of the top leaders of the Girl Scouts, favored the idea of integration and was rather instrumental in getting the two scout organizations to integrate. Afterward she studied the effects of the integration as her thesis at the Institute for Educational Research at the University of Oslo.

The study showed that before the integration, many women had been troop leaders and other leaders of the Girl Scouts. After the integration almost all troops were led by men—the former women leaders had become assistant leaders.

But even more important facts were revealed by the analysis of the types of *activities* that were allowed to continue and dominate the new mixed-sex organization. Analysis of the activities in the former Girl Scouts as compared to the activities in the former Boy Scouts revealed that the activities of the girls were of a more cooperative nature than those of the boys. The boys had activities where they competed more against each other or against other groups of boys or other troops. Their activities were more achievement-oriented. They received decorations and outward recognition when passing certain tests. Analysis of the types of activities that were allowed to live on in the mixed-sex scout movement revealed clearly that the activities were those of the boys. The competitive activities of the boys became the activities for both the girls and the boys. The cooperative activities of the girls were lost. The integration had been on the boys' terms.

Runa Haukaa and I have shown that co-educational gymnastics as they have recently been practiced in Norway cater more to the needs of boys than of girls. When boys and girls are allowed to choose between various types of physical exercises, we find that girls very often choose both more individual and less competitive activities, such as jazz gymnastics and dance, boys choose both more collective and frequently more competitive activities, such as football or soccer. In co-educational gymnastics the girls have to learn to play football or soccer while the boys do not have to learn to dance or do jazz gymnastics (Brock-Utne & Haukaa, 1980; Brock-Utne, 1982a, 1982b).

Studies from Norway show that women are almost as physically active as men (40 percent against 45 percent of the total adult population; Fasting, 1982) when physical activity includes hiking (the most popular physical activity in Norway) and gymnastics, which is often organized by housewives. But when we look at competitive sports there are very few women who are organized in sports clubs and compete. Organized sports, according to the physical education researcher Kari Fasting (1982), means male sports. Most of the money that goes to organized sports goes to males.

We may summarize our findings here by noting that:

- Girls more than boys tend to equalize rewards, while boys more than girls try to establish dominance hierarchies and oneupmanship.
- Girls more than boys tend to choose more cooperative sport activities, while boys more than girls tend to choose more competitive games and sport activities.

Organized sports, as Fasting (1982) points out, means male sports and discrimination against women: they get less of the resources and have little influence on the type of activities given high priority.

An analysis of the discrimination of women in sports is normally done from a liberal feminist perspective, where a concept such as equality is a core concept. Though my perspective is more of a radical feminist perspective, I also think it is important that we document how women are discriminated against in sports—as everywhere else in society—how women have been kept out of *some* sports, and how little women get of the available physical space and resources. An interesting study using this perspective was done at the University of Tromsø some years ago (Andreassen & Mortensen, 1982), showing the uneven distribution of space in the athletics hall between boys and girls having physical education together. When the boys entered the hall first, they would regularly occupy the whole hall, throw long-distance balls at each other, and shout to the boys at the other end of the hall. When the girls entered, they had to cluster together in a small group. If the girls entered first, however, they would occupy only *half* of the hall, leaving the rest to the boys.

But if an analysis is made from a more radical feminist perspective, we would ask, as I mentioned in the chapter on feminist perspectives, not so much about the distribution of the pie as about the basic recipe. What is this pie made from, of which we want a bigger share? What sort of power concept are we dealing with in organized sports, the concept of power-over (power as dominance) or the feminist concept of power-to (power as competence)? Are we, through sports, giving youngsters an education for violence? Are we training them more for war than for peace? I am afraid that a more lengthy and thorough analysis of the institution of sports than I can undertake here would leave us with the conviction that the question may have to be answered in the affirmative. Today the values embedded in organized sports are not very different from those instilled in young males during military training. I shall here deal with violence in sport activists, not spectators, by differentiating between direct violence, which leads to instant deaths or maiming for life, and indirect violence, which creates winners and losers and loss of self-esteem. I shall end on a more optimistic note pointing to the fact that physical activity *can* be viewed in the feminist way of power as competence, as pleasure and joy.

Direct Violence—The Cult of Danger and Courage

A couple of years ago the sport pages of the Norwegian newspaper *Dagbladet* (24, October 1986) contained some glossy pictures of men in fast cars and attractive girls watching them. The headlines which were in big, capital letters read: "These courageous men . . . " and in somewhat smaller letters "and their beautiful women." The article deals with the car race contest in Estoril, Portugal, and starts this way: "This week-end they are gathered in the big final contest, all the courageous men who are risking their lives in the missile-like formula 1 cars and the beautiful women who surround them and shed their warm light on this event." As a researcher at the Albert Einstein College of Medicine has shown, the cult of danger and risk-taking going into the concept of masculinity may be dangerous to the health of males and shorten their lives (Harrison, 1978). Males are much more accident-prone than females; they are, for instance, involved in motor vehicle accidents leading to deaths or maiming for life almost three times as often as females (Harrison, 1978, p. 76).

There are risk sports other than car-racing—for example, boxing, climbing, canoing in powerful waterfalls, parachuting off steep mountains, like the Troll wall (Trollveggen). "The more people who die when parachute-jumping from the Troll wall, the more people want to jump from that mountain," the newspapers could tell us last year.

It is forbidden to jump off the Troll wall, but this fact is constantly under attack from parachutists and climbers. One could, of course, argue that one may try to convince people they ought not to jump off the Troll wall but still be against forbidding them to do so. But in the Norwegian debate on this subject a couple of years ago those who did not want to forbid the jumping did not argue against jumping either. On the contrary: "The adventure and excitement may be so big that it may be worth risking one's life for," said a Norwegian professor of philosophy (Naess, 1985).

I argued against him, pointing out that we are not self-sufficient human beings, we exist in relation to other people. Most of us have somebody who is attached to us, who would mourn our death. Our lives do not belong solely to ourselves. Our lives belong also to those who care about us and to a society that has invested resources in us. It is much worse to be left behind when the one you love dies than to die yourself. (The debate about the jumping off the Troll wall can be found in the Norwegian newspaper *Dagbladet*, Brock-Utne 1985b, 1985c; also, Breivik, 1985; Naess, 1985; Stigen, 1985. See also the last chapter in Brock-Utne, 1986.)

There is ample evidence that violence in sports is learned behavior, rather than some "natural" tendency rooted in male biology (Doyle, 1983; Messner, 1985, with further references; Pleck, 1982). Mike Messner demonstrates how this violence leads not only to deaths and low life expectancy among retiring athletes, but also to permanent injuries and a tendency to abuse alcohol and other drugs (Messner, 1985). The permanent injuries are caused by an obedience to the "no pain, no gain" philosophy of many coaches and athletes. Boys are taught that to endure pain is courageous, to survive pain is manly. Don Sabo (1985) has shown how what he calls the pain principle is defended by the social organization of sports. And he asks us to look at stress-related illnesses among older athletes or former athletes and how the machismo aspects of their roles lower their life expectancies. He tells that the average life expectancy of National Football League players (American football) in the United States is 54, nearly two decades below the overall male mean! (Sabo, 1985, p. 11).

The pain priniciple is also at work in the military which is an institution with a lot of similarities to organized sports. Here men are taught to endure physical hardship, to risk their lives, to be brave and courageous. Gwynne Dyer (1985) in his book *War* (also a television series in Canada and the United States) quotes Captain Pingree in the U.S. Marine Corps talking to his recruits:

> You have an enemy here at Parris Island. The enemy that you are going to have at Parris Island is in every one of us. It's in the form of cowardice. The most rewarding experience you're going to have in recruit training is standing on line every evening, and you'll be able to look into each other's eyes, and you'll be able to say to each other with your eyes: "By God, we've made it one more day! We've defeated the coward." (Dyer, 1985, p. 114)

The cult of danger and courage seems to go into the stuff that men are made of. We find it in organized sports and in the military.

Indirect Violence—The Cult of Power as Dominance

"Except for war, there is nothing in American life—nothing—which trains a boy better for life than football." These well-known words were uttered by Robert Kennedy as attorney general (Clinch, 1973, p. 266). And indeed the similarities between the socialization—we may even call it indoctrination—going on in the military and in athletic competitions on the sports fields are many. Both the military and organized sports aim at making an individual both loyal to his group, team, or gang *and* competitive. Individual competition is promoted through ranks, medals, assorted rewards, and assignments. William Arkin and Lynne Dobrofsky (1978) have shown how the military creates both a sense of loyalty with the military and at the same time promotes the values of competition, aggression, and fighting to win. Basic military training involves an intense period of indoctrination whose purpose is not really to teach the recruits basic military skills, but rather to change their values and their loyalties. "I guess you can say we brainwash them a bit," admitted a U.S. Marine drill instructor (Dyer, 1985, p. 105).

Men are not born fighters, are not aggressive and competitive by nature. They are made that way through powerful institutions which have specialized in masculine socialization. The combat soldier is a properly socialized male. So is the athlete. In many ways the athletic role, just like the role of the military man, can be seen as the prototype of the male role. It separates the men from the boys. Peter Stein and Steven Hoffman (1978), who have made a study of sports and the male role, found that the athletic role caused stress and role strain for both athletes and nonathletes. The athletes' preoccupation with and emphasis on high-level performance and winning were the underlying reasons for their experiencing role strain. The nonathletes, on the other hand, were faced with their inability to make it in the world of their male peers and experienced feelings of failure, of not being "real men."

Feigen Fasteau (1975), who writes about the male machine and how sports provide the training ground for that machine, shows how fathers pressure their sons to do well in athletics. In one study he refers to, only 1 out of 20 fathers did not want his boys to be good athletes (Aberle & Naegele, 1952, here taken from Fasteau, 1975). Success as athletes was seen as a sine qua non of manhood. Also, the fathers Fasteau (1975, p. 106) interviewed thought sports were important for their sons because they would be taught how to compete in a rough world and how to get along with other people. But *does* sport actually build character? And, if it does, what *kind* of character? Two psychologists who have studied the effects of athletic competition on personality for eight years and tested approximately 15,000 athletes from the high school gym to the professional level concluded: "We found no empirical support for the tradition that sport builds character. Indeed, there is evidence that athletic competition limits growth in some areas" (Ogilvie & Tutko, 1971, p. 61, here taken from Fasteau, 1975, p. 106). The same researchers found that men who survive our culture's highly competitive, star-oriented sports system for the most part have personalities that conform to the traditional male stereotype: high in achievement need, respectful of authority, dominant among peers, self-controlled, and low in sensitivity to other people. The researchers also sometimes found players who had very good physical skills with immense character strengths but who did not make it in sports. They say about these players: "They seem to be so well put together emotionally that there is no neurotic tie to sport'' (Ogilvie & Tutko, 1971, p. 63). And Fasteau (1975, p. 107) asks: Could it be that such men are so well put together that, among other things, they simply don't need athletic success to feel adequate as men?

The two researchers found that men who were permanent managers of well-known sport teams cherished the following values: absolute team loyalty, unquestioning obedience to authority, respectful fear and hatred of the opposition, disregard of individual injury and suffering—all justified in the name of victory (Ogilvie & Tutko, 1971). To me these seem to be exactly the same values that go into a warrior, a good combat soldier. So the comparison Robert Kennedy made was not far-fetched.

His father, Joseph Kennedy, whose dedication to the precepts ''win at all costs'' and ''second place is losing'' is well-documented, made heavy use of athletic competition to inculcate these values into his children. If they lost races, they were sharply scolded and sometimes sent in disgrace to eat dinner in the kitchen (Clinch, 1973, p. 31).

Marc Feigen Fasteau (1975, pp. 112–114) shows how American presidents over and over use the language of competitive sports to justify their actions. That is a language men understand. And they reduce complex real-life problems of choosing objectives and weighing human costs to the simplistic imperatives of a competitive game.

Men have been taught the simplistic language of competitive sports and have become fascinated by it, though most of them participate in the competitions once removed—as spectators on the field or even more likely in front of the television in their armchairs. The main psychic payoff by watching competitive games on television is in talking about it with other men, either *at* the time or later. Besides the weather, sport is virtually the only topic of casual conversation that crosses class barriers for men and talking about sports events signals to them that despite social and economic differences, they are still *men*. But viewing competitive sports on television, apart from creating both hostility and solidarity between men, also seems to increase the likelihood of men using violence against each other or against women and children.

Physical Activity as Pleasure and Joy

I promised to end on a more optimistic note and I shall here look at the feminist concept of power as power-to, as competence, as pleasure.

My family and I live right on the fjord and in the summer we swim every day. I often swim long distances with a good neighbor. One summer while we were both sitting outside writing we would pause in the middle of the day and swim a kilometer together. The distance never seemed far to me because we were always keeping pace with each other, discussing what we were both involved in writing. One day another friend came and wanted to swim the same distance with me. We had hardly begun swimming before she decided she wanted to see who was the best swimmer and could get to the other side in the shortest time. I said I was not interested in racing her yet when she started, I somehow caught up, but did not enjoy that swimming at all; for the first time I felt that the distance was tremendously long, and I was completely exhausted when I reached the other side. It took me a long time to recover. It gave no joy, no extra gain I could use in my work which I normally did swimming with my neighbor.

I have given a personal example here but I know there are athletic coaches and sports researchers who think the same way about physical activity as I do. Much of this work has been spearheaded by women researchers (Fasting, 1982; Felshin, 1974; Hall, 1979) following a variety of feminist analytical perspectives. This fact should not surprise us. Women, especially if they are feminists, are more likely to detect patriarchal values in the institutions under study. As Don Sabo (1985, p. 24) has well remarked: "The fish are the last ones to discover the ocean." But he himself is an excellent example showing that some fish have begun to test the waters. And there *are* other men researchers using feminist perspectives to understand sports. I hope their number is growing. Terry Orlick (Orlick & Betterill, 1975; Orlick, 1978a, 1978b, 1982) has, for instance, written books about sports without competition, how we can all become winners. It would be a fascinating task to explore how rules of games could be changed to enhance cooperation instead of competition. One might for instance decide that a game with two teams would not end until the two teams were even, that is, have obtained the same number of goals. Why structure amateur sport so that many of the participants and would-be participants lose rather than gain from the experience? Why make it into a copy of patriarchy where a few men get to the top stepping on other men and on women and children? People learn and gain confidence from facing challenges that, with effort, they can meet, not from struggling in a system geared to the interests and abilities of the very few.

Boys learn to be competitive or cooperative just like girls do. In a whole book scrutinizing the relationship between organized sports and the formation of male identity in our Western world the co-editors conclude that sports seems to be the training ground for machismo, and that we shall have to redefine sports if we want to work for a more peaceful world (Sabo & Runfola, 1980, p. 252). Through one article after another the notion that humans evolve through relentless competition with nature and each other is shown to be false. Another false myth is also killed: that human beings, especially males, are born competitors. They are not. Competition is learned. Examples are given of the games of many cultures having no competitive element whatsoever. In his article called "Winning isn't Everything. It's Nothing" George Leonard (1980, pp. 259–266) tells about a popular game known as taketak which is played by the Tangu people of New Guinea. It involves throwing a spinning top into massed lots of stakes driven into the ground. There are two teams. Players of each team try to touch as many stakes with their tops as possible. In the end, however, the participants play not to win but to draw. The game must go on until an exact draw is reached. This requires great skill, since players sometimes must throw their tops into the massed stakes without touching a single one. Taketak expresses a prime value in Tangu culture, that is, the concept of moral equivalency, which is reflected in the precise sharing of foodstuffs among the people. In the same article George Leonard writes about the Stone Age peoples that survive in remote corners of the world and who are "until we meddle with them, usually gentle and sensitive, with a fine ecological sense" (Leonard, 1980, p. 261). He mentions that the Tasaday tribe of Mindanao in the Philippines have no words for "hate" or "fight." They are described as cooperative and loving—men and women alike.

DO WE EDUCATE GIRLS FOR PEACE AND BOYS FOR WAR?

I started out the discussion of peace education from a feminist perspective by posing the question: Do we educate girls for peace and boys for war? Using radical and socialist feminist perspectives I could also ask: Are some boys trained to dominate other boys and girls in our patriarchal society? Are boys taught to be aggressive and taught to compete more than girls are? Are girls taught to be gentle, caring and cooperative? Is this upbringing the reason that we find many more women opposed to nuclear weapons and the military buildup than we find men? Would the world be a better, a more just, less violent, more peaceful world had boys been given the same upbringing that girls are given?

In this chapter I have tried to shed some light on the above questions by referring to studies and discussing the socialization process as it goes on within the nuclear family unit, through the choice of toys and games, through the media, especially television, and the institution of sports.

From the studies I have gone through, it appears that boys in our culture, more than girls, are taught to compete and to display aggressive behavior. The typical child can and will exhibit behavior that is either "masculine" or "feminine" but the adults to whom the child is exposed will reinforce only that behavior which they deem appropriate to the child's sex. And in our Western industrialized world they deem it appropriate for girls to please, to defer, to wait while boys are encouraged to build a concept of self-esteem based on tangible accomplishments, to compete and excel. The way parents behave toward their children, the toys they are given, the tasks they are expected to perform, the behavior that is punished or rewarded generally seems to foster more aggressiveness in boys than in girls. Studies referred to also seem to indicate that there is a stronger correlation between aggressive behavior and the viewing of televised violence for boys than for girls. As mentioned, this finding may stem from the fact that violent TV shows offer more rewarding models for boys than for girls to identify with.

I issued a warning that aggressive behavior at a microlevel where the aggressive behavior is usually a result of aggressive feelings does not necessarily correlate with aggressive behavior at a macrolevel where such behavior may be displayed without any aggressive feelings. I also referred to a study showing that it might be easier for mothers belonging to the middle or upper classes to educate their sons to refrain from participating in organized violence or in training to use violence at a national and international level than it is for working-class or resourceless mothers to do the same. These mothers may not see any other way out for their sons.

Even though we may conclude from the studies I have referred to that in our society boys are taught to compete more than girls are and are encouraged to watch and participate in more violent behavior while girls are taught more to care, to nurture, be docile and pleasing, we cannot therefore conclude that girls are educated for peace and boys for war. Neither can we conclude that if boys were just given the upbringing now given to girls there would have been no wars. As I have shown in this chapter, there are at least two important reasons why we cannot make the above conclusions.

First of all, peace, as shown in my second chapter, though it means justice and equality—the absence of structural violence—also means the absence of direct violence when of a collective kind called war. There seem to be a lot of other qualifications going into the good soldier than the inclination to show violent and aggressive behavior, qualifications such as obedience and loyalty, willingness to take orders, to conform. These qualifications seem to be developed in girls just as much, even more, than in boys. Boys having been given the upbringing of girls might not be any less inclined to join the military or to become good soldiers.

Second, one of the studies I refer to seems to indicate that women may support wars, as least as enthusiastically as men, but for other reasons—not because a boundary or right has been violated but to end oppression of a weak group by a stronger one. More studies looking into the differing attitudes of men and women toward war are needed.

As far as I see it the best peace education is not to give the education now given to girls to both sexes. That education may not lead to less wars since girls are so well trained in obeying orders and deferring to others. The best peace education would be an education that is neither the typical education of girls nor the typical education of boys. It would be an education where children were taught to care, share, and relate to other human beings and animals, as girls are taught today, and at the same time were educated to stand up for their rights, to assert themselves, as boys are taught today. It would be an education where children were taught to be nonconformists, to think for themselves, be critical of authorities and orders. It would be an education where they were taught to rely on themselves, to protest against wrongs, to show courage—not by risking their lives but by standing up for the rights of oppressed groups, to show civil courage by protesting against wrongs done to themselves or to others.

An education for peace would not be merely an education giving girls more of a boy's education and boys more of a girl's education. It would be a different type of education, of socialization for both boys and girls. It would entail the development of competence in nonviolent conflict solutions, in power-to and a doing-away with strong competition, power-over. It would mean girls' refusing to become feminine in the sense where femininity means the acceptance of playing a serving and secondary role, obeying husbands and other men having power over them. It would mean boys' refusing to become masculine when masculine means having power over other people, mostly women, being aggressive, and not showing emotions.

At the outset of this chapter I defined peace education and I asked: Would a feminist peace education be defined differently? Having made the discussion I have during this chapter I would like to add one sentence to my earlier definition.

> Peace education tries to do away with rigid sex role socialization and the training into femininity or masculinity.

Sex role socialization seems to be such an important part of all socialization and so related to learnings going into attitudes furthering conformity, loyalty, violence, competition, caring and relating, that it seems necessary to combat such socialization, especially of a rigid kind. With Erling Lars Dale (1986) we might ask how it is possible to keep the caring and tender aspects in the personalities of many women and at the same time make them strong, able to lead independent lives, to protest, and to stand up for their rights? And how is it possible to keep the assertiveness in many males and still make them care more for others, relate to each other, and to children and women?

Are the caring and tender aspects many women get through their socialization just meant to be part of the personality of the oppressed, meant to please the oppressor? Maybe the whole of women's culture is only a product of women's victimage and powerlessness? When women are gentle, quiet, smiling, this may be looked at as the proper behavior for the oppressed ones in any structure. There are sometimes good reasons *not* to be gentle, to break away from the stereotype of the feminine woman, to protest and strike. Such behavior has been discouraged in girls.

In our society both boys and girls are trained to conform, conform to the group, be loyal to authorities, to do like everyone else does. The sex role socialization is powerful to maintain such an aim. It is likely that to create a viable peace culture we shall have to do away with both the rigid and typical male role and the rigid and typical female role. But our society functions in such a way that individuals who try to break away from these roles are punished—girls by not being regarded as feminine and pleasant partners for males, boys by being labeled a sissy or a girl. Because of the denigration of women and girls in patriarchy it seems to be even more difficult for boys not to conform to the sex role stereotypes than it is for girls. There seems to be even stronger pressure on boys to conform; pressure is exerted by fathers, peers, television, and the powerful institution of sports. Competitive sports create conformist robots. To compete with someone, you must agree to run on the same track, to do what he is doing, to obey the same set of rules. The only way you'll differentiate yourself is by doing precisely the same thing slightly faster or better. Through competition, one becomes increasingly like the person with whom one competes.

Doing away with rigid sex role socialization is not only a women's question. It is as much a male question, a task for humankind—an essential task for any peace education.

6

Feminist Perspectives on Peace Education in the Formal Sector

PEACE EDUCATION IN A FORMAL SCHOOL SETTING

It is a thought-provoking fact that the same countries responsible for the main threats facing humankind today, ecocide and genocide, are also the ones having the populations with the highest formal education or schooling. In fact, the two superpowers of the world, the United States and Russia, are also the countries that rank highest in the world when it comes to how much schooling the population has gone through (Galtung, 1975, p. 86).

One cannot assume that this statistical correlation is a causal one, that the more formal education a population gets, the more it will start producing arms and polluting the environment. Yet the correlation warrants thinking about the *type* of formal education given in the highly industrialized world today: What is the role of schooling in shaping norms relating to war and the environment?

Applying insights developed through my discussion of the peace concept I would like to ask: What would a peace education within the formal school system look like? Using our definition of peace it would ideally have to be an education without both direct and indirect violence. But using such a strict definition, it almost follows that peace education is not possible in the normal school setting where indirect violence seems to be an integral part of the system. It would appear that schools should be disregarded as settings where peace education can take place. Such a radical conclusion may be easily drawn and is easy to argue for. Schools are important socializing agents, how important may be debated. But it is a sad conclusion to draw that they, given the structure most of them have, cannot serve peace education. A more constructive approach may be to ask: Even though schools are problematic institutions from a peace education viewpoint, even though bureaucratic limitations are severe and indirect violence exists, what is it still possible to do to promote some degree of peace education in schools?

In many schools all over the world direct violence from teachers toward pupils is still used as a disciplinary method, a way of teaching kids their lessons. In the Nordic countries corporal punishment in schools is now forbidden, but it was in frequent use in the last century. And when visiting Britain ten years ago, I was struck by the fact that in all of the many headmaster offices I visited there were whips for spanking the children. Not long ago Britain abolished the permission for teachers and headmasters to discipline children through physical violence.

And even where corporal punishment in schools is forbidden, there is a lot of direct violence going on in schools, especially among the boys at recess. Many children get scars for life, mostly of a psychological nature. Most of them are subjected to structural violence affecting the mind through oppression and alienation. Is there reason to believe that one social class or one gender is more oppressed than the other or more alienated in the present system of formal schooling?

In Röhrs' (1983) book on peace education Johan Galtung is cited as not believing much in peace education within the normal, competitive school system. I tend to agree with Galtung that it is difficult to teach peace in a setting where children are taught to compete against each other. In many countries, including my own, children are given grades according to a relative scale. That means that a certain percentage of the children will always receive bad grades. They are not able to get a better grade unless one of their classmates gets a worse grade. It was not originally the intention that the relative grading system be used down to the class level, but in practice it has been, and many instances are known where teachers who had not followed the relative distribution in their classes (had given too many good grades, for instance) were summoned to the headmaster and asked to redo their original grading to be more in line with the normal distribution.

But even when it is applied to large numbers, the theory behind it is a good illustration of structural violence. One does not wonder when educational researchers find that the same percentage who get the lowest grades in schools also dislike school and want to quit. The children who get the lowest grades often also get deep psychological wounds, they lose their self-esteem and the esteem of teachers and parents, often, also of schoolmates. Some of them try to fight back by misbehaving and downgrading the values of the school, others just withdraw and sometimes develop psychosomatic diseases of various kinds.

The whole schooling situation is normally one of dominance. This seems to be so even when the official school ideology is one of dialogue and reform pedagogics. This has been well demonstrated by two Swedish educational researchers, Staf Callewaert and Bengt A. Nilsson (1980), who went into several eighth grade classrooms in a school in a middle-sized town in the south of Sweden. They sat in on lessons in many subjects, taught by different teachers, in a school officially adhering to dialogue-centered ideas and reform pedagogical thinking. The analysis of the observations and the taped lessons showed that traditional classroom teaching dominated, independent of teacher, subject, grouping, and so forth. The researchers found that the dominance of the teacher's verbal utterances against the total of pupils' utterances was 10 to 1 and that the dominance of the questioning ritual which structures the whole verbal interaction in school was almost unchanged in comparison to traditional didactics. The very few utterings being made by pupils were mostly just a word or two or a sentence as a response to something asked by the teacher. In just 1 percent of all classroom communication was the talking initiated by the students, and in those cases it was defined by the teacher mostly as irrelevant talk or disturbance. We have a vast amount of research showing that boys talk more than girls in class, normally two-thirds of the student talk is taken up by the boys. Some researchers have shown that the teachers pay more attention to boys. Inga Wernersson (1977) shows for instance that the reason why teachers talk more to boys is that they demand the teacher's attention. In the lower grades because the boys make noise and misbehave, much of the teacher's talk directed to them is scolding, but in higher grades the boys ask more questions and actually get more help from the teachers than the girls do. Other researchers have shown that it is the boys who interrupt the teachers and grab their attention rather than the teachers who initially pay more attention to the boys (Nielsen & Larsen, 1985). It is difficult to teach about equality between states large and small when there is so little equality between teachers and pupils, to teach about the equality of the sexes when the boys in the class are allowed to dominate the girls. Is it at all possible to teach democracy in a highly authoritarian school or university?

In another article on peace education Johan Galtung (1975, p. 81) discusses this dilemma and asks: "Will it not merely sound hypocritical?—or even worse, remain empty words that are nullified through the much stronger message of verticality and dominance being normal and acceptable, conveyed through the structure itself?"

Again—it is not difficult to agree with Galtung and discard the school as a hopeless case. One might as well give up trying to introduce peace education in formal school settings. But there are teachers all over the world who do not give up on the idea of working with peace education in schools. Are they just naive? Do they work without any prospect of success? I like to think that they have some prospects of succeeding. I see one condition for success as essential: that the tendencies counteracting peace education, the messages of verticality and dominance in school, be made part of the curriculum of peace education, that they be analyzed and used as vivid examples of structural violence drawn from the students' own school days. The consequences of such violence may be analyzed by the students themselves and parallels drawn to other cases around the world, also to violence between countries and within a country. Combining such analysis with the radical feminist perspective, we may come to see that the dominance hierarchies Galtung is talking about are patriarchal structures, structures built up so that a few men are taught to and feel justified to dominate women and also other men. We may see that what working-class kids and girls generally may experience as oppression on the individual and personal level really is a structural violence. When all the personal experiences are gathered together and analyzed, the political structures are easier to detect.

Applying a radical feminist perspective to an analysis of peace education within a formal school setting, what would such a peace education look like? The radical feminist perspective questions the values governing existing structures, the basic recipe they are made from. It asks about the type of power demonstrated in schools. Is it more of a power-over than a power-to? Are children taught more to dominate or to be dominated rather than given a competence to cope with this world? Using a socialist feminist perspective we may ask not only how girls are taught to be dominated by boys but also how some kids in the class learn that they will be the directors and others learn that they are dumb and will get only jobs with low salary or go directly into the ranks of the unemployed. Using a woman of color perspective, we may also ask whether teaching in schools or the structure of certain academic fields such as science presupposes that people of some races are worth less than people from other races? From any feminist perspective we would ask whether school girls have other attitudes toward peace, in my wide definition of the concept, than school boys have.

After having briefly looked at a survey on gender differences in attitudes toward peace, I shall divide the rest of the chapter into two parts. Merely for analytical purposes I have divided the chapter into one part dealing with the factual knowledge transmitted in school, the official curriculum, and another part dealing with the attitudes and norms shaped or strengthened in school, mostly through the hidden curriculum (Brock-Utne & Haukaa, 1980; Brock-Utne, 1988a). In reality it is difficult to make such a division because all factual information also conveys attitudes and norms. If history is taught as a long series of wars, youngsters may learn that wars have always existed, that violence pays, maybe even that wars are excitement. If science is taught "for its own sake" (Brock-Utne, 1985a, p. 116) without its detrimental effects taken into account, this teaching may just strengthen cultural norms already conveyed to youngsters, especially boys, of disregarding, yes even admiring danger (Brock-Utne, 1986b, 1987a, 1987b; Nader, 1981; Sabo, 1985). One part of this chapter deals with the more cognitive aspects of the knowledge transmitted in schools, not disregarding that this knowledge given or not given is also shaping attitudes and norms. Questions are asked about the teaching of nonviolent conflict solutions. Questions about science teaching are also being asked: Is there reason to believe that youngsters are taught a narrow-minded science where the human, ecological, and ethical consequences of scientific and technological innovations are not taken into account?

Knowledge, along with attitudes and norms, is shaped by actual information given or not given. But norms are also shaped through the whole structure and setup of education. The second part of this chapter deals with this structure. Is there reason to believe that the mostly hierarchical structures of our schooling systems encourage obedience and loyalty instead of opposition to authority and critical thinking?

Is there reason to believe that formal education is a force shaping norms conducive to patriarchal and militarist thinking? The militarist mind, according to Kjell Skjelsbæk (1979, p. 222) filters the world through concepts like: strength–weakness, victory–defeat, supremacy, destruction, revenge, threat, loyalty, and obedience. The use of some concepts to the detriment of others will often be rooted in a world view or in the choice of certain values. Patriarchy is sometimes defined as: "a system of values developed through male experience: competition, hierarchy, aggression, alienation from the earth, denial of emotion and the objectification of other whether it be sex, race or class" (Reardon, 1985, p. 37). Could education create values, norms, concepts which, according to Skjelsbæk (1979), are noncongruent with the militarist mind, norms like trust, forgiveness, construction, reconciliation, empathy? Could education plant seeds of doubt about the direction in which the world is heading? The last part of this chapter will discuss this possibility. What are the chances that schools could become places where pleasure is experienced, where youngsters are taught the joys of sharing, are taught to take care of each other, of the weak ones in society, of plants and animals, of nature?

THE TYPICAL PEACE-ORIENTED SCHOOL STUDENT

In a thought-provoking paper presented at the Eleventh General Conference of IPRA reporting on a survey conducted in Swedish schools Stig Lindholm (1986, p. 16) describes the typical peace-oriented gymnasium school student, according to the survey, in this way . . . "She is most often a girl . . . She considers the risk of nuclear war to be very great, but at the same time she believes that she herself can help to prevent it and that this can be better done through the peace movement than through national defense. She is prepared to reduce her living standard to make the world more just and she believes that non-violent methods—at least to some extent—can be used to defend Sweden. She also thinks that the peace movement has accomplished something in terms of promoting world peace and she wants to have peace and conflict education as a subject in her schools." After having described this peace-oriented school student—a prototype who emerged through the survey—Stig Lindholm expresses a sincere wish: "Let us wish this girl all success in persuading her fellow students to join her in the efforts to learn more, to discuss means and ways of acting and to act."

The survey was conducted on 1,080 students from four gymnasium schools outside of Stockholm, 50 percent girls and 50 percent boys. The students were asked about their attitudes to questions concerning nuclear warfare, the peace movement, national defense and also concerning indirect violence like the injustices in the world. Some of the results from this survey were so interesting that I would like to repeat them here for a discussion of them.

How great is the risk that nuclear weapons will be used in warfare?			Can you contribute to the prevention of a nuclear war?	
	Very great	Not so great	Yes	No
Girls	51	40	52	42
Boys	29	59	36	59

The numbers are percentages.

As we see, girls judge the risk that nuclear weapons will be used in warfare to be greater than boys do (22 percent difference) yet they at the same time believe more in their own capacity to contribute to the prevention of nuclear war (16 percent). In many ways this result is rather sensational. It somehow contradicts what one would expect, since women in our society normally have less traditional power than men do.

When it comes to *how* girls and boys feel they can help prevent a nuclear war, there is also a clear difference between the sexes. The same goes for the use of nonviolence in the defense of Sweden.

Can you help prevent a nuclear war by supporting: the peace movement? national defence?			Are non-violent methods (those of Gandhi) applicable to the defence of Sweden?		
	Peace movement	National defence	Yes	To some extent	Not at all
Girls	78	10	8	64	22
Boys	52	25	7	40	49

The numbers are percentages.

There are, of course, several ways to interpret these results. Stig Lindholm says that what he has done is "to highlight the well-established correlation between sex and attitudes to peace issues and to emphasize the importance of further investigations and conclusions" (Lindholm, 1986, p. 13). He quotes the Finnish researcher Riitta Wahlström (1985), who also found sex differences in a similar investigation and concluded that girls are more peaceful than boys. She explains her results by pointing to the fact that boys more than girls are educated to embrace models of violence and the elements of the militaristic culture. One may also maintain that the way girls and boys have answered the above questions may partly be a function of what one may call anticipatory socialization. The boys know that they, in some few years, are expected to do their military service and there adhere to and be part of the official defense policy in Sweden.

The girls are not met with such expectations. The answers they give may be based not only on their different experiences up until then, their different socialization, but also on the socialization they anticipate to get in a couple of years and which they are already adjusting their attitudes to receive. If this is the case, we have yet another example showing that it is possible to have people change attitudes by forcing them to perform some acts and then count on the likelihood that they will change their attitudes to be in better harmony with the acts they are performing.

But an interesting question which none of these investigations throws any light on would be: What characterizes those boys who believe that the risk that nuclear weapons will be used in warfare is very great (29 percent), that *they* can contribute to the prevention of a nuclear war (36 percent), that they can help prevent a nuclear war by supporting the peace movement (52 percent) and that nonviolent methods are applicable to the defense of Sweden—at least to some extent (47 percent)? How do these boys differ from the rest? Why has the education which has led other boys to hold that nonviolent methods are not at all applicable to the defense of Sweden (49 percent) not had the same effect on these boys? Do they belong to a different social group? Do they have parents who have actively counteracted educational influences other boys have picked up in sports or the media? Do they have an especially close relationship to their mother or to their father?

When it comes to the girls, Wahlström (1985) finds that a strong self-concept is connected with a positive attitude to the possibilities of the private citizen to do something to prevent war. This strong self-concept of the girls is also correlated with active peace work. There is something in this finding which seems contradictory. On the one hand, the correlation between sex and attitudes to peace issues is explained by pointing at the different education given girls and boys. On the other hand, the traditional education of a girl does not embrace the creation of a strong self-concept. The finding of Wahlström, if it is confirmed in further investigations, seems to raise some interesting questions: Maybe those girls and women dedicating themselves to peace work belong to those who have opposed the traditional socialization of females in our society?

When Wahlström does not find any correlation between self-concept and peaceful or nonpeaceful attitudes when it comes to the boys, this may not be so surprising. There may be factors other than a strong self-concept, factors which would break with the traditional socialization of boys, such as empathy, which might show a stronger correlation.

We need to go further than establishing over again the "well-established correlations between sex and attitudes to peace issues." We shall have to look at factors characterizing the girls and boys who gave the various answers. The most interesting group to look at may be the peace-oriented boys. How do they differ from the rest? Maybe we shall find that the most peace-oriented pupils are neither the typical feminine girls (they seldom have strong self-concepts) or the typical masculine boys. If this is the case, then certainly changes in sex role socialization are of great consequence for peace education.

The survey Lindholm reports on also asks the students' opinions on peace education as a subject to be introduced in schools. As expected the more peace-oriented students were most eager to have peace education in school. Peace education had not been well defined as far as can be seen from Lindholm's report but the students have probably interpreted it as education *about* peace—disarmament, development, human rights—not a change in the regular curriculum and even less in the structure of the school.

When I shall now look into the values and attitudes transmitted by the school and which have relevance for peace education, I shall not look at topics introduced as "peace education" but rather at some subjects which transmit values of great importance for attitudes concerning peace and war, development and scientific "progress." I have singled out history and science. I shall then look more generally at attitudes transmitted through the hidden curriculum of schooling.

WHAT ATTITUDES TOWARD THE WORLD ARE SHAPED THROUGH THE OFFICIAL CURRICULUM?

Through the Teaching of History

Not only the news media (Eysenck & Nias, 1978; Schmid & de Graaf, 1982) but also history books (Krügler & Parkman, 1985, p. 111) consistently focus on results achieved by violence. Moreover, Christopher Krügler and Patricia Parkman (1985), from Harvard University's Program on Nonviolent Sanctions in Conflict and Defense, find that history books give more attention to violent struggles that fail to achieve their objectives than to nonviolent struggles that succeed. There is, in fact, a vast history of nonviolent sanctions. Gene Sharp defines nonviolent sanctions as pressures that do not kill or threaten physical harm but which, nonetheless, thwart opponents' objectives and cause them to alter their behavior (Sharp, 1980, p. 289). He has himself described 85 major cases where nonviolent sanctions have been used (Sharp, 1971). Yet the conflicts which have been solved through nonviolent means are both underresearched and made invisible in history. Krügler and Parkman (1985) show through their analysis that when both a violent and a nonviolent action have been used in a conflict, the violent one is the one that is described in history, yes even the one celebrated, as in the case of the uprising against the dictatorship of Martinez in El Salvador in 1944. The violent action of April 2 was not successful in getting the dictator to resign. The nonviolent action of May 9 *was* successful. Yet April 2 is celebrated, not May 9! When violent sanctions fall short of achieving their objectives, the conclusion is not drawn that violence has been tried and found wanting. Instead, military analysts ask what conditions favored the winner, and where did the loser go wrong? The assumption is not made that there is something wrong with the whole use of violence. When nonviolent struggles are not successful, however, it is easily concluded that nonviolence is not useful. Questions should be asked about ways of improving nonviolent means of conflict resolution. In most cases where nonviolent sanctions have been used they have been improvised under harsh conditions, with little or no advance preparation on the part of those using them.

Elise Boulding has, on several occasions, argued convincingly for the teaching of skills in nonviolent conflict solutions at all levels of formal schooling and in adult education (Boulding, 1982, 1986a). In an article in the Bulletin of the Atomic Scientists she deplores the declining civilian competence in conflict resolution and holds that our whole educational system should be geared toward creating more confidence and competence in conflict resolutions by means other than violence (Boulding, 1982). When the capabilities for nonviolent problem-solving are not developed at lower levels in the education system, it gets more difficult to develop them later on. Formal education, it seems, does little to teach youngsters nonviolent conflict solutions or to train their capacity for visionary thinking. And history books concentrate on the violent solution to conflicts between states, on wars, and underscore the fact that statistically the normal relationship between states is one of non-war, or peace, and that most conflicts in the world, both between people on the microlevel and between states, are solved through nonviolent means. School children could learn more about the nonviolent solutions of conflicts, less about the violent ones. This would also necessitate more research on these conflict resolutions and a rewriting of history. As history is presently taught, important phenomena like the effective use of nonviolence and the important role of women are made invisible, hidden, forgotten (Spender, 1982). And if a woman has devoted her life to nonviolent conflict solving, to peace and disarmament she is kept invisible, if not to her own generation then to the next generations. Such has been the fate of one of the greatest peace heroes in this century, the Austrian writer and political activist Bertha von Suttner (1843–1914). Without her there would have been no Nobel Peace Prize, yet Nobel, who took the money for the prize from his profits on weapons and dynamite, is remembered (Brock-Utne, 1985a, pp. 37–45). At last, there seems to be some literature on Bertha von Suttner's fascinating life and work coming up (Hamann, 1986). Is there a hope that she will be reintroduced in history books?

There is a need for a history of nonviolent actions, a need to move these actions from the hidden history to the official one, into the history books. But it is extremely important that this be done in a scientific manner where part of this history, the actions started and led by women, are not to be left in the hidden history. That would make such a necessary rewriting of history incomplete. It should be remembered that Mahatma Gandhi stressed over and over again that he had learned most of his nonviolent tactics from the British suffragettes (Gandhi, 1939, 1940). He insisted that there had to be 60 percent women in all peace marches if they were to remain peaceful (Gandhi, 1939).

Through the Teaching of Science

Science is another important school subject shaping cultural norms to technical progress, to scientific research, and to the use of the environment. Mark Oliphant (1982, p. 192), himself a professor of physics, stated at a Pugwash conference that every advance in methods of mass destruction has been made, not in response to demands from the armed services, but from proposals put forward by men of science. All nuclear weapons originated in this way, as did all the guidance systems for the vehicles which deliver them. Indeed, in relation to the nuclear arms race, which feeds on the continuous input of scientific innovation and technological skill, these factors have acquired a momentum of their own. There seems to be much truth in the statement that nowadays technology dictates policy, that new weapons systems emerge, not because of any military or security requirements, but because of the sheer impetus of the technological process. Lord Zuckerman (1980), for many years chief scientific adviser to the British government, claims in his book on scientific advisers and nuclear weapons that when it comes to nuclear weapons the military chiefs on both sides usually serve only as a channel through which the men in the laboratories transmit their views. Lord Zuckerman holds that it is the man in the laboratory—not the soldier, sailor, or airman—who at the start proposes that for this or that arcane reason it would be useful to improve an old or devise a new nuclear warhead. He finds that it is the scientist, the technician, who is at the heart of the arms race, not the commander in the field. It is the scientist who starts formulating a so-called military need. Most scientists get on with what they look at as an interesting and challenging task, without much concern for the social, political, or economic consequences of their success. Sean MacBride (1978, p. 91), Nobel Prize winner and former Minister of Foreign Affairs of Ireland, calls these scientists who are not concerned about the ethical and political implications of their research the "alienated" scientists. It seems important to take a closer look at the way the harder sciences are taught, not only in institutes of higher learning like engineering colleges, technical schools and universities, but also in secondary schools. To what degree are the human and social consequences of technological innovations taken into account? Is physics, for instance, taught as a narrow subject where students learn methods and technicalities but not to evaluate technology in terms of its effects on humans and the environment?

The fact that girls do not choose physics as a curricular option in school or tend to drop out of physics at the university level may be analyzed from different perspectives. From a more liberal feminist perspective, one in which the concept of equality is central, one may ask what is wrong with girls since they drop out of physics. One would try to find means to have girls choose that subject and stay in it. From a more radical feminist perspective one would rather ask what is wrong with the teaching of physics that it causes girls to drop out of the subject?

An interesting project in science teaching has been conducted from this radical feminist perspective by two male physicists at the University of Oslo (Lie & Sjöberg, 1984; see also Sjöberg, 1982). They started their studies assuming that when girls dropped out of physics in such great numbers there might be something wrong with physics rather than with the girls.

They made an analysis both of textbooks used and of attitudes toward physics held by girls and boys. They selected the four most frequently used textbooks in chemistry and physics through grades 4 to 9 in the Norwegian compulsory school system. Here they both found that girls were actively discriminated against, hardly mentioned, or portrayed as sex objects, and they found that concrete examples were taken from experiences boys had, not experiences that girls had. They have formulated their criticism of the context of the textbooks in three points:

1. A regular discrimination of women
2. Preferential treatment of boys through the examples given
3. Indirect discrimination of women through the image conveyed of the subject, the type of knowledge selected

They maintain (Lie & Sjöberg, 1984, pp. 35–36) that it should be easy to do something with point 1. Here the discrimination is easy to document and could easily be eradicated. It is also comparatively easy to do something with point

2. One example may be replaced by a different one building more on the experiences of girls. Some innovative work would have to be done but there is no need for a fundamental change of the curriculum. When it comes to point 3, however, there is a great need for a fundamental change, a restructuring of the curriculum. While the two first points are easy to detect through an analysis of the textbooks, the third one they arrived at also through questionnaires administered to the students. They found that the students, but especially the girls, look at physics as too abstract, difficult, far from the lives of ordinary people. They would like to know more about the human and social consequences of technological innovations. They would like to know about these consequences for human beings and for the environment, both the good ones and the bad ones. They do not get to know about this, even though the stated aims for the teaching of science contain nice words about the learning of principles of ecological balance, learning to live in harmony with nature, the significance of science for production and daily life, and so on. But the textbooks and, as far as the researchers have been able to detect especially through their questionnaires, the actual teaching in school is not in accordance with the stated aims. The students get a narrow science devoid of social consequences, a narrow physics—and the girls drop out of it. Many boys also do. Maybe those who stay on did not have such social interests to start with. Anyway they get trained in a narrow thinking.

The two physicists maintain that the values actually taught through science in the Norwegian compulsory schools today are "almost the opposite values of those girls are socialized to adhere to. And those values we see as important values which also ought to be instilled in boys!" (my translation, taken from p. 112). As socially concerned physicists, they see a restructuring of science teaching as necessary not only because it would benefit girls and draw more women to science, but also because such a new science would be a better science for all, would make us see the consequences of modern technology on the environment and on human beings.

In a provoking paper on science education Robin Burns (1986) maintains that science is not only *male* science developed by men; those men were white. Science is also racist. One way in which the racism of science can be specifically understood is through its use in imperial expansion and continued domination of developing countries by the industrialized ones. Robin Burns sees the control of scientific resources as a key factor of scientific domination as racism. She refers to cases which have been uncovered, especially within agriculture and medicine, where scientific results have been suppressed because they are not in the interests of dominant commercial enterprises. In the selection of particular sorts of science for support and development, and in the failure of science to provide a value base for alternative processes, it is open to such manipulation. She also argues that the whole rhetoric of scientific cooperation for development is based on an "aid" model which is inherently inegalitarian and asymmetrical, the Western (or Eastern) scientist helping the "Southerner" to solve *his* problems with *their* methods. The resources and environment of Third World countries are exploited by multinational corporations undertaking scientific production free from the legal constraints, production safeguards, strong labor unions or environmentally concerned pressure groups of the countries in which they developed their techniques. "No longer merely the resource-provider for industrialization, the third world has become its scientific testing-ground as well, from the testing of drugs to the testing of nuclear bombs" (Burns, 1986, p. 13). This testing is racist as it implies that the lives of those affected by the testing are of less worth than the lives of those in the home countries of the testers.

In the policy recommendations following their study Lie and Sjøberg (1984) are advocating a new science teaching, teaching of a science many female scientists and also male scientists like Brian Easlea (1981, 1983) call a female science.

Several female scientists have tried to outline what a female science would look like. Such a science is in the making and has not yet been fully developed. But it is clear that such a science takes on a holistic approach, is listening to nature and not exploiting her. A theoretical basis for a feminist science can be found in some of the books on green politics (Spretnak, 1986; Spretnak & Capra, 1986) and on ecofeminism (see Caldecott & Leland, eds., 1983, especially King, 1983, and Leland, 1983). Ecofeminism is about connectedness and wholeness of theory and practice. It asserts the special strength and integrity of every living thing. Ecofeminists insist that if we learned better ways of living in harmony with the earth there would be no energy shortage. If we employed our knowledge and technology toward a greater understanding of ecology, we could learn to use the clean energy resources and power provided by nature–earth, sun, wind, and sea. Ecology is universally defined as the study of the balance of all life on earth. The feminine principle outlined in feminist philosophy is the striving toward balance and interrelationship (see, for instance, Leland, 1983, p. 72). It follows from this that feminism and ecology are inextricably connected.

Evelyn Fox Keller (1985) examines in her *Reflections on Gender and Science* how the making of men and women has affected the making of science. She sees the dominant science of our time as the result of connections between mind, nature and masculinity. She shows that the history of science evidences tension and struggle between scientific explanations that stress hierarchies, control and unidirectional causal patterns—a masculine science—and those that stress interconnectedness, multiple interactions, and directional paths—a female science. These two explanations stem from different views of nature, domination, and control. In the first one, epitomized by Bacon, science is a mastery of man over nature. In the other associated with the Platonic knower, the scientist is part of nature, seeing phenomena from inside, relying on cooperation between nature's web and one's place within it.

If we want to think about how science might be different, envision a female science, a good guide would be the biologist Barbara McClintok, as described both by Keller (1985) and by Bleier (1984). Barbara McClintok's work challenged the "master molecule theory" that locates genetic control in a single molecule within a hierarchical organization. Her theory of genetic "transposition" posits instead that elements can move from one chromosomal site to another. The real heresy of her argument is the inference that genetic reorganization can result from signals external to DNA, from the cell, the organism, even from the environment. At the heart of McClintok's theory is a respect for complexity and for individual differences of phenomena. According to Keller this "serves both as a clue to new modes of connectedness in nature, and as an invitation to engagement in nature" (Keller, 1985, p. 163). McClintok does not adhere to a division between subject and object, self and other, mind and nature but rather works with concepts like connections, relatedness, even feeling and intuition. The biologist Ruth Bleier (1984) likewise sees it as an important task for all feminist scientists to question and examine all dualisms, all dichotomous ways in which nature and human activities are described, analyzed, and categorized. "The relationship of culture to nature is not necessarily oppositional, the relationship of the knowing subject to the studied subject is not necessarily the dualistic one of activity and passivity or domination and subordinance. These dualisms resonate metaphorically with the female-male dichotomy throughout our literary, artistic, scientific, and other cultural expressions" (Bleier, 1984, p. 200). Bleier finds that scientists who envision a new science, a female science, must have the ability to listen, to be aware and perceptive (abilities often cultivated more in women than in men), appreciate process and interaction. They must, in the words of Barbara McClintok as Bleier (1984, p. 206) cites her, "let the material speak to you" and have "a feeling for the organism, whether that material or organism is another human being, a chimpanzee, genes, or the unexpected signals from a radiotelescope." This new science involves an appreciation of the complexity of all phenomena and the constancy of only the process of change. It involves a science taking human, social and ecological factors into account.

This female science or some would prefer to call it "new science" or "human science" is not advocated only by female scientists. I have mentioned the two Norwegian physicists Svein Lie and Svein Sjöberg and the British physicist Brian Easlea adhering to the same view. Also, Sergei Kapitza, professor of physics in Moscow, deplores the lack of a broad and integrated approach to the teaching of physics.

Unfortunately, the way science is taught, usually dividing everything into separate subjects, does not lead to a systematic approach. This lack of interdisciplinary thinking looms even larger when we consider the connections between the humanities and science, the dichotomy usually designated as "the two cultures" (Kapitza, 1982, pp. 247–248). Kapitza feels that the symptoms of fear and apathy demonstrated by escapism and lack of interest shown by the younger generation in some countries may be related to this lack of an integrated approach in our educational system. He asks: "To what extent can the whole issue of the emergence of irrationality be traced to defects in modern education, to a lack of a more general scientific and social outlook, without which it is very difficult to start thinking in a new way not only on matters of disarmament, but also on the social impact of science and technology?" (Kapitza, 1982, p. 248). It should be added that the lack of interdisciplinarity is much more pronounced at the higher levels of formal education than at the lower ones. The most holistic and integrated teaching can be found in the kindergartens and the lower levels of the elementary school, the most narrow and compartmentalized in the universities and other institutes for higher learning. Also, some of the most holistic subjects carry the least prestige. A subject where conservation, maintenance and care of the environment is taught is home economics. This subject is usually a curricular option and opted for mostly by girls. It also carries low prestige and does not give high formal qualifications for further studies and work.

WHAT ATTITUDES TOWARD THE WORLD ARE SHAPED THROUGH THE HIDDEN CURRICULUM OF THE SCHOOL?

When history is taught as a series of wars, and science is taught without taking ecological and human consequences into account, this teaching naturally influences the attitudes and norms that are being transmitted. The actual content of textbooks would not have been such an issue had formal education encouraged critical thinking and opposition to authority—had it encouraged an independent search for knowledge by students and teachers together, sharing and cooperation. Again—such pedagogics may be found in good kindergartens, but is found less and less the higher one climbs on the ladder of formal education. It is a common observation, often made by student-teachers in teacher training, that the number of spontaneous questions coming from a child goes rapidly down the higher up in the school system one gets. When a child first meets school she or he will ask the grown-up all sort of questions out of curiosity. The child asks someone that he or she presumes knows more about questions the child would like answered. But after some years of schooling the pupil does not ask questions out of curiosity anymore because that student has learned that in schools *teachers* ask questions, not pupils. And teachers ask questions they already know the answers to themselves. They do not ask out of curiosity. They ask questions mostly to control their students, to determine whether they have acquired the right "deposits" in their brains—to use a word from the Brazilian educator, Paulo Freire (1972). Or the teachers ask questions to "motivate" the pupils for the learning that is going to take place. The teachers, who *know* what this learning is, which the students do not, ignore some of the answers to their questions because they fall outside the area of intended learning and pick up others that conform to what is in the teacher's mind. This has been well demonstrated by a group of Danish educational researchers (*Skoledage*, 1979). The type of questions encouraged in students are mostly questions asking for further information, not questions that are truly critical of the whole learning taking place. Such questions are looked at as signs of disobedience. They are interruptions of the teaching process.

The Learning of Obedience and Loyalty

And through the years of schooling students learn to become obedient because if they are not, they can be met by all types of sanctions, the worst being the lowering of their school grades. And bad grades again mean less chances of progressing up the educational ladder. Conformity to rules, obedience and loyalty seem to be part of the hidden curriculum of formal education. Through likely sanctions the "right" kind of information is stored in the students, deposited as in a bank, according to Paulo Freire (1972). He sees the banking concept of education, characterized by attempts to control thinking and action and to lead students to adjust to the world as it is, as necrophilic (Freire, 1972, p. 51). That is, it is nourished by love of death, not life.

It seems that obedience to authority and loyalty to rules make up a big part of the hidden curriculum of formal education. This is analyzed by educational researchers (Alvater, 1971; Brock-Utne, 1982b; Illeris, 1976). But it is not normally admitted by those administering the educational system. They want the school to foster some cherished values in children like democratic thinking, cooperation, creativity, and a critical awareness, and somehow refuse to see that the means used in school are incongruent with the aims. It resembles what is going on in the game of disarmament. Disarmament has become talk, negotiations, words—often spoken by men from the foreign ministries while the military buildup consists of deeds, money, acts—often decided upon by men in the defense departments, military experts, and men in the weapons research laboratories. In disarmament talks, especially in the UN, nice aims may be agreed upon but in actual day-to-day politics states do not select means that are congruent with these aims.

The Learning of Competitiveness

Though the value of cooperation may be stressed in official school curricula, the system of exams and grades, stars and class rankings, defeats such an aim and furthers the value of competition instead. In many Western capitalist countries grades are given according to a normal distribution curve which means that a certain percentage of the student body will get failing or bad grades. This in reality means that a student who is constantly getting one of these lowest grades is unable to advance in the system unless she or he steps on someone else, unless someone else gets a worse grade, is downgraded. The hidden learning here is that in order to get ahead yourself, you have to step on your brother or sister. The structural violence is built into the system.

Competition, oneupmanship, seems to be one of the key norms regulating behavior within the formal educational system, mostly taught through the hidden curriculum. And competition increases during the school years as the sorting of students into their proper places in society picks up.

Johan Galtung (1975, p. 89) claims that the main function of a teacher in a schooling system is not to educate, but to sort people, and they are sorted both horizontally and vertically. They are sorted into boxes which fit into the social structure. Examining this sorting function of schooling he concludes: "It may well be that schooling is a major factor responsible for oppression" (Galtung, 1975, p. 89).

At the higher levels of education the basic sorting has been done, but the competition still goes on. And it carries over into adult life, a race between individuals and groups of individuals, between states and groups of states. A race for higher prestige, more money, to win, to be best and strongest. In all the explanations given for the continuing arms race, competition seems to be one of the main driving forces. Either competition between military blocs as some theorists see the arms race, or competition within one side with the other side trying to catch up, or competition within both sides, driven by internal forces. This theory is named bilateral autism (Wiberg, 1981, p. 139).

Wiberg (1981b) stresses that these three models each by itself may be insufficient as explanations of the arms race while certain combinations, maybe quite complicated combinations, provide better explanations. It is a difficult methodological problem to systematically compare the relative strength of external or action-reaction factors to those driven by internal forces.

Competition between the United States and the Soviet Union certainly plays a large part in the accelerating arms race, but there is reason to believe that it is used mostly to motivate taxpayers to spend more money on the perfection of instruments for death and destruction. It may be that the competition going on between scientists and military branches within each country plays an even bigger role than the competition between the superpowers. In the case of nuclear weapons, the Americans are so far ahead of the Russians in almost every aspect of the technological race that they don't really need to compete with them. They've got each other. One of the reasons for developing the Pershing II medium-range missile for instance seems to have been that the Army's Pershing I was becoming outdated and the Army was faced with the prospect of "losing the last vestiges of nuclear missile turf to the enemy: the U.S. Air Force and U.S. Navy," according to defense observers Alexander Cockburn, James Ridgeway, and Andrew Cockburn (Mansueto, 1983, p. 113).

The formal educational system both in the NATO and the WCT countries is highly competitive and is likely to produce individuals questing to be the first discoverers, the heads of laboratories, the chief and most important researchers. The theory of bilateral autism becomes plausible when looking at the formal educational systems.

When Virginia Woolf (1938) maintained that the universities shaped norms that might easily lead to war, she was writing about the harsh competition of the universities together with the segmented kind of knowledge taught.

IS THERE A LIGHT IN THE TUNNEL?

Formal education, as it has been outlined here, may seem like a dark tunnel filled with suffering, pain, and structural violence. Is there some light to be seen somewhere in the tunnel? Any place where part of the visions about a new education as advanced by Virginia Woolf (1938) have come true?

Virginia Woolf tells about a woman who was asked by an educated man how women could help men prevent war. The woman decided that it would be necessary that women be educated if they were to help prevent war, but not through an education like the one now given. She pictured a new type of college where there would be no competition, no grades, and the aim would not be to specialize and segregate knowledge but to combine it. Knowledge should be combined so that the consequences of any innovation for human life are not only known but also desired. In such a college there would be sharing of ideas, joy and pleasure, caring for animals and plants and living beings. There would not be dominance and traditional power-plays.

In the first part of this chapter some lights have been shown. A couple of researchers are doing research into nonviolent resolutions of conflicts. Their number should be drastically increased and their findings be part of the teaching of history. History books should be rewritten and the hidden history of nonviolence and of the lives of women be made open, be part of the curriculum. Another policy recommendation would be to have the teaching of constructive thinking and conflict management as part of the normal school curriculum. There are books that could be used for such teaching (for instance, Masters & Houston, 1972) and that could be translated into several languages and adapted to various levels of schooling. It might also be a good idea to have educators and historians from various antagonist countries meet and try to select some good examples together of nonviolent conflict solutions. Such exercises, when done by dedicated and competent people, may turn into very useful textbooks giving another outlook on history.

Nonviolent conflict solutions can be taught also within a normal school setting where the teacher uses her or his own class as a laboratory. A Norwegian teacher in the lower secondary school has shown how her class, with a high percentage of working-class kids and children of migrants, solved problems they met in their daily lives in the classroom, in the intermissions, and in the corridors of school (Halvorsen, 1982). Becoming conscious of conflicts among themselves and between them and parents or teachers helped the pupils see solutions to the conflicts and trained their conflict imagination. Grades were downplayed to a minimum. But since they had to pass the regular exams they were at least helped, through a critical awareness, to see what grades did to the climate of their group. In his thorough discussion of peace as a task for educators the West German Professor Hermann Röhrs (1983) maintains that the success of peace education in schools should be measured more by the way pupils behave toward one another in the schoolyard and the classroom than by the amount of learning they are able to reproduce about the arms race or disarmament (Röhrs, 1983, p. 193).

Another light was shown in the dark tunnel of the first part of this chapter when a new science, a "female" science, was envisioned. And there were actually some male physicists who had seen the light. They should be given time and money to work together with female scientists, who are also critical of current science teaching and trying to build up a new science.

Also within peace research, there seem to be alternative ways of thinking which ought to be tried and given space. Elise Boulding (1980) found, in a study of women peace researchers, that they wanted other priorities for peace research than the current ones. They found that there had been too much mindless weapon counting going on, too little research on the human and social consequences of the arms race and too little research on nonviolent resolutions to conflict. Since 1981 a group of women within the International Peace Research Association have formed a network and conducted seminars. (See Brock-Utne, Traylor, & Aas, eds., 1986.) In the IPRA conference in Sussex in May 1986, this network conducted sessions to which men were invited. Exactly the same number of men as women attended (16 of each). The men present had, like the women, read feminist theory and were concerned also with masculine socialization for aggression, with the personal as political, with seeing the connections between the various levels of analysis. Papers were presented on feminist peace education, on the effects of the military on the lives of women, on the use of sexual imagery in weapons research, on the role of women in peace movements. The papers were interesting but even more interesting was the discussion which followed their presentation in which the participants tried to combine insights from weapons research, political science, and education with those developed in feminist theory. We started discussing explanations from feminist perspectives and found new themes that had to be developed, such as what the whole existence of various feminist perspectives meant for feminist analysis of peace and peace education.

This meeting of minds within peace studies and feminist studies may prove very beneficial to both fields. Another light in the dark. In the second part of the chapter no examples have been given of formal education shaping norms conducive to necessary disobedience toward authority or of furthering cooperation, sharing and joy instead of competition. Some examples could have been given of small private schools where parents and teachers are striving to realize values other than those transmitted through the normal school system. But these schools are mostly at the elementary level and their numbers very limited, their effects uncertain. Also, within the formal educational system there have been experiments in cooperation and sharing, teamwork between teachers, group work between pupils, grading kept to a minimum. In a four-year educational action research project it was shown that lower secondary schools belonging to the same formal educational system and being located in the same municipality with the same economic resources had very different school cultures (Brock-Utne, 1981; Brock-Utne, 1988d). Where one school had a lot of exams and separate subjects, the other school placed little emphasis on exams and had an integrated approach to teaching. When teachers in the upper secondary schools received students from these two schools they could often tell from which school they came from the questions being asked. The students from the traditional school mostly asked questions to assure that they got the homework assignments right. The students from the other school asked questions like: Why study that subject at all? Why do you want us to learn that? What is the point?

There are also examples of college and university studies built on cooperation and sharing, studies that are interdisciplinary, problem-oriented, and where students work in groups, even take their exams in groups and where the grade is only passed or not passed (Brock-Utne, 1988, 1988a).

Some educational theorists claim that those who try to create a green oasis in the gray educational desert are just fooling themselves (Callawaert & Kallos, 1978). Education will always be a function of society, an instrument for the state and for the elite to maintain control. Education cannot change unless the whole structure of society changes, they maintain. They see it as a task for educational researchers to analyze how education functions to maintain the existing power structure of society, the ruling values and norms. But to initiate change in this system they see as futile and, for an educational researcher, as counterproductive.

To this criticism one may answer that structures are built up of people and that changes must be worked for at micro-, meso-, and macrolevels at the same time. Radical feminist thinking sees the personal as political.

Personal changes have political significance and political changes have personal consequences. Even though the task of educational researchers may be to analyze how formal education functions to maintain the status quo and the control of the elites, one way to do precisely that would be to try to create alternatives, green oases within the system. That is one way of testing the limits of the system. And at the same time some more, and extremely needed, critical thinkers may emerge from these green plots.

REFERENCES

Aberle, David, and Kaspar, Naegele. 1952. "Middle-Class Fathers' Occupational Role and Attitudes Toward Children." *American Journal of Orthopsychiatry*. Vol. 22.

Abzug, Bella. 1984. *Gender Gap: A Guide to Political Power for American Women*. Boston: Houghton Mifflin.

Alexander, Susan. 1984. *Why Nuclear Education: A Sourcebook for Educators and Parents*. Cambridge, MA: Educators for Social Responsibility.

Alger, Chad, and Stohl, Michael, (eds.). 1988. *A Just Peace Through Transformation*. Boulder, CO: Westview Press.

Alvater, Elmar. 1971. *Materialen zur Politischen Ökonomi des Ausbildungssektors*. Erlangen: Politladen.

Andersen, Margaret. 1983. *Thinking About Women, Sociological and Feminist Perspectives*. New York: Macmillan Publishing Co.

Anderson, Marion. 1982a. *The Empty Pork Barrel: Unemployment and the Pentagon Budget*. 2d ed. Lansing, MI: Employment Research Associates.

Anderson, Marion. 1982b. *Neither Jobs, nor Security: Women's Unemployment and the Pentagon Budget*. Lansing, MI: Employment Research Associates.

Andreassen, Odd, (ed.). 1982. *Nedrustning*. (Disarmament). Oslo: Universitetsforlaget.

Andreassen, Geir and Mortensen, Elin. 1982. En studie av sammenhengen mellom kjønn, atferd og dominans i felles-undervisning av jenter og gutter i kroppsøvningsfaget. Universitetet i Tromsø. *Grunnfagsoppgave*. Vår 1982. (A study of the interrelationship between sex, behavior and dominance in the co-education of girls and boys in athletics. Reported 1982).

Anker, Nini Roll. 1945. *Kvinnen og den Svarte Fuglen*. (The women and the black bird.) Reprinted in 1982. Oslo: Aschehoug.

Arcana, Judith. 1983. *Every Mother's Son. The Role of Mothers in the Making of Men*. London: The Women's Press.

Arditti, Rita; Brennan, Pat; and Cavrak, Steve. 1980. *Science and Liberation*. Boston: South End Press.

Arditti, Rita; Duelli Klein, Renate; and Minden, Shelley, (eds.). 1984. *Test-tube Women. What Future for Motherhood?* London: Pandora Press.

Arkin, William, and Dobrofsky, Lynne. 1978. "Military Socialization and Masculinity." *Journal of Social Issues*. 34:1, pp. 151–168.

Ålvik, Trond, (ed.). 1986. Et Alternativ Etableres. (An Alternative Study is Established.) Lillehammer: *Oppland Distriktshøg-skoles Skriftserie*. No. 60.

Ås, Berit. 1975. "On Female Culture: An Attempt to Formulate a Theory of Women's Solidarity and Action." *Acta Sociologica*. 18: 2/3.

Ås, Berit. 1981. "A Five-Dimensional Model for Change. Contradictions and Feminist Consciousness." *Women's Studies International Quarterly.* 4:1, pp. 101–115.
Baker, Robert, and Ball, Sandra. 1969. *Violence and the Media.* A staff Report to the National Commission on the Causes and Prevention of Violence. Washington, DC: U.S. Government Printing Office.
Bandura, A. 1973. *Aggression: A Social Learning Analysis.* Englewood Cliffs, NJ: Prentice-Hall.
Bandura, A. 1959. *Adolescent aggression. A study of the influence of child training practices and family interrelationship.* Englewood Cliffs, NJ: Prentice-Hall.
Bandura, A. 1977. *Social Learning Theory.* Englewood Cliffs, NJ: Prentice-Hall.
Bard, Merton. 1974. "The Study and Modification of Intra-familia Violence." In Suzanne Steinmetz and Murray Strauss (eds.), *Violence in the Family.* New York: Dodd, Mead & Co.
Barrow, Isaac. 1970. *The Usefulness of Mathematical Learning Explained and Demonstrated.* 1743. Frank Cass.
Befring, Edvard. 1980. Pedagogikk (Pedagogics). In *Pax Leksikon.* Oslo: Pax Forlag. pp. 104–108.
Bellak, Leopold, and Antell, Maxine. 1974. "An Intercultural Study of Aggressive Behavior on Children's Playgrounds." *American Journal of Orthopsychiatry* (Cited in Holliday, 1978). 44: 503.
Bellow, Linda; Berry, Carolle; Cunningham, Joyce; Jackson, Margaret; Jeffreys, Sheila; and Jones, Carol. 1983. *Breaching the Peace. A Collection of Radical Feminist Papers.* London: Only Women Press, Ltd., pp. 18–22.
Belotti, Elena Gianini. 1973. *Dalla parte delle bambine.* Milano: Gianiacomo Feltrinelli Editore, 1973. Norwegian edition: *Slik former vi jentene.* (The making of girls). Oslo: Gyldendal Norsk Forlag, 1976.
Bendict, Ruth. 1934. *Patterns of Culture.* Boston: Houghton Mifflin.
Bergom Larsson, Maria. 1979. "Women and Technology in Industrialized Countries." pp. 47–69. In Michael Young (ed.), *Knowledge and Control.* London: Collier MacMillan.
Bernard, Jessie. 1981. *The Female World.* New York: The Free Press.
Berndt, Ronald. 1962. *Excess and Restraint.* Chicago: University of Chicago Press.
Bertell, Rosalie. 1985. *No immediate danger? Prognosis for a radioactive earth.* London: The Women's Press.
Bleier, Ruth. 1984. *Science and Gender: A Critique of Biology and Its Theories on Women.* Oxford: Pergamon Press.
Borrelli, Mario, and Haavelsrud, Magnus. 1983. The Development of the Concept of Peace Education Within the Archipelago of Peace Research. *Monograph.* 80 pp. Presented at the 10th IPRA conference, Gyor, Hungary.
Boulding, Elise. 1976. *The Underside of History.* Boulder, CO: Westview.
Boulding, Elise. 1978. "Las Mujeres y la Violencia Social (Women and Social Violence)." In *Revista Internacional de Ciencias Sociales.* (International Social Science Journal). Paris: UNESCO. 30:4.
Boulding, Elise. 1980. "The Role of Women in the Development of Peace Research." In *The Role of Women in Peace Movements, in the Development of Peace Research and in the Promotion of Friendly Relations Between Nations.* Paper presented by UNESCO to the World Conference for the United Nations Decade for Women, Copenhagen, July 14–30, 1980, pp. 45–54.
Boulding, Elise. 1984. Focus on: The Gender Gap. *Journal of Peace Research,* 21:1, pp. 1–3.
Boulding, Elise. 1986a. Från Vision till Verklighet. (From Vision to Reality). *Fredsårsdelegationens skriftserie.* No. 2.31 p. Published by the Swedish government, can be had for free (in Swedish). Address: Fredsårsdelegationen. Box 161 21. 103 23 Stockholm.
Boulding, Elise. 1986b. "Educating for Peace: A Feminist Perspective on Peace, Research and Action." Bookreview. *The Journal of Higher Education.* September/October 1986. 57:5, pp. 552–554.

Boulding, Kenneth. 1978. *Stable Peace.* Austin: University of Texas Press.

Boulding, Kenneth. 1985. *Human Betterment.* Beverly Hills: Sage Publications.

Brain, P. F., and Benton, D., (eds.). 1981. *Multidisciplinary Approaches to Aggression Research.* Amsterdam: North Holland Biomedical Press. (Here taken from Lagerspetz, 1983).

Breaching the Peace. 1983. A Collection of Radical Feminist Papers. London: Only Women Press Ltd.

Breivik, Gunnar. 1985. Norsk Risikopolitikk. (Norwegian politics on risk-talking). *Kronikk Dagbladet,* 24 September.

Brock-Utne, Birgit, and Haukaa, Runa. 1980. *Kunnskap uten Makt. Kvinner som Lärere og Elever.* (Knowledge without Power. Women as Teachers and Students). Oslo: Universitetsforlaget. (Norwegian University Press). Reprinted in 1981 and 1984. German edition in 1986: *Wissen ohne Macht.* Giessen: Focus Verlag.

Brock-Utne, Birgit. 1981. *Ungdomsskoler i Utvikling.* (Innovative secondary schools). Oslo: Universitetsforlaget.

Brock-Utne, Birgit. 1981a. *The Role of Women as Mothers and Members of Society in the Education of Young People for Peace, Mutual Understanding and Respect for Human Rights.* Commissioned paper for a UNESCO expert meeting on the role of women in peace education. New Delhi, India, December 7–11, 1981. ED-81/CON. 609/2. A more extensive version can be identified as *PRIO publication S-12/81.*

Brock-Utne, Birgit. 1981b. *Disarmament Education as a Distinct Field of Study.* Paper presented at the 9th IPRA General Conference, Toronto, Canada, session on Peace Education, June 21–26 (pp. 253–267). In Y. Sakomoto and R. Klaassen (eds.) *Key Issues of Peace Research.* Proceedings of the IPRA Ninth General Conference.

Brock-Utne, Birgit. 1981c. Kvinner i Fredsarbeid. In H. Sivertsen, F. Stockholm, & L. Vislie (eds.) *Kvinne viser vei.* (A Woman leads the way). Festschrift to Eva Nordland. Oslo: Aschehoug.

Brock-Utne, Birgit. 1982a. "What are the Effects of Curricular Options?" In *Sex Stereotyping in Schools,* edited by Council of Europe. Swets & Zeitlinger-Lisse.

Brock-Utne, Birgit. 1982b. "Girls and the Hidden Curriculum of the Compulsory School." *Tidsskrift för Nordisk Förening för Pedagogisk Forskning.* (Journal for the Nordic Society for Educational Research, No. 1–2, 1982. Special issue on women and education).

Brock-Utne, Birgit. 1982c. "Ett Kvinneperspektiv på Norsk Forsvarspolitikk." (A Feminist Perspective on Norwegian Defense Policy). *PRIO publikasion P-6/82.*

Brock-Utne, Birgit. 1982d. "Gewaltfrei Denken. Zur Rolle der Frauen in der Friedensforschung." (Non-Violent Thinking. On the Role of Women in Peace Research). In C. Randzio-Plath (ed.) *Was Geht uns Frauen der Krieg an?* Hamburg: Rowohlt Verlag.

Brock-Utne, Birgit. 1982e. Rauhan Kasvatus. *"Rauha saa Alkunsa Naisten Mielissa."* (Women and Peace. "Peace starts in the Minds of Women.") Helsinki: Naiset Rauhan Puolesta.

Brock-Utne, Birgit. 1982f. Hvorfor Fredsundervisning i Norsk Skole og Voksenopplæring? (Why Peace Education in Norwegian Schools and Adult Education?) pp. 11–23. In Hansjordet (ed.) *Skole for Fred.* (Schools for Peace). Oslo: Det Norske Samlaget.

Brock-Utne, Birgit. 1982g. Hvordan kan utdanningsverket brukes til å fremme nedrustning? (How can the formal schooling system be used to serve disarmament?) pp. 247–258. In Andreassen (ed.) *Nedrustning.* (Disarmament). Oslo: Universitetsforlaget.

Brock-Utne, Birgit. 1983a. Likestilt til å Drepe. (Equal to kill). *Ny Tids Kronikk.* 13 April.

Brock-Utne, Birgit. 1983b. "Are Universities Educating for War?" Keynote lecture held at Johann Wolfgang Goethe-University, Frankfurt am Main, Federal Republic of Germany, September, 1983 in connection with the IV International Congress of the European Association for research and development in higher education, Oslo. Published in the EARDHE proceedings, edited by Ulrich Petter Ritter and Hans Peter Kühn, Frankfurt am Main. September 1984.

Brock-Utne, Birgit. 1983c. *Education as the Key to Equal Participation of Women in the Devel-*

opment Process. Commissioned paper prepared on request for the Nordic seminar on WOMEN IN DEVELOPMENT held near Helsinki, November 9–11, 1983. Also published in Troil, Margaretha von (ed.) *Women in Development.* Helsinki: Publication of the Office of the Prime Minister. 1984:4.

Brock-Utne, Birgit. 1983d. *Research on Women and Peace.* Prepared on request for the expert group meeting on the participation of women in promoting international peace and cooperation held in Vienna, December 5–9, 1983.

Brock-Utne, Birgit. 1983e. "Symmetric Peace Education as Advanced by Anatol Pikas—A Critique and an Analysis." *International Review of Education.* 29:3, pp. 345–353.

Brock-Utne, Birgit. 1983f. "A Last Word about Symmetric Peace Education—A Response to a Rejoinder." *International Review of Education.* 29:3, pp. 355–357.

Brock-Utne, Birgit. 1984. "The Relationship of Feminism to Peace and Peace Education." *Bulletin of Peace Proposals.* 15:2, pp. 149–154. Also published in T. Carson, and H. Gideonse (eds.) *Peace Education and the Task for Peace Educators.* New York: A World Council for Curriculum and Instruction Monograph.

Brock-Utne, Birgit. 1985a. *Education for Peace. A Feminist Perspective.* New York: Pergamon. A Korean edition appeared in 1986 and a Norwegian edition in 1987; an Italian will appear in 1989. The Norwegian edition is published by Folkereisning mot Krigs forlag, the Italian edition by Edizione Gruppo Abele. The English edition has been reprinted in 1987.

Brock-Utne, Birgit. 1985b. Livsfarlig Mannsideal. (Life-endangering Masculinity). *Kronikk, Dagbladet,* 12 September.

Brock-Utne, Birgit. 1985c. Risiko og Dumdristighet. (Risktaking and Foolishness) *Utspill, Dagbladet,* 10 October.

Brock-Utne, Birgit. 1986a. Kvinner og Fred på Forum, på den Offisielle Konferansen og Framover. (Women and Peace at "Forum", the Official Conference and in the Future). *PRIO Inform, 4/86.*

Brock-Utne, Birgit. 1986b. The Peace Concepts through Three U.N. Women's Decade Conferences. *PRIO Working Paper, 1/86.* Also published in: *The Journal of World Peace.* Spring 1986. Minnesota.

Brock-Utne, Birgit. 1986c. Feminist Perspectives on Peace Research. *PRIO-Report. 17/86.*

Brock-Utne, Birgit. 1986d. *En Mors Tåre, Vi Som Mister Våre Barn på Veiene.* (A Mother's Tear. We Who Lose Our Children on the Highways). Oslo: Ida Forlag.

Brock-Utne, Birgit. 1986e. Broren på Lillehammer. (The Brother at Lillehammer) pp. 255–269. In T. Ålvik (ed.) *Et alternativ etableres.* (An alternative study is established). Lillehammer: *Oppland Districktshøgskoles Skriftserie,* No. 60.

Brock-Utne, Birgit. 1987a. Sports, Masculinity and Education for Violence. *PRIO-Reports. 1/87.*

Brock-Utne, Birgit. 1987b. Når Feminister Oppdrar Sønner. (When Feminists Educate Sons). In B. Brock-Utne and S. Bjørnar (eds.) *Når Gutter Blir Menn.* (When Boys Grow into Men). Oslo: Universitetsforlaget.

Brock-Utne, Birgit. 1988a. Formal Education As a Force in Shaping Cultural Norms in Relation to War and the Environment, pp. 83–101. In A. Westing (ed.) *Cultural Norms to War and the Environment.* Oxford: Oxford University Press.

Brock-Utne, Birgit. 1988b. "Disarmament Education: The European Evolution." pp. 112–129. In D. Ray (ed.) *Peace Education.* London: Third Eye.

Brock-Utne, Birgit. 1988c. "The Development of Peace and Peace Education Concepts through Three UN Women's Decade Conferences." pp. 170–190. In C. Alger and M. Stohl (eds.) *A Just Peace Through Transformation.* Boulder, CO: Westview Press.

Brock-Utne, Birgit. 1988d. "What is Educational Action Research?" pp. 253–259. In S. Kemmis, and R. McTaggart (eds.) *The Action Research Reader.* Australia: Deakin University Printery.

Brock-Utne, Birgit. 1989. "Gender and Cooperation in the Laboratory." *Journal of Peace Research*. No. 1.

Brock-Utne, Birgit; Traylor, Julianne; and Aas, Solveig, (eds.). 1986. Women, Militarism and Disarmament—a conference report. p. 213 *PRIO-Reports. 6/86.*

Brock-Utne, Birgit, and Sarnes, Bjørnar, (eds.). 1987. *Når Gutter Blir Menn.* (When Boys Turn into Men). Oslo: Universitetsforlaget.

Bronfenbrenner, Urie. 1958. "The Study of Identification through Inter-Personal Perception." In *Person Perception and Interpersonal Behavior.* Stanford, CA: Stanford University Press.

Brownmiller, Susan. 1975. *Against Our Will: Men, Women and Rape.* New York: Simon and Schuster.

Brunet, Odette, and Lezine, Irene. 1966. *I Primi Anni del Bambino.* Roma: Armando. (Cited in Belotti, 1973).

Burns, Robin. 1981. Continuity and Change in Peace Education. *Bulletin of Peace Proposals.* 2, pp. 115–123.

Burns, Robin. 1982. *Development, Disarmament and Women: Some New Connections.* Paper delivered at Victorian Association for Peace Studies, March 1982.

Burns, Robin. 1986. *Women, Science Education and Action for Peace.* Paper presented to the IPRA Conference, University of Sussex, April 14–18, 1986. School of Education. La Trobe University, Bundoora, Victoria 3083 AUSTRALIA.

Buss, Arnold. 1971. "Aggression Pays." In J. Singer (ed.) *The Control of Aggression and Violence,* New York: Academic Press.

Butcher, N. (1969). "MMPI Characteristics of Externalizing and Internalizing Boys and their Parents." In J. Butcher (ed.) *MMPI Research Developments and Clinical Applications.* New York: McGraw-Hill. (Cited in Holliday, 1978).

Buvinic, Mayra. 1981. Introduction to "Women and Development: Indicators of their Changing Role." *Socio-economic Studies,* Paris. UNESCO. No. 3.

Caldecott, Leonie, and Leland, Stephanie, (eds.). 1983. *Reclaiming the Earth: Women Speak Out for Life on Earth.* London: The Women's Press.

Callawaert, Staf, and Kallos, Daniel. 1976. Den Rosa Vågen i Svensk Pedagogik. (The Pink Wave in Swedish Pedagogics). *Forskning om Utbildning.* No. 1. 1976.

Callewaert, Staf, and Nilsson, Bengt A. 1980. *Skolklassen Som Socialt System. Lektionsanalyser.* (The School Class As a Social System. Analysis of Lessons). Kristianstad: Lunds Bok och Tidskrifts AB.

Carloni, Alice Stewart. 1981. "Sex Disparities in the Distribution of Food within Rural Households." *Food and Nutrition.* 7, p. 1.

Carpenter, Susan. 1977. *A Repertoire of Peacemaking Skills.* Boulder, CO: Consortium on Peace Research, Education, and Development.

Carroll, Berenice. 1972. "Peace Research: The Cult of Power." *Journal of Conflict Resolution.* 6 (4), pp. 585–616.

Carson, Rachel. 1964. *The Silent Spring.* London: Penguin Books.

Carson, Terrance, and Gideonse, Hendrik D., (eds.). 1987. *Peace Education and the Task for Peace Educators.* New York: A World Council for Curriculum and Instruction Monograph.

Chodorow, Nancy. 1978. *The Reproduction of Mothering, Psychoanalysis and the Sociology of Gender.* Berkeley. Los Angeles, London: University of California Press.

Cisse, Jeanne M. 1975. "Woman, The First Teacher." *Prospects.* 3, pp. 347–352.

Clinch, Nancy G. 1973. *The Kennedy Neurosis.* New York: Grosset and Dunlap.

Cohen, L. J., and Campos, J. J. 1974. "Father, Mother and Stranger as Elicitors of Attachment Behaviors in Infancy." *Development Psychology.* X, pp. 146–154.

Dale, Erling Lars. 1986. *Oppdragelse Fri fra Mor og Far.* (Education Freed from "Mother" and "Father"). Oslo: Gyldendal.

Daly, Mary. 1979. *Gyn/Ecology.* London: The Women's Press.

Davis, Elisabeth Gould. 1971. *The First Sex*. New York: Putnam's Sons. Later reprinted by Penguin Books.

Deem, Rosemary. 1978. *Women and Schooling*. London: Routledge & Kegan Paul.

Degler, Carl. 1981. What the Women's Movement Has Done to American History. In E. Langland and W. Gove (eds.) *A Feminist Perspective in the Academy*. Chicago: University of Chicago Press.

Detre, Thomas, et al. 1974. "The Nosology of Violence." In *Neural Basis for Violence and Aggression*, edited by Fields and Sweet. (Cited in Holliday, 1978).

Dinnerstein, Dorothy. 1977. *The Mermaid and the Minotaur*. Harper Colophon Books.

DiPietro, J. 1977. *Rough and Tumble Play: A Function of Gender*. Unpublished manuscript. Stanford University, Psychology Department. (Cited in Maccoby, 1980).

Doyle, J. A. 1983. *The Male Experience*. Dubuque, IA: William C. Brown.

Dumas, L. J. 1981. "Disarmament and Economy in Advanced Industrialized Countries—The US and the USSR." *Bulletin of Peace Proposals*. 12:1, pp. 1–100.

Dyer, Gwynne. 1985. *War*. New York: Crown Publishers, Inc.

Easlea, Brian. 1981. *Science and sexual oppression. Patriarchy's confrontation with woman and nature*. London: Weidenfeld and Nicholson.

Easlea, Brian. 1983. *Fathering the Unthinkable. Masculinity, Scientists and the Arms Race*. London: Pluto Press.

Eckhardt, William. 1980. The Causes and Correlates of Western Militarism. pp. 323–355. In A. Eide and M. Thee (eds.) *Problems of Contemporary Militarism*. London: Croom Helm.

Edwards, C. P., and Whiting, B., 1977. *Sex differences in Children's Social Interaction*. Unpublished report to the Ford Foundation. (Cited in Maccoby, 1980).

Eglin, Josephine. 1982. Cited in *Feminism and the Peace Movement: The Universalistic Nature of the Struggle against Injustice and Violence*. Paper. University of Bradford. England.

Ehrenreich, Barbara. 1984. The Politics of Talking in Couples: Conversus Interruptus and other Disorders. pp. 73–76. In A. Jaggar and P. Rothenberg *Feminist Frameworks, Alternative Theoretical Accounts of the Relationships between Men and Women*. New York: McGraw-Hill Book Co.

Eide, Asbjørn, and Thee, Marek, (eds.). 1980. *Problems of Contemporary Militarism*. London: Croom Helm.

Eisler, Riane, and Loye, David. 1986. Peace and Feminist Theory: New Directions. *Bulletin of Peace Proposals*. 17:1, pp. 95–101.

Elster, Jon. 1979. *Ulysses and the Sirens*. Cambridge: Cambridge University Press.

Enerstvedt, Regi. 1979. *Mennesket—Kiønn og Personlighet*. (The Human being—Sex and Personality). Oslo: Forlaget Ny Dag.

Engels, Friedrich. 1970. (Originally published in 1942): *The Origin of the Family, Private Property and the State*. New York: International Publishers Company, Inc., pp. 87–145.

Enloe, Cynthia. 1983. *Does Khaki become You? The Militarisation of Women's Lives*. London: Pluto Press.

Erikson, Eric. 1951. "Sex Differences in Play Configurations of Preadolescents." *American Journal of Orthopsychiatry*. 21, p. 667. (Cited in Holliday, 1978).

Eron, Leonard, et al. 1974. "How Learning Conditions in Early Childhood—Including Mass Media—Relate to Aggression in Late Adolescence." *American Journal of Orthopsychiatry*. 44, p. 412. (Cited in Holliday, 1978).

Ethelberg, Eva. 1983. *Kvindelighedens Modsigelse*. (The Contradiction of Femininity). Copenhagen: Antropos.

Ethelberg, Eva. 1985. Självkänsla Kontra Realiltet—Ett Dilemma för Psykologin och för Kvinnorna. (Self-assurance Versus Reality—A Dilemma in Psychology and for Women). *Kvinnovetenskaplig Tidskrift*. No. 1, pp. 4–16.

Etzioni, Amitai. 1967. Non-conventional Uses of Sociology as Illustrated by Peace Research. In P. Lazarfeld, W. Sewell, and H. Wilensky (eds.) *The Uses of Sociology.* New York: Basic Books.

Eysenck, H. J., and Nias, D. K. B. 1978. *Sex, Violence and the Media.* London: Maurice Temple Smith.

Fabbro, David. 1978. Peaceful Societies: An Introduction. *Journal of Peace Research.* 15:1.

Fall, Elimane. 1987. Football—Ferveur, Fanatisme, Violence et Chauvinisme. *Jeune Afrique.* 1375 (13), pp. 48–49.

Fasteau, Marc Feigen. 1975. *The Male Machine.* New York: Delta Books.

Fasting, Kari. 1982. "Female Sports—Equal but Different." *Tidsskrift for Nordisk Forening for Pedagogisk Forskning.* 1–2/1982. Special issue on sexism and education. pp. 45–56. (*Journal of the Nordic Society for Educational Research*) Sweden.

Felshin, J. 1974. Social Commentary. Chapter 7. In W. W. Gerber, et al. *The American Women in Sport.* Boston: Addison Wesley.

Firestone, Shulamith. 1970. *The Dialectic of Sex: The Case for Feminist Revolution.* New York: William Morrow.

Forcey, Linda Rennie. 1984. Making of Men in the Military: Perspectives from Mothers. *Women Studies International Forum.* 7:6, pp. 477–486.

Freire, Paulo. 1972. *Pedagogy of the Oppressed.* New York: Penguin Books.

French, Marilyn. 1986. *Beyond Power. On Women, Men and Morals.* London: Abacus.

Freud, Sigmund. 1964. (Originally published in 1933). *New Introductory Lectures on Psychoanalysis.* (The chapter on "Femininity," pp. 158–184). London: Norton and Company.

Galsworthy, John. 1933. *The Forsythe Saga.* New York: Scribner.

Galtung, Johan. 1964. Editorial. *Journal of Peace Research.* 1.

Galtung, Johan. 1967. In *Alternativer-5 års Fredsdebatt.* (Alternatives: Five Years of Peace Debate). Oslo: Pax Forlag. p. 209.

Galtung, Johan. 1968. Peace Research. In *The Social Sciences—Problems and Orientations.* pp. 194–200. Mouton/UNESCO.

Galtung, Johan. 1969. Violence, Peace and Peace Research. *Journal of Peace Research.* 6:3.

Galtung, Johan. 1975. "Peace Education: Problems and Conflicts." In Haavelsrud (ed.) *Education for Peace-Reflection and Action.* Guildford: IPC Science and Technology Press.

Galtung, Johan. 1979. "Fredsforskning." (Peace Research). In *Pax Leksikon.* 2, pp. 439–440. Oslo: Pax Forlag.

Galtung, Johan. 1981a. Social Cosmology and the Concept of Peace. *Journal of Peace Research.* XVIII:2, pp. 183–197.

Galtung, Johan. 1981b. Disarmament Education: A Partial Answer. In M. Haavelsrud (ed.) *Approaching Disarmament Education.* Guildford: Westbury House.

Galtung, Johan. 1985. Twenty-five Years of Peace Research: Ten Challenges and Some Responses. *Journal of Peace Research.* 22:2, pp. 141–158.

Gandhi, Mahatma. 1939. "Swaraj through Women." *Harijan 2* (December 1939).

Gandhi, Mahatma. 1940. What is Women's Role? *Harijan 24* (February 1940).

Garbo, Gunnar. 1984. Over Alle Grenser. Den Internasjonale Informasjonsformidlingen, Mediesamfurnet og Utviklingslandene. (Beyond Limits. International Communication, The Media Society and the Developing Countries). *Aktuelle Utenrikspolitiske Spørsmål. No. 27.* Oslo: Det Kongelige Utenriksdepartement.

Garcia, Celina. 1981. Androgyny and Peace Education. *Bulletin of Peace Proposals.* 2, pp. 163–178.

Gardner, Howard, and Perkins, David. 1982. Harvard's Project Zero Studies the Numerous Artistic Intelligence. *Behavior Today.* 13:17, May 3.

Gast, Sonja van der. 1981. "Women Against Nuclear Weapons." In *Women of Europe in Action for Peace.* Conference report from a conference held in the Netherlands, November 27–28, 1981, sponsored by Women's International League for Peace and Freedom.

Gelder, Lindsy Van, and Carmichael, Carrie. 1975. "But What About Our Sons?" *Ms.* October 1975.

Gerber, W. W., et. al. 1974. *The American Women in Sport.* Boston: Addison Wesley.

Giele, J. Z., and Smock, A. C. 1977. *Women: Roles and Status in Eight Countries.* New York: John Wiley & Sons.

Gil, David. 1973. *Violence against Children.* Cambridge: Harvard University Press.

Gilder, George. 1973. *Sexual Suicide.* New York: Quadrangle Books.

Gilligan, Carol. 1982. *In a Different Voice. Psychological Theory and Women's Development.* Cambridge: Harvard University Press.

Glueck, Eleanor, and Sheldon. 1950. *Unravelling Juvenile Delinquency.* Cambridge: Harvard University Press.

Goldstein, Jeffrey, and Arms, Roberg. 1971. "Effects of Observing Athletic Contests on Hostility." *Sociometry.* 34, p. 83. (Cited in Holliday, 1978).

Goodenough, E. W. 1957. "Interest in Persons as an Aspect of Sex Differences in the Early Years." *Genetic Psychology Monographs.* 55, pp. 287–323.

Graff, Harvey. 1981. *Literacy and Social Development in the West: A Reader.* New York: Cambridge University Press.

Green, Frankie. 1983. "Not Weaving but Frowning." In *Breaching the Peace.* A Collection of Radical Feminist Papers. London: Only Women Press, Ltd.

Green, Richard. 1974. "The Behaviorally Feminine Male Child." In *Sex Differences in Behavior,* edited by Richard Friedman. (Cited in Holliday, 1978).

Green, Richard. 1976. "One Hundred Ten Feminine and Masculine Boys: Behavioral Contrasts and Demographic Similarities." *Archives of Sexual Behavior.* 5, pp. 425–446.

Haavelsrud, Magnus. (ed.). 1975. *Education for Peace Reflection and Action.* Guildford: IPC Science and Technology Press.

Haavelsrud, Magnus. (ed.). 1981. *Approaching Disarmament Education.* Guildford: Westbury House.

Haavind, Hanne. 1982. Makt og Kjærlighet i ekteskapet. (Power and Love in Marriage). In Haukaa, Hoel, Haavind (eds.) *Kvinneforskning—Bidrag Til Samfunnsteori.* Oslo: Universitetsforlaget.

Halberstam, David. 1972. *The Best and the Brightest.* New York: Random House.

Hall, Ann. 1979. Sport and Gender: A Feminist Perspective on the Sociology of Sport. Ottawa: *CAHPER Sociology of Sport Monograph Series.*

Halvorsen, Anne. 1982. Krig, Fred, Nedrustning Angår Alle Ungdomsskolelärere. (War, Peace, Disarmament Concern All Secondary School Teachers). In H. Hansjordet (ed.) *Skole for Fred.* (Schools for Peace). Oslo: Det Norske Samlaget.

Hamann, Brigitte. 1986. *Bertha von Suttner. Ein Leben für den Frieden.* Piper Verlag.

Hansjordet, H., (ed.). 1982. *Skole for Fred.* (Schools for Peace). Oslo: Det Norske Samlaget.

Hantover, Jeffrey. 1978. The Boy Scouts and the Validation of Masculinity. *Journal of Social Issues.* 34:1, pp. 185–195.

Harrison, James. 1978. "Warning: The Male Sex Role May Be Dangerous to Your Health." *Journal of Social Issues.* 34:1, pp. 65–86.

Hartmann, Heidi. 1984. The Unhappy Marriage of Marxism and Feminism: Toward a More Progressive Union. pp. 172–189. In A. Jaggar and P. Rothenberg (eds.) *Feminist Frameworks.* New York: McGraw-Hill Book Co.

Haukaa, Runa. 1979. Sosial Bevegelse og Sosial Teori. (Social Movements and Social Theories). *Sosiologi i dag* nr. 2.

Haukaa, Runa. 1982a. Women's Studies: Pedagogic and Educational Dilemma. *Tidsskrift för Nordisk Förening för Pedagogisk Forskning.* No. 1–2/1982.

Haukaa, Runa. 1982b. *Bak Slagordene. Den Nye Kvinnebevegelsen i Norge.* (Behind the Slogans, The New Feminist Movement in Norway). Oslo: Pax Forlag.

Haukaa, Runa, and Haavind, Hanne, (eds.). 1982. *Kvinneforskning—Bidrag Til Samfunnsteori. (Women Studies—Contributions to a Theory of Society).* Oslo: Universitetsforlaget.

Hawke, C. C. 1950. "Castration and Sex Crimes." *American Journal of Mental Deficiency.* 55, p. 220. (Cited in Holliday, 1978).

Hite, Shere. 1976. *The Hite Report,* chapter on "Redefining Sex." New York: Macmillan Publishing Company.

Holliday, Laurel. 1978. *The Violent Sex. Male Psychobiology and the Evolution of Consciousness.* Guerneville, CA: Bluestocking Books.

Holter, Harriet, (ed.). 1982. *Kvinner i Fellesskap. (The Collectivity of Women).* Oslo: Universitetsforlaget.

Hooks, Bell. 1984. *Feminist Theory—From Margin to Center.* Boston, MA: South End Press.

Horowitz, B., and Kishwar, Madhu. 1982. "Family Life—The Unequal Deal." *Manushi.* 11.

Hoskins, Betty, and Holmes, H. Bequaert. 1984. "Technology and Prenatal Femicide." In R. Arditti, R. Klein, and S. Minden (eds.) *Test-tube Women. What Future for Motherhood?* London: Pandora Press.

House of Commons. 1976. *Report on Violence in Marriage.* 8:4.

Hunter, Derek. 1984. *Peace through Education.* London, Philadelphia: The Falmer Press.

Hutt, Corinne. 1972. *Males and Females.* Harmondsworth: Penguin.

Höivik, Tord. 1971. "Social Inequality: The Main Issue." *Journal of Peace Research.* 8:4.

Höivik, Tord. 1985. Fra Kanoner til Brød. (From Cannons to Bread). Kronikk (Chronicle). *Dagbladet.* 28 November.

Illeris, Knud. 1976. *Problemorientering og Deltagerstyring.* (Problem-centered and Participatory Learning). København: Munksgaard.

Ishida, Takeshi. 1969. "Beyond the Traditional Concepts of Peace in Different Cultures." *Journal of Peace Research.* VI:2, pp. 133–145.

Jacklin, C. N., and Maccoby, E. E. 1978. "Social Behavior at 33 months in Same-sex and Mixed-sex Dyads." *Child Development* 49, pp. 557–569.

Jaggar, Alison, and Struhl, Paula R. 1978. *Feminist Frameworks. Alternative Theoretical Accounts of the Relations between Women and Men.* New York: McGraw-Hill Book Company.

Jaggar, Alison, and Rothenberg, Paula. 1984. *Feminist Frameworks: Alternative Theoretical Accounts of the Relations between Women and Men.* New York: McGraw-Hill Book Company.

Jalmert, Lars. 1979: *Små Barns Sociale Utveckling.* (The Social Development of Small Children). Stockholm. Norwegian edition: *Små Barns Sociale Utvikling.* Oslo: Pax Forlag, 1980.

Janssen-Jurreit. 1976. *Seximus, Uber die Abtreibung der Frauenfrage.* (Sexism: The Male Monopoly of Thought). München/Wein: Carl Hanser Verlag. An abbreviated version has been translated into Swedish: *Sexism: Manssamhällets Ideologi Och Historia.* Stockholm: Norstedt Trykkeri, 1979; *Sexism-The Monopoly of Male Thought.* London: Pluto Press, 1982.

Johnson, Miriam. 1977. "Androgyny and the Maternal Principle." *School Review,* 1, pp. 50–69.

Kapitza, Sergei. 1982. Social Consciousness and Education for Disarmament. In J. Rotblat (ed.) *Scientists—the Arms Race and Disarmament.* London: Taylor and Francis, Ltd.

Kelkar, Govind. 1983. *Women and Structural Violence in India.* Paper presented at the UNESCO/IPRA consultation on women, militarism and disarmament in Gyor, Hungary, August 25–28, 1983.

Keller, Evelyn Fox. 1985. *Reflections on Gender and Science.* New Haven: Yale University Press.

Kemmis, Stephen, and McTaggart, Robin, (eds.). 1988. *The Action Research Reader.* Australia: Deakin University Printery.

Kempe, C. H., and Helfer, R. 1968. *The Battered Child.* Chicago: University of Chicago Press.

King, Ynestra. 1983. The Eco-Feminist Imperative (pp. 9–15). In L. Caldecott and S. Leland (eds.) *Reclaiming the Earth.* Women Speak Out for Life on Earth. London: The Women's Press.

"Kjerringråd" 1980. *Kjerringråd.* (Norwegian Feminist Academic Journal). No. 1, 1980.

Klemesrud, Judy. 1979. "How Feminists Bring up their Sons." *New York Times*. 27, p. 8.
Knight, G. P., and Kagan, S. 1977. "Development of Prosocial and Competitive Behaviors in Anglo-American and Mexican-American Children." *Child Development*. 48, pp. 1394–95.
Kolakowski, Leszek. 1966. *Mennesket uten Alternativ. Om Det Mulige og Umulige i å være Marxist*. Oslo: Gyldendal. Fakkel.
Kronsberg, Sandora. 1981. "An Investigation of Parent Intervention Behavior with Toddler Boys and Girls." Doctoral Dissertation. University of Oregon.
Kruegler, Christopher, and Parkman, Patricia. 1985. "Identifying Alternatives to Political Violence: An Educational Imperative." *Harvard Educational Review*. 55:1, February 1985, pp. 109–117.
Lagerspetz, Kirsti. 1981. Combining Aggression Studies in Infra-humans and Man. In P. F. Brain and D. Benton (eds.) *Multidisciplinary Approaches to Aggression Research*. Amsterdam: North Holland Biomedical Press.
Lagerspetz, Kirsti. 1982a. TV-våldets Inverkan på Åskådarens Aggressivitet. (The effect of TV-Violence on the Aggressivity of the Viewer). *Societas Scientiarum Fennica Årsbok—Vuosikiria*. LX (1982) B, N: o 1, pp. 67–80.
Lagerspetz, Kirsti. 1982b. An international investigation of televised violence and aggression in children. *The Nordicom Review of Nordic Mass Communication Research*. 2/1982.
Lagerspetz, Kirsti. 1983. Beror krigen på människans aggression? (Do wars stem from the aggressivity of man?) *Nordisk Psykologi*, 35 (3), pp. 225–236.
Lamb, Michael. 1977. "The Development of Parental Preferences in the First Two Years of Life." *Sex Roles*. 3, pp. 495–497.
Lamb, Michael. 1978. "The Father's Role in the Infant's Social World." In J. H. Stevens and M. Mathews (eds.) *Mother/Child Father/Child Relationship*. New York: National Association for the Education of Young Children.
Lamb, Michael. 1981. *The Role of the Father in Child Development*. New York: Wiley.
Lamb, Michael, and Lamb, Jamie. 1976. "The Nature and Importance of the Father-Infant Relationship. *The Family Coordinator*. 25, pp. 379–387.
Langer, Susanne. 1958. *Filosofi i ny Tonart*. Stockholm: Almqvist & Wiksell.
Langland, Elizabeth, and Gove, Walter, (eds.). 1981. *A Feminist Perspective in the Academy—The Difference it Makes*. Chicago and London: The University of Chicago Press.
Lansky, L. M. 1956. Patterns of Defense Against Conflict. Unpublished Doctoral Dissertation, University of Michigan. (Cited in Lynn, 1976).
Lazarsfeld, Paul; Sewell, William; and Wilensky, Harold, (eds.). 1967. *The Uses of Sociology*. New York: Basic Books.
Lefkowitz, M. M.; Eron, L. D.; Walder, L. O.; and Huesmann, L. R. 1977. *Growing Up to Be Violent. A Longitudinal Study of the Development of Aggression*. Oxford: Pergamon Press. (here taken from Lagerspetz, 1982a).
Leland, Stephanie. 1983. Feminism and Ecology: Theoretical Connections. pp. 67–73. In L. Caldecott and S. Leland (eds.) *Reclaiming the Earth. Women Speak Out for Life on Earth*. London: The Women's Press.
LeMaire, L. 1956. "Danish Experience Regarding the Castration of Sexual Offenders." *Journal of Criminal Law and Criminology*. 47, p. 294. (Cited in Holliday, 1978).
Leonard, George. 1980. Winning isn't Everything. It's Nothing. pp. 259–266. In D. Sabo, and R. Runfola (eds.) *Jock—Sports and Male Identity*. Englewood Cliffs, NJ: Prentice Hall.
Lie, Svein, and Sjöberg, Svein. 1984. *Myke Jenter i Harde Fag*. (Soft Girls in Hard Science). Oslo: Universitetsforlaget.
Liebert, Robert. 1974. "Television and Children's Aggressive Behavior: Another Look." *American Journal of Psychoanalysis*. 34, p. 99. (Cited in Holliday, 1978).
Liljeström, Rita; Svensson, G.; Liljeström, G.; Mellström; and Furst, G. 1976. *Roller i Omvandling*. (Sex Roles in Transition). (Sou 1976:71). Stockholm: Liber.

Lindholm, Stig. 1981. Paradigms, Science and Reality. On Dialectics, Hermenutics and Positivism in the Social Sciences. *Research Bulletins from the University of Stockholm, IX.*

Lindholm, Stig. 1985. *Kunnskap: Från Fragment til Helhetssyn.* Stockholm: Liber Förlag.

Lindholm, Stig. 1986. A Thousand Students on War, Peace and Peace Education. *Paper.* 23 pp. Presented at the 11th General Conference of IPRA, University of Sussex, April 13–18, 1986.

Lutz, Dieter. 1984. *Weder Wehrkunde noch Friedenserziehung?* (Neither Security Studies nor Peace Education?) Baden-Baden: Nomos Verlagsgesellschaft.

Lynn, D. B. 1976. "Fathers and Sex-role Development." *The Family Coordinator* XXV: 4, October.

MacBride, Sean. 1978. "Brainwashing with a Good Clean Bomb." In *Suicide or Survival? The Challenge of the Year 2000.* Paris: UNESCO.

Maccoby, Eleanor. 1980. *Social Development, Psychological Growth and the Parent-child Relationship.* New York: Harcourt Brace Jovanovich.

Maccoby, E. E., and Jacklin, C. N. 1974. *The Psychology of Sex Differences.* Stanford: Stanford University Press.

Mansueto, Connie. 1983. "Take the Toys from the Boys. Competition and the Nuclear Arms Race." p. 114. In D. Thompson (ed.) *Over our Dead Bodies.* London: Virago.

Mark, Vernon Hershel, and Ervin, Frank R. 1970. *Violence and the Brain.* San Francisco: Harper & Row.

Masters, Robert, and Houston, Jean. 1972. *Mind Games: The Guide to Inner Space.* New York: Viking Press.

McAllister, Pam. 1982. *Reweaving the Web of Life. Feminism and Non-Violence.* Philadelphia: New Society Publishers.

Mead, Margaret. 1935. *Sex and Temperament in Three Primitive Societies.* New York: Morrow.

Mead, Margaret. 1978. *Male and Female.* New York: Penguin Books.

Merchant, Carolyn. 1980. *The Death of Nature.* San Francisco: Harper & Row.

Messner, Mike. 1985. "The Changing Meaning of Male Identity in the Lifecourse of the Athlete." *The Arena Review.* November, Vol. 9, Number 2, pp. 31–60.

Milgram, Stanley. 1975. *Obedience to Authority. An Experimental View.* New York: Harper & Row.

Mill, John Stuart. 1970. (Originally published in 1851): On the Subjection of Women. From *"Essays on Sex Equality"* by John Stuart Mill and Harriet Taylor Mill, edited by Alice Rossi. Chicago and London: University of Chicago Press, pp. 125–156.

Miller, Alice. 1980. *Am Anfang war Erziehung.* Suhrkamp. Danish translation in 1984: I Begyndelsen var Opdragelsen. (In the Beginning There was Education). København: Hans Reitzels Forlag.

Mitchell, Juliet. 1974. *Psychoanalysis and Feminism.* New York: Pantheon Books.

Moberg, Eva. 1986. Är Krig Naturligt? (Have Wars Always Existed?) *Fredsårsdelegationens Skriftserie.* No. 1. 1986. p. 24. Published by the Swedish government. Can be had for free (in Swedish) Address: Fredsårsdelegationen, Box 161 21, 103 23 Stockholm.

Montagu, Ashley, (ed.). 1978. *Learning Non-Aggression. The Experience of Non-Literate Societies.* New York: Oxford University Press.

Morgan, Robin. 1980. "The First Feminist Exiles from the USSR." *Ms.* November 1980.

Morgan, Robin, (ed.). 1984. *Sisterhood is Global.* New York: Anchor Books.

Moyer, Kenneth. 1974. "A Physiological Model of Aggression." In *Neural Bases for Violence and Aggression.* Warren H. Green. (Cited in Holliday, 1978).

Mussen, P., and Rutherford, E. 1963. "Parent-child Relations and Parental Personality in Relation to Young Children's Sexrole Preferences." *Child Development.* 34, pp. 589–607.

Nader, Laura, and Maretzki, T. W., (eds.). 1973. *Cultural Illness and Health. Essays in Human Adaptation.* Washington DC: American Anthropological Association.

Nader, Laura. 1981. "Barriers to thinking new about energy." *Physics Today.* February 1981, pp. 10, 100, 104.

Nance, John. 1975. *The Gentle Tasaday.* New York: Harcourt Brace Jovanovich.

Nathan, O., and Nordon, H. 1980. *Einstein on Peace.* New York: Simon and Schuster.

Newcombe, Hanna. 1986. New Ways to Choose Leaders. *Paper* presented to the IPRA Conference, University of Sussex, April 14–18, 1986.

Newland, Kathleen. 1979. *The Sisterhood of Man.* New York/London: Worldwatch Institute.

Nielsen, Harriet Bjerrum, and Larsen, Kirsten. 1985. Piger og Drenge i Klasseoffentlig-heden. (Girls and Boys in the Public Space of the Classroom). *Rapport no. 2.* Oslo: Pedagogisk Forskningsinstitutt.

Nietzsche, Friedrich. 1969. (Originally published in 1885) English edition. *Thus spoke Zarathustra.* New York: Penguin Books.

Nordland, Eva. 1948. *Sammenhengen Mellom Sosial Atferd og Oppdragelse.* (The Relationship between Social Conduct and Socialization). Oslo: Aschehoug.

Nordland, Eva. 1968. *Mors Egen Gutt.* (Mother's Own Boy). Bergen: J. W. Eide A/S Offsettrykkeri.

Nordland, Eva. 1985. What Does Security Mean to Women? *Paper* given at the Halifax conference: Women negotiating for Peace. June 5. Mimeo.

Næss, Arne. 1985. Valgt og Tvungen Risiko. (Chosen versus Forced Risks). *Kronikk Dagbladet.* 23 September.

Ogilvie, Bruce, and Tutko, Thomas. 1971. "Sport: If You Want to Build Character, Try Something Else." *Psychology Today.* October 1971.

Oliphant, Mark. 1982. "Comment on the social responsibilities of scientists." In J. Rotblat, (ed.) *Scientists, the Arms Race and Disarmament.* London: Taylor and Francis Ltd.

Olweus, Dan. 1969. *Prediction of Aggression. On the Basis of a Projective Test.* Stockholm: Skandinaviska Testførlaget.

Olweus, Dan. 1978. *Aggression in Schools: Bullies and Whipping Boys.* New York: Halsted Press.

Orlick, Terry, and Betterill, Cal. 1975. *Every Kid Can Win.* Chicago: Nelson-Hall.

Orlick, Terry. 1978a. *The Cooperative Sport and Games Book. Challenge without Competition.* New York: Pantheon. In Swedish, 1978: *Alla Vinner!* Stockholm: W&W.

Orlick, Terry. 1978b. *Winning through Cooperation. Competitive Insanity—Cooperative Alternatives.* Washington: Acropolis.

Orlick, Terry. 1982. *The Second Cooperative Sports and Game Book. Over 200 Brand New Non-Competitive Games for Kids and Adults Both.* New York: Pantheon.

Parsons, Talcott. 1964. *The Social Systems.* The Free Press of Glencoe.

Pedersen, Nina. 1980. Integrering av Pike—og Gutte—Speiderne av Norges Speiderforbund. (The Integration of the Girl Scouts and Boy Scouts of the Norwegian Scout Association). *Hovedoppgave.* (Thesis). Institute for Ed. Research. University of Oslo.

Pietilä, Hilkka. 1985. Tomorrow Begins Today—Alternative Development with Women in the North. *Working paper* presented at the ICDA/ISIS Workshop in Forum 85 Nairobi 10.-19.7.1985. UN Association, Helsinki, Finland.

Pikas, Anatol. 1983a. "Symmetric Peace Education." *International Review of Education.* 29:3, pp. 333–344.

Pikas, Anatol. 1983b. "Symmetric Peace Education—A Rejoinder and a Response." *International Review of Education.* 29:3, pp. 354–355.

Pizzey, Erin. 1974. *Scream Quietly or the Neighbors will Hear.* Harmondsworth: Penguin.

Pleck, Joseph. 1982. *The Myth of Masculinity.* Cambridge, MA: MIT Press.

Pletanek, Vaclav. 1987. "Den Blodige Onsdagskvelden." (The Bloody Wednesday Night). Oslo: *Dagbladet.* May 13, 1987, pp. 24–25.

Pope, C., and Whiting, B. 1973. "A Cross-Cultural Analysis of Sex Differences in the Behavior of

Children Aged Three to Eleven." *Journal of Social Psychology*. 91, p. 171. (Cited in Holliday, 1978).

Randzio-Plath, Christa, (ed.). 1982. *Was Geht uns Frauen der Krieg An?* Hamburg: Rowohlt Verlag.

Rathenow, Hanns-Fred, and Smoker, Paul. 1983. *Peace Education in Great Britain*. Lancaster, UK: Workshop Report No. 1, Nov. 1983, Richardson Institute for Conflict and Peace Research.

Ray, Douglas, (ed.). 1988. *Peace Education. Canadian and International Perspectives*. London: Third Eye.

Reardon, Betty. 1981. Militarism and Sexism. UME Connexion. Vol. IX. No. 3. Fall 1981. UME Connexion c/o Educational Ministries/ABC. Valley Forge, PA.

Reardon, Betty. 1982. *Sexism and the War System*. Paper written for the Institute for World Order.

Reardon, Betty. 1985. *Sexism and the War System*. New York, London: Teachers College Press.

Reardon, Betty. 1988a. *Comprehensive Peace Education. Educating for Global Responsibility*. New York: Teachers College Press.

Reardon, Betty. 1988b. *Educating for Global Responsibility*. New York: Teachers College Press.

Redner. 1982. An Interview with Kenneth Boulding. *Social Alternatives*. 1.

Reed, Evelyn. 1970. "Women Caste, Class or Oppressed Sex?" From *Problems of Women's Liberation*. New York: Pathfinder Press, pp. 64–67.

Reithaug, Tone. 1983. Kjønnsforskjeller i Språkbruk Ved Overgang fra Barnehage til Skole. (Sex Differences in Language Usage on the Transition from Kindergarden to School). *Tidsskrift for Nordisk Forening for Pedagogisk Forskning*. 3–4.

Rheingold, H. L., and Cook, K. V. 1975. "The Content of Boys and Girls Rooms as an Index of Parents' Behavior." *Child Development*. 46, pp. 459–563.

Rich, Adrienne. 1977. *Of Woman Born, Motherhood As Experience and Institution*. London: Virago.

Roberts, Barbara. 1983. "No Safe Place: The War against Women." *Our Generation*. 15(4), pp. 7–26.

Roberts, Barbara. 1984. "The Death of Machothink: Feminist Research and the Transformation of Peace Studies." *Women's Studies International Forum*. 7:4, pp. 195–200.

Roggencamp, Viola. 1984. "Abortion of a Special Kind: Male Sex Selection in India." In R. Arditti, R. Klein and S. Minden (eds.) *Test-tube Women. What Future for Motherhood?* London: Pandora Press.

Rotblat, Joseph, (ed.). 1982. *Scientists, the Arms Race and Disarmament*. London: Taylor and Francis Ltd.

Rubin, Gayle. 1984. The Traffic in Women: Notes on the "Political Economy" of Sex. In A. Jaggar and P. Rothenberg (eds.) *Feminist Framework. Alternative Theoretical Accounts of the Relations between Women and Men*. New York: McGraw-Hill Book Co.

Rubin, Josephine. 1981. A feminist world, please. *Paper* Presented to the Ninth General Conference of IPRA, Orilla, Canada, June 21–26.

Röhrs, Hermann. 1983. *Frieden—Eine Pädagogische Aufgabe. Idee und Realität der Friedenspädagogik*. (Peace—an educational task. Ideas and reality in peace education). Agenter Pedersen: Westermann.

Sabo, Donald, and Runfola, Ross, (eds.). 1980. *Jock—Sports and Male Identity*. Englewood Cliffs, NJ: Prentice-Hall.

Sabo, Don. 1985. "Sport, Patriarchy and Male Identity: New Questions About Men and Sport." *The Arena Review*. November. 9:2, pp. 1–30.

Sakamoto, Yoshikazu, and Klassen, Ruth, (eds.). 1981. *Key Issues of Peace Research. Proceedings of the IPRA Ninth General Conference*.

Samhälskunnskap och samhällssyn. 1976. (Knowledge about and attitudes towards society) En internationell studie. Stockholm. Utbildningsförlaget. Skolöverstyrelsen 1976. This Swedish study is part of a bigger project undertaken by the UNESCO Institute in Hamburg. Here the attitudes of youngsters from various countries to important social and global questions were measured.

Schmid, Alex P., and de Graaf, Janny. 1982. *Violence as Communication. Insurgent Terrorism and the Western News Media*. London, Beverly Hills: Sage Publications.

Schuman, Howard; Inkeles, Alex; and Smith, David. 1969. "Some Psychological Effects and Non-Effects of Literacy in a New Nation." *Economic Development and Cultural Change*. 16, October 1969.

Sears, R. R.; Maccoby, E. E.; and Levin, H. 1957. *Patterns of Child Rearing*. New York: Row, Peterson.

Sharp, Gene. 1971. *Exploring Nonviolent Alternatives*. Boston: Porter Sargent.

Sharp, Gene. 1980. *Social Power and Political Freedom*. Boston: Porter Sargent.

Silvermann, Alan. 1986. "Some Reflections on Peace Education: A View from the Male Side." *Working paper* presented to the IPRA conference in Sussex, April 14–18, 1986.

Singer, Jerome, (ed.). 1971. *The Control of Aggression and Violence*. New York: Academic Press.

Sivard, Ruth Leger. 1981. *World Military and Social Expenditures*. Leesburg, VA: World Priorities.

Sivertsen, Helge; Stockholm, Finn Børre; and Vislie, Lise, (eds.). 1981. *Kvinner Viser Vei*. (A Woman Leads the Way). Festschrift to Eva Nordland. Oslo: Aschehoug.

Sjöberg, Svein. 1982. "Soft Girls and Hard Science." *Tidsskrift for Nordisk forening for Pedagogisk Forskning. The Journal of the Nordic Society for Educational Research*. No. 1–2. Published at the University of Lund.

Skjelsbaek, Kjell. 1979. Militarism, Its Dimensions and Corollaries: An Attempt at Conceptual Clarification. *Journal of Peace Research*. 16:3, pp. 213–229.

Skoledage I og Skoledage 2.: (School Days 1 and School Days 2). 1979. København: Unge Pædagoger.

Smoker, Paul. 1981. "Small peace." *Journal of Peace Research*. 2, pp. 149–157.

Spender, Dale. 1980. *Man-made Language*. London: Routledge and Kegan Paul.

Spender, Dale. 1981a. *Men's Education—Women's View: Writers and Readers*. London: Publishing Cooperative.

Spender, Dale. 1981b. *Men's Studies Modified. The Impact of Feminism on the Academic Disciplines*. Oxford: Pergamon Press.

Spender, Dale. 1982. *Women of Ideas and What Men Have Done to Them*. London, Boston, Melbourne: Routledge and Kegan Paul.

Spretnak, Charlene. 1983. "Naming the Cultural Forces that Push Us Toward War." *Journal of Humanistic Psychology*. 23:3, pp. 104–114.

Spretnak, Charlene. 1986. *The Spiritual Dimension of Green Politics*. Santa Fe, NM: Bear & Company.

Spretnak, Charlene, and Capra, Fritjof. 1986. *Green Politics. The Global Promise*. Santa Fe, NM: Bear & Company.

Stanford, Barbara. 1983. "Fear of Success and Hope for Survival: An Analysis of the Relationship Perspective in Three U.S. Peace Education Projects." *Paper*. 34 pp. Presented at the 10th IPRA conference, Gyor, Hungary, August 1983.

Stark, Rodney, and McEvoy, James. 1970. "Middle-Class Violence." *Psychology Today*.

Stein, Peter, and Hoffman, Steven. 1978. "Sports and Male Role Strain." *Journal of Social Issues*. 34:1, pp. 136–150.

Steinmetz, Suzanne K., and Strauss, Murray A., (eds.). 1974. *Violence in the Family*. New York: Dodd, Mead and Company.

Stevens, J. H., and Mathews, M., (eds.). 1978. *Mother/Child—Father/Child Relationships*. New York: National Association for the Education of Young Children.

Stiehm, Judith. 1982. "The Protected, the Protector, the Defender." *Women Studies International Forum*. 5 (3/4), pp. 367–376.

Stigen, Anfinn. 1985. "Stopp Vanviddet! (Stop the Crazyness!) *Dagbladet*. 12 September.

Strauss, Murray. 1974. "Some Social Antecedents of Physical Punishment." In S. Steinmetz, and M. Strauss (eds.) *Violence in the Family*. New York: Dodd, Mead and Company.

Strauss, A. 1978. *Negotiations: Varieties, Contexts, Processes and Social Order*. San Francisco: Jossey-Bass.

Sørensen, Bjørg Åse. 1982. Ansvarsrasjonalitet. (Caring rationality). In H. Holter (ed.) *Kvinner i Fellesskap*. (The Collectivity of Women). Oslo: Universitetsforlaget.

Thairu, Kihumbu. 1975. *The African Civilization*. Nairobi: Kenya Literature Bureau.

Thee, Marek. 1982. "The Race in Military Technology." p. 51. In J. Rotblat (ed.) *Scientists—The Arms Race and Disarmament*. London: Taylor & Francis Ltd.

Thee, Marek. 1983. "Swords into Ploughshares: The Quest for Peace and Human Development." *International Labour Review*. 122:5, September–October.

Thompson, Dorothy. 1983. *Over our Dead Bodies. Women against the Bomb*. London: Virago Press.

Thorsson, Inga. 1978. *Nedrustning-Utvikling*. Fra FN's spesialsesjon i 1978. *FN-Sambandet Oslo. (Disarmament-development. From the UN Special Session in 1978).*

Thorsson, Inga. 1984. *In Pursuit of Disarmament*. Stockholm: Liber.

Thygesen, B. 1971. "Faderens Betydning for Kønsrolleudviklingen." (The Importance of the Father for Sex role Development). *Nordisk Psykologi* XXIII, pp. 275–289.

Tiger, Lionel, and Fox, Robin. 1971. "Give and Take," from *The Imperial Animal*, pp. 60–67.

Tornes, Kristin. 1981. "Sex typing and Schooling." In *A Report on the Educational Research Workshop held in Hønefoss*, Norway, May 5–8, 1981. Also published in *Sex Stereotyping in Schools*. Edited by Council of Europe: Swets & Zeitlinger—Lisse.

Tromp, Hylke. 1980. Introduction to the *UNESCO Yearbook on Peace and Conflict Studies*. UNESCO, Paris.

UNESCO. 1987. "A Multidisciplinary Study of the Origins and Forms of Violence in Sports Activities and in Particular Its Social and Educational Aspects Together with Appropriate Remedial Action." Paris: *15. April, 126 Ex/14, Item 5.2.2.* of the provisional agenda.

Vargas, Ines. 1983. *Women and Violence. PRIO Working paper 17/83*. Oslo: International Peace Research Institute of Oslo.

Vellacott, Jo. 1982. "Women, Peace and Power." In P. McAllister (ed.) *Reweaving the Web of Life: Feminism and Non-Violence*. Philadelphia: New Society Publishers.

Vetterling-Braggin, Mary. 1981. *Sexist Language: A Modern Philosophical Analysis*. Totowa, NJ: Littlefield Adams.

Wahlström Riitta. 1985. "De Ungas Uppfattning om Krig och Fred." (Young People's Perceptions of War and Peace). *Nordisk Psykologi*. 37:4, 1985.

Wernersson, Inga. 1977. "Könsdifferentiering i Grundskolan." (Sex Differentiation in the Elementary School). *Göteborg Studies in Educational Sciences*. 22. Göteborg: Göteborg Universitet.

Westing, Arthur, (ed.). 1988. *Cultural Norms War and the Environment*. Oxford: Oxford University Press.

Whiting, B. B., and Whiting, J. W. M. 1973. "Altruistic and Egoistic Behavior in Six Cultures." In L. Nader and T. W. Maretzki (eds.) *Cultural Illness and Health: Essays in Human Adaptation*. Washington, DC: American Anthropological Association.

Whiting, B. B, and Whiting, J. W. M. 1975. *Children of Six Cultures*. Cambridge: Harvard University Press.

Wiberg, Håkan. 1981a. "Journal of Peace Research 1964–1980—What Have We Learnt about Peace?" *Journal of Peace Research. 18/2, pp. 11–148.*

Wiberg, Håkan. 1981b. "Dilemmas of Disarmament Education." In M. Haavelsrud (ed.) *Approaching Disarmament Education*. Guildford: Westbury House.

Wiberg, Håkan. 1984. "The Peace Research Movement." In Friedensbewegungen und

Wirkungen. *Wiener Beiträge zur Geshichte der Neuzeit. Band 11/84.* Wien: Verlag für Geschichte und Politik.

Wiberg, Håkan. 1987. "Fred och Konflikt." (Peace and conflict). In *Konfliktteori och Fredsforskning.* (Theory of conflict and peace research). Stockholm: Esselte Studium (second edition).

Williamson, Nancy. 1978. *Boys or Girls? Parents Preference and Sex Control.* Washington, DC: Population Reference Bureau. (Cited in Newland, 1979).

Wilson, Edward. 1978. *On Human Nature.* Cambridge: Harvard University Press. ch. 6.

Wolfgang, M., and Strohm, R. B. 1956. "The Relationship Between Alcohol and Criminal Homicide." *Quarterly Journal of Studies of Alcohol.* 17.

Woolf, Virginia. 1938. *Three Guineas.* London: The Hogarth Press. New York 1977.

Wright, Quincy. 1942. *A Study of War.* Chicago: Chicago University Press.

Young, Michael. 1979. *Knowledge and Control.* London: Collier MacMillan.

Ziman, John. 1982. "Basic Principles." In *Scientists—The Arms Race and Disarmament.* London: Taylor and Francis Ltd.

Zuckerman, Lord. 1980. *Science Advisers and Nuclear Weapons.* London: The Menard Press.

Zur, O. Morrison, and Zaretsky, E. 1985. "Men, Women and War. Gender and Differences in Attitudes towards War." *Paper* presented at the Western Psychological Association Meetings, April 1985, San Jose, California. Requests for reprints: O. Zur. 2212 Derby Street, Berkeley, CA 94705.

Index

Accidents, as structural violence, 45–46
Aggression
  absence of in various cultures, 101
  as behavior and emotion, 95
  behavior versus feelings, 121
  biological factor, question of, 128–29
  children, 10
  definition of, 93–94
  fathers' effect on sons, 130–31
  frustration-aggression theory, 103–4
  males, 17–18
  potentialities for, 102–3
  socialization into, 119–28
  threshold of inhibition and, 98–99
  war and, 95–96
Aggression in Schools (Olweus), 96–97
Analysis
  primary analysis, 5–6
  secondary analysis, 5
Andersen, Margaret, 31
Anderson, Marion, 55–56
Androgen levels, in men, aggression and, 124–25
Antagonism, between men and women, development of, 21
Antell, Dr. Maxine, 132
Arkin, William, 148
Arousal hypothesis, 139
Attitude formation, social behavior and, 99–106
Ås, Berit, 62

Bandura, A., 103–4
Bellak, Dr. Leopold, 132
Belotti, Elena, 109–10, 114, 115, 133
Benedict, Ruth, 101
Bernard, Jessie, 29–30
Bertell, Rosalie, 60, 86
Beyond Power (French), 23–25
Big Breadwinner Hog, 141
Birth imagery, 32
Bleier, Ruth, 168
Borrelli, Mario, 84, 85, 87
Boulding, Elise, 1, 5, 41, 50–51, 103, 163, 173
Boys
  bullies versus whipping boys, 96–98
  changing social/educational environment of, 127
  egoistic behaviors in, 143–44
  sports/games of, 144
Brownmiller, Susan, 51
Burns, Robin, 30, 68, 87, 166
Buss, Arnold, 121

Callewaert, Staf, 157
Caring
  "rationality" of, 69
  teaching of, 11
Carmichael, Carrie, 111–12
Carroll, Berenice, 25–26
Chain of command, military, compared to patriarchal family, 116
Childbearing/rearing, 6, 32, 60
Child care, 33, 37, 114
Children
  aggression, 10
  choosing sex of, son preference and, 110–11
  male children, limiting number of, 125–26
Chodorow, Nancy, 32, 33, 119

Cisse, Jeanne Martin, 115
Co-feminists, 28
Competitiveness, taught through hidden curriculum, 171–72
Compilation research, 5
Comprehensive Peace Education (Reardon), 81
Conservative feminist perspective, 17–18
  definition of, 16
"Converus Interruptus and Other Disorders" (Ehrenreich), 63
Copenhagen document, 44, 70–77, 189–90
Critical thinking, 10

Daly, Mary, 29, 49, 51, 107
Davis, Elisabeth Gould, 127
Degler, Carl, 15
de Graaf, Janny, 140–41
Detre, Thomas, 120
Dialectical approach, to peace education, 85
Dialectic of Sex, The (Firestone), 32
Direct violence, sports/games, 146–47
Disinhibition hypothesis, 139
Distribution of resources, 58–60
Dobrofsky, Lynne, 148
Dominance, 30–31
  power as, 25, 26
  in school settings, 156
"Dowry deaths", 50
Dyer, Gwynne, 147

Easlea, Brian, 15, 32, 68, 167–68
Eckhardt, William, 30
Eco-feminists, 33
Edelman, Marian Wright, 56
Education
  definition of, 74–75
  socialization and, 75–76
  See also Formal school settings; Hidden curriculum; Peace education
Egoistic behaviors, in boys, 143–44
Ehrenreich, Barbara, 63–64
Eisler, Riane, 30
Elster, Jon, 104
Empirical approach, to peace education, 74
Engels, Friedrich, 44
Enloe, Cynthia, 52, 68
Erikson, Erik, 122, 143
Eron, Leonard, 138–39
Ervin, Frank, 102
Estrogen
  hormonal interference by, 127
    effect on male aggression, 127–28
Ethelberg, Eva, 105–6
Evolutionary approach, to peace education, 85–88
Eysenck, H. J., 136, 138, 140, 162

Fabbro, David, 99
Family institutions
  peace education within, 107–33
    fathers' role, 128–33
    feminist mothers of sons, 111–16
    "ideal mother" and "ideal soldier", 116–19
    mothers' role, 107–11
    socialization into violence and aggression, 119–28
Fasteau, Marc Feigen, 148–49
Fasting, Kari, 145
Fathers
  effect on sons' aggression, 130–31
  role in peace education, 128–33
  role in sex-stereotyping, 129–30
  time spent with children, 130
Female ethos, 30
"Female science", 173
Feminist frameworks, distinction between, 16–17
Feminist mothers of sons, 111–16
Feminist Perspective in the Academy, A (Langland/Grove), 15
Feminist perspectives
  combination of, 35–38
  conservative feminist perspective, 17–18
  definition of, 2
  liberal feminist perspective, 18–20
    definition of, 16

Marxist feminist perspective, 20–22
definition of, 16
of peace education, 73
personal threat to men from, 69
radical feminist perspective, 22–31
definition of, 16
formal school settings, 158
socialist feminist perspective, 31–34
definition of, 16
variations of, 34
Feminist researchers, "rationality" of caring adhered to by, 69
Firestone, Shulamith, 32
Fishman, Pamela, 63
Food distribution, 58–60
Football, violence of, 142–43
Forcey, Linda Rennie, 118–19
Formal school settings
nonviolent conflict situations, teaching of, 163
peace education in, 155–59
radical feminist perspective, 158
See also Education
Formal sector, peace education in, 11–13, 155–75
Forward-Looking Strategies from Nairobi, *See* Nairobi document
Fox, Robin, 17, 127
Freire, Paulo, 170
French, Marilyn, 23–28, 32–33
Freud, Sigmund, 17
Frustration-aggression theory, 103–4
Fuller, Buckminster, 126, 127

Galtung, Johan, 40–41, 44, 155–58, 171
Garbo, Bunnar, 137
Gelder, Lindsy van, 111–12
Gender differences
in attitudes toward war, 119
peace education, 82–83
Gender neutrality, 1–2
breaking of, 2
Gender-specific socialization, 7
Genital mutilation, 49–50
Gilder, George, 117
Gilligan, Carol, 15, 119
Girls, socialization of, 11
Green, Dr. Richard, 127, 134
Grove, Walter, 15
Gyn/Ecology (Daly), 107

Haavelsrud, Magnus, 84–85, 87
Haavind, Hanne, 21
Haukaa, Runa, 29, 144, 158
Hidden curriculum
attitudes shaped through, 169–72
competitiveness, 171–72
loyalty, 170
obedience, 170
in schools, 12
See also Education; Schools
History, attitudes shaped through teaching of, 162–64
Hite, Shere, 19
Hoffman, Steve, 148
Hoivik, Tord, 4, 46, 57
Holliday, Laurel, 17, 18, 86, 123–26, 127, 132, 133, 138–39, 141
Hooks, Bell, 34–35
Housework, unpaid, 29, 62, 114
Hutt, Corinne, 120

"Ideal mothers"
and "ideal soldiers", 116–19
perspectives of, 118
training of, 117
Indirect violence, sports/games, 147–49
Infant/preschool mortality, 46, 60–61
Infants/pre-schoolers, aggression, 128
International Peace Research Association, 173–74
Inter-sex conversation, crisis in, 63–64

Jaggar, Alison, 16, 20, 34
Jalmert, Lars, 128

Kapitza, Sergei, 169
Keller, Evelyn Fox, 167
Klemesrud, Judy, 113
Knowledge without Power (Brock-Utne/Haukaa), 35–36
Kronsberg, Sandora, 122
Krugler, Christopher, 162, 163

Lagerspetz, Kirsti, 94–95, 139
Lamb, Jamie, 130
Lamb, Michael, 129–30
Langland, Elizabeth, 15, 16
La Rocque, Gene R., 126, 127
Leisure time, women versus men, 62–63
Leonard, George, 150–51
Liberal feminist perspective, 18–20
  definition of, 16
Liebert, Dr. Robert M., 138
Lie, Svein, 167–68
Lindholm, Stig, 5, 14, 83, 159–61
Loyalty, hidden curriculum of, 12, 170
Loye, David, 30

MacBride, Sean, 165
McClintok, Barbara, 168
Male devaluation, of "feminine" things, 131
Male ethos, 30
Males
  aggression, 17–18
  male solidarity, 31
  masculine socialization, 148
  See also Aggression
Mark, Vernon, 102
Marriage, 114–15
Marxist feminist perspective, 20–22
  definition of, 16
Messner, Mike, 147
Mexico document, 44, 70–71, 88–89
Milgram, Stanley, 98
Military
  chain of command compared to patriarchal family, 116
  training, 117
  women's support of, 36
Military spending, 53–57
  loss of jobs and, 55–56
  versus poverty, 56
  women's attitudes toward, 53–54
Mill, Harriet Taylor, 18
Mill, John Stuart, 18–19
Mixed-sex conversations, men's/women's contributions to, 63
Montagu, Ashley, 93–94, 101, 102
Morgan, Robin, 65
Mothers
  relationship between daughters and, 114
  role in child punishment, 132
  role in peace education, 107–11
Moyer, Kenneth, 141

Nairobi document, 3–4, 9, 44, 72, 90–92
Namelessness, as trait of mothers/soldiers, 117
National Organization of Women, *See* NOW
Negative peace, 8, 41–44
  summarizing table, 47
Nias, D. K. B., 136, 138, 140, 162
Nilsson, Bengt A., 157
No Immediate Danger? (Bertell), 60
Nonformal sector, peace education in, 10–11, 107–54
Nonsexist education, by feminist mothers of sons, 111–12
Nonviolent conflict solutions, teaching of, 163, 173
Nonviolent tools of feminism, 27
Norwegian Council for Equality, 20
NOW (National Organization of Women), 20
Nuclear weapons, deaths from, 60
Nurturing, fathers' role in, 131

Obedience
  hidden curriculum of, 12
  taught through hidden curriculum, 170
  teaching of, 10–11
  of women, 19
Oliphant, Mark, 164
Olweus, Dan, 95–98
"On the Subjection of Women" (Mill), 18–19
Oppression, 31, 73
  sexual, 28
Organized violence, versus unorganized violence, 44–45
Orlick, Terry, 150

Paid labor, 62
Parkman, Patrica, 162, 163
Parsons, Talcott, 25
Patriarchy
analysis of, 29
higher status of males in, 69
patriarchical language, 27–28
revolution against, 26–27
strength of, 3
theory of, 29, 33
Peace
definition of, 39–41, 43
feminist perspectives on, 7–9
negative peace, 8, 41–44
summarizing table, 47
positive peace, 9, 39, 44–65
summarizing table, 47
preliminary table of concept, 43
Peace education, 12, 107–33
approaches to, 84–88
dialectical approach, 83
evolutionary approach, 85–88
structural approach, 83
changing the world through, 109–10
as controversial concept, 79–80
definition of, 74–76
educating girls for peace/boys for war, 151–55
as education *about* peace, 77–78
as education *for* peace, 78–79
empirical approach, 74
feminine perspectives on, 9
in formal sector, 11–13, 155–75
in nonformal sector, 10–11, 107–54
girls' versus boys' education, 151–54
level of information, 83–84
readiness to act on, 83–84
recent developments in, 80–84
sports/games, 143–51
direct violence, 146–47
indirect violence, 147–49
physical activity as pleasure/joy, 149–51
taking gender into account, 82–83
television's role in, 135–43
theoretical approach, 74
through choice of toys, 133–35
within family institution, 107–33
See also Family institutions, peace education within
Peace-oriented school student, 159–62
Peace research, 66–67
criticism of, 3
research groups, 68–69
Perspective, definition of, 14
Physical violence, 2, 42, 48–51
definitions of, 2
war concept and, 43
Plan of Action from Mexico, *See* Mexico document
Play patterns, children, 121–22
Political violence
rape and, 51–52
women's plight during, 51
Positive peace, 9, 39, 44–65
summarizing table, 47
Poverty, versus military spending, 56
Power, 6
as competence, 25
cult of, 25
as dominance, 25, 26
pleasure and, 26–28
trouble caused by concept of, 24
Private reproductive society, 22
Private violence, definition of, 3
Programme of Action from Copenhagen, *See* Copenhagen document
Punishment, father's role in, 132

Radical feminist perspective, 22–31
central idea of, 27
definition of, 16
formal school settings, 158
Rape, political violence and, 51–52, 65
Rathenow, Hanns-Fred, 80
Reardon, Betty, 49, 51, 68, 81–82, 87, 109, 116
Reed, Evelyn, 21
Refugees/displaced persons, statistics, 59
Reithaug, Tone, 122
"Report of the Committee on the Status of Women in India", 61

Repression, 61–64
Reproduction, controlling men through, 32
Research, male perspective in, 14–15
Resources, distribution of, 58–60
Roberts, Barbara, 2–3, 42, 44
Rohrs, Hermann, 82, 173
Rothenberg, Paula, 16, 20, 34
Rubin, Gayle, 31, 32

Sabo, Don, 147, 150, 158
Schmid, Alex P., 140–41
Schools
  attitudes shaped through curriculum, 9, 162–69
    history, 162–64
    science, 164–69
  peace-oriented school student, 159–62
  See also Education; Hidden curriculum
Science
  attitudes shaped through teaching of, 164–69
  feminist analysis of, 12
Sexism
  as belief system, 109
  compared to racism, 109–10
Sex roles, socialization and, 153–54
Sex-stereotyping, fathers' role in, 129–30
Sex and Temperament in Three Primitive Societies (Mead), 99
Sexuality, men's control of women's, 29
Sexual liberation, 19
Sexual oppression, 28
Sharp, Gene, 25, 26, 163
Silverman, Alan, 15
Sivard, Ruth Leger, 57
Sjøberg, Svein, 167–68
"Small Peace" (Smoker), 99–100
Smoker, Paul, 80, 99–100
Social behavior, attitude formation and, 99–106
Socialist feminist perspective, 31–34
  definition of, 16
  variations of, 34
Socialization, 15
  education and, 75–76
  of girls, 11
  into violence and aggression, 119–28
  processes, 75
  sex roles, 153–54
Social learning theory, 139–40
Social Power and Political Freedom (Sharp), 25
Son preference, 110–11
Sons research project (Brock-Utne), 113
Spender, Dale, 36, 64, 163
Sports/games
  aggression in, 141–43
  direct violence, 146–47
  indirect violence, 147–49
  physical activity as pleasure/joy, 149–51
Spretnak, Charlene, 113–14
Steinfeld, Jesse, 137
Stein, Peter, 148
Structural approach, to peace education, 85
Structural violence, 44–45
  accidents as, 45–46
  phenomena, 46
Submission, of girls, 114–15
Suttner, Bertha von, 164

Television
  "bad guys" versus "good guys", 141
  psychic payoff of watching sports/games on, 149
  role models produced by, 10
  role in peace education, 135–43
Thairu, Kihumbu, 34
Thorsson, Inga, 57
Three Guineas (Woolf), 108
Threshold of inhibition, aggression and, 98–99
Tiger, Lionel, 17, 126, 127
Toddlers, *See* Infants/pre-schoolers
Torture toys, 134
Toys
  "feminine" versus "masculine" sets of, 128–29
    experiment, 128–29

peace education through choice of, 133–35
torture toys, 134
Training
of "ideal mothers", 117
military, 117

Unorganized violence, versus organized violence, 44–45
UN Women's Decade conferences, 9, 63, 65, 74
Copenhagen document, 70–77, 189–90
Mexico document, 70–71, 88–89
Nairobi document, 72, 90–92
peace concept, development of, 70–72, 88–92
U.S. National Conference on Child Abuse and Neglect, statistics, 44

Vargas, Ines, 51
Vindication of the Rights of Women, A (Wollstonecraft), 18
Violence
football and, 142–43
natural inhibitions against, 140
socialization into, 119–28
in sports, 142–43, 147
television and, 135–43
U.S. national commissions on, 136–37
Violence and the Brain (Mark/Ervin), 102
Violence as Communication (Schmid/de Graaf), 140–41
Violence in the Family (Bellak/Antell), 132–33
Violent Sex, The (Holliday), 123–24, 132

Wahlstrom, Riitta, 161–62
War
concept of, 42–43
relationship between aggression and, 95–96
women's contribution through education, 52
Watson, Lyall, 126
Wernersson, Inga, 157
"What We Have Learnt About Peace" (Wiberg), 40
"What the Women's Movement Has Done to American History" (Degler), 15–16
Wiberg, Hakan, 40–44, 46, 67, 105, 171
Williamson, Nancy, 110
Wilson, Edward, 17
"Winning Isn't Everything. It's Nothing" (Leonard), 150–51
Women
obedience of, 19
security, 2
woman-headed households, 108–9
as world rulers, 126–27
See also Female ethos; Feminist frameworks; Feminist perspectives; Feminist researchers
Women of color, definition of, 34
Women of color perspective, 6, 34–35
definition of, 16
Women writers, 64–65
Woolf, Virginia, 108, 172
Woolstonecraft, Mary, 18
World Military and Social Expenditures (Sivard), 57
Wright, Quincy, 39

Zuckerman, Lord, 164–65

About the Author

Birgit Brock-Utne is an Associate Professor at the Institute for Educational Research at the University of Oslo, Norway. She has studied in the United States at Stanford University and the University of Illinois, where she received her Masters in Education. Her main academic interests are peace education and research, feminist studies, educational innovation, and curriculum development. She has written several books, including *Educating for Peace: A Feminist Perspective*. She has been a guest researcher at the International Institute of Peace Research, Oslo, and is widely known as a peace educator and peace activist in Norway. In addition, Birgit Brock-Utne has served as a consultant to many international organizations, including UNESCO, OECD, the European Council, the International Peace Research Association, the Nordic Council, and the United Nations. Currently, she holds the position of Professor of Education at the University of Dar es Salaam, Tanzania.

THE ATHENE SERIES
An International Collection of Feminist Books
General Editors: Gloria Bowles, Renate D. Klein, and Janice Raymond
Consulting Editor: Dale Spender

MEN'S STUDIES MODIFIED The Impact of Feminism on the Academic Disciplines
Dale Spender, editor

WOMAN'S NATURE Rationalizations of Inequality
Marian Lowe and *Ruth Hubbard*, editors

MACHINA EX DEA Feminist Perspectives on Technology
Joan Rothschild, editor

SCIENCE AND GENDER A Critique of Biology and Its Theories on Women
Ruth Bleier

WOMAN IN THE MUSLIM UNCONSCIOUS
Fatna A. Sabbah

MEN'S IDEAS/WOMEN'S REALITIES Popular Science, 1870-1915
Louise Michele Newman, editor

BLACK FEMINIST CRITICISM Perspectives on Black Women Writers
Barbara Christian

THE SISTER BOND A Feminist View of a Timeless Connection
Toni A.H. McNaron, editor

EDUCATING FOR PEACE A Feminist Perspective
Birgit Brock-Utne

STOPPING RAPE Successful Survival Strategies
Pauline B. Bart and *Patricia H. O'Brien*

TEACHING SCIENCE AND HEALTH FROM A FEMINIST PERSPECTIVE
A Practical Guide
Sue V. Rosser

FEMINIST APPROACHES TO SCIENCE
Ruth Bleier, editor

INSPIRING WOMEN Reimagining the Muse
Mary K. DeShazer

MADE TO ORDER The Myth of Reproductive and Genetic Progress
Patricia Spallone and *Deborah L. Steinberg,* editors

TEACHING TECHNOLOGY FROM A FEMINIST PERSPECTIVE
A Practical Guide
Joan Rothschild

FEMINISM WITHIN THE SCIENCE AND HEALTH CARE PROFESSIONS
Overcoming Resistance
Sue V. Rosser

RUSSIAN WOMEN'S STUDIES Essays on Sexism in Soviet Culture
Tatyana Mamonova

TAKING OUR TIME Feminist Perspectives on Temporality
Frieda Johles Forman, editor, with *Caoran Sowton*

RADICAL VOICES A Decade of Feminist Resistance from *Women's Studies International Forum*
Renate Klein and *Deborah L. Steinberg*, editors

THE RECURRING SILENT SPRING
H. Patricia Hynes

EXPOSING NUCLEAR PHALLACIES
Diana E.H. Russell, editor

THE WRITING OR THE SEX? or why you don't have to read women's writing to know it's no good
Dale Spender

FEMINIST PERSPECTIVES ON PEACE AND PEACE EDUCATION
Birgit Brock-Utne